111 Job Interview Questions and Answers to Land Your Dream Job

111 Job Interview Questions and Answers to Land Your Dream Job

111 Most Common Job Interview Questions with Expert Tips, Guides, and Insights to Answer Them

Be.Bull Publishing Group
Mauricio Vasquez

Toronto, Canada

Authors:
Be.Bull Publishing Group
Mauricio Vasquez

First Printing: August 2024

ISBN-978-1-998402-65-6 (Paperback)
ISBN-978-1-998402-66-3 (Hardcover)
ISBN-978-1-998402-67-0 (Ebook)

INTRODUCTION

Welcome to "111 Job Interview Questions and Answers to Land Your Dream Job" your ultimate guide to navigating the challenging world of job interviews with confidence and poise. Whether you are a recent graduate stepping into the professional world for the first time or an experienced professional seeking new opportunities, this book is designed to equip you with the tools and insights needed to excel in any interview scenario.

Job interviews can be daunting. The stakes are high, the competition is fierce, and the pressure to make a lasting impression can be overwhelming. However, with the right preparation and mindset, you can turn any interview into an opportunity to showcase your unique strengths and secure the job you desire. This book aims to demystify the interview process by providing you with a comprehensive collection of 111 common interview questions, along with detailed guidance on how to respond effectively.

Why this book?

In today's competitive job market, standing out from the crowd requires more than just a polished resume and a well-written cover letter. Employers are looking for candidates who not only possess the necessary skills and experience but also demonstrate a strong fit with their company culture and values. This book is designed to help you articulate your qualifications and convey your enthusiasm in a way that resonates with interviewers.

Each question in this book is accompanied by:

- Tips: Practical advice on approaching each question, highlighting key points to consider and common pitfalls to avoid.
- Response Framework: A structured outline to help you craft a comprehensive and compelling answer.
- Key Takeaways: Essential insights to reinforce your understanding and ensure you are well-prepared.
- Sample Answer: A model response to illustrate how you can effectively apply the tips and framework in a real interview scenario. See Appendix No 2

How to use this book?

This book is structured to provide you with a systematic approach to interview preparation. Each section focuses on a specific category of questions, ranging from personal background and career aspirations to technical skills and situational challenges. By breaking down the questions into manageable sections, you can focus on honing your responses one step at a time.

Here's how to make the most of this book:

1. Read through each question: Familiarize yourself with the questions you might encounter. Understanding the rationale behind each question will help you anticipate what interviewers are looking for.
2. Study the tips: Pay close attention to the practical advice provided for each question. These tips help you highlight key information and avoid common mistakes.
3. Use the response framework: Follow the structured outline to organize your thoughts and ensure your answers are coherent and impactful.
4. Learn from the sample answers: Analyze the model responses to see how the tips and framework come together. Use these examples as a guide to formulate your unique answers.

5. Practice, Practice, Practice: Rehearse your responses to build confidence and ensure you can deliver them naturally during the interview. Consider practicing with a friend or mentor who can provide feedback.

The path to success

Preparing for a job interview is about more than memorizing answers to common questions. It's about understanding your story, articulating your value, and connecting with the interviewer meaningfully. This book will guide you through this process, helping you to present your best self and make a lasting impression.

Believe in your abilities and strive for excellence. Your hard work will yield remarkable results. Take pride in your work and give it your best. Your commitment to excellence can set you apart. As you embark on this journey, remember that each interview is an opportunity to learn and grow. With thorough preparation and a positive mindset, you can turn the interview process into a rewarding experience that leads to your dream job.

Welcome to the journey of mastering the interview. Let's begin.

Dear Reader,

Thank you for taking the time to read my book. Your feedback is incredibly valuable, not just to me but also to future readers who are looking for reliable resources to help them in their job search.

By leaving a review, you can help others make an informed decision and ensure that the content continues to improve and meet the needs of readers like you. Your insights can make a difference.

To share your thoughts, please scan the QR code below, which will take you directly to the review page.

I sincerely appreciate your support and the time you've taken to contribute your thoughts.

Best regards,

Mauricio Vasquez

PS. If you're looking to elevate your job search and interview preparation, our latest book is a must-have. It offers a step-by-step guide on harnessing the power of Artificial Intelligence and ChatGPT, specifically tailored for job seekers.

TABLE OF CONTENTS

CHAPTER 1

INTRODUCTION AND PERSONAL BACKGROUND

1. TELL ME ABOUT YOURSELF.

Tips

1. **Be Relevant:** When answering this question, it is crucial to tailor your response to the specific job you are applying for. Highlight your most relevant skills and experiences that align with the job description. This shows the interviewer that you have taken the time to understand the role and how your background fits into it. Discussing aspects of your career that directly relate to the job can make a strong impression, as it demonstrates your suitability for the position. Additionally, try to anticipate what the interviewer might be most interested in hearing about, based on the job requirements and company culture.

2. **Be Concise:** Although it's important to provide enough detail to be informative, keeping your answer to around 1-2 minutes ensures that you remain engaging and to the point. Avoid going off on tangents or including too much unrelated information. Instead, focus on key highlights and major accomplishments. Practice your response to make sure it flows smoothly and sticks to the important points. This not only helps in keeping the interviewer's attention but also shows that you can communicate effectively and respect their time.

3. **Show Progression:** Your response should illustrate your career progression, showing how each role has built upon the previous ones and prepared you for this position. Begin with your educational background or first relevant job and move forward chronologically, highlighting promotions, increased responsibilities, and key learning experiences. This narrative helps the interviewer understand your career journey and see how your experiences have culminated in your current expertise. It also provides context for your professional growth and development.

4. **End with the Present:** Conclude your response by explaining why you are excited about this particular role and how it fits into your career path. This helps to bring your story full circle and demonstrates that you are forward-thinking. Emphasize what specifically drew you to this company and position, and how you see it as the next logical step in your career. By ending on a note of enthusiasm and future aspirations, you leave the interviewer with a positive impression of your motivation and fit for the role.

Response Framework

1. **Brief Introduction:** Start with your name and a high-level summary of your professional background. Mention how long you've been in your current position and any notable titles or responsibilities. This provides a quick snapshot of who you are and sets the stage for deeper details. For example, "My name is Jane Doe, and I have over eight years of experience in marketing, with a focus on digital strategies and content creation."

2. **Highlight Relevant Experience:** Discuss 2-3 key roles or experiences that are most relevant to the job you are applying for. For each role, provide a brief overview of your responsibilities and major accomplishments. Use specific metrics or examples to illustrate your impact. For instance, "At XYZ Company, I led a team that increased our social media engagement by 30% and drove a 20% increase in lead generation through targeted campaigns."

3. **Connect to the Role:** Explain why you are interested in this position and how your background makes you a great fit. Discuss any specific aspects of the job or company that attracted you and how they align with your career goals. This demonstrates that you have done your homework and are genuinely

interested in the role. For example, "I am particularly excited about this opportunity at your company because of your commitment to innovation and sustainability, which are areas I am passionate about."

4. **Future Aspirations:** Mention what you hope to achieve in this role and how it fits into your long-term career goals. This shows that you are thinking ahead and are committed to your professional growth. For example, "In this role, I hope to leverage my skills to drive impactful marketing campaigns and contribute to the company's growth, while continuing to develop my expertise in digital strategy."

Key Takeaways

1. **Relevance is Key:** Focus on the parts of your background that are most relevant to the job you are applying for. This demonstrates that you have carefully considered how your experiences align with the job requirements and are well-prepared for the role. It also shows that you understand what the employer is looking for and can articulate why you are a good fit.

2. **Conciseness Matters:** Keep your response clear and to the point to maintain the interviewer's interest. Avoid unnecessary details and focus on delivering a compelling narrative that highlights your key qualifications and experiences. Practicing your response can help ensure that you stay within a reasonable time frame while covering all important points.

3. **Showcase Growth:** Demonstrate how your past experiences have prepared you for this role. Highlight your career progression, key learnings, and how each step has contributed to your current skill set. This not only shows your capability but also your dedication to continuous improvement and professional development.

4. **Align with the Job:** Make sure to align your skills and experiences with the job requirements. Clearly articulate how your background makes you a suitable candidate for the position and how you can add value to the company. This helps the interviewer see the direct connection between your past achievements and future potential in their organization.

2. WALK ME THROUGH YOUR RESUME.

Tips

1. **Be Structured:** Present your resume in a logical, chronological order. Start with your educational background, then move through each job role, highlighting key responsibilities and achievements. This helps the interviewer follow your career progression and understand your professional journey.

2. **Be Detailed but Relevant:** While it's important to provide a comprehensive overview, focus on the most relevant experiences that align with the job you're applying for. Highlight achievements and responsibilities that demonstrate your suitability for the role. Avoid overloading the interviewer with too much information; instead, prioritize what best showcases your qualifications.

3. **Use Metrics:** Whenever possible, quantify your achievements. This makes your contributions more tangible and impactful. Numbers and data points help illustrate your successes clearly and make your experience more relatable and credible.

4. **End with the Present and Future:** Conclude with your current role and what you are looking for in your next opportunity. This provides a smooth transition from your past experiences to your future aspirations, showing the interviewer your career trajectory. This also ties your past experiences to the role you are applying for, emphasizing your growth and forward-thinking mindset.

Response Framework

1. **Begin with Education:** Start your resume walkthrough by briefly mentioning your highest level of education, including the degree obtained, the institution's name, and any honors or relevant achievements. This sets the stage by establishing your academic foundation and how it prepared you for your professional journey.

2. **Discuss Your Career Start:** Next, introduce your first significant role in the industry, including the company name, your job title, and the duration of your tenure. Focus on the key responsibilities you held and any noteworthy achievements. This helps illustrate the skills and experiences you developed early in your career, showcasing your initial growth and areas of specialization.

3. **Highlight Career Progression:** Move chronologically through your subsequent roles, giving a brief overview of each position. For each role, mention the company, your title, the duration, and your core responsibilities. Highlight specific achievements, focusing on how your responsibilities evolved and how you made impactful contributions. This section should emphasize your career progression and the increasing complexity of your roles over time.

4. **Detail Your Current Role:** Describe your current position, including the company you work for, your job title, and your primary responsibilities. Highlight any major accomplishments, special projects, or leadership roles you've undertaken. This part of your walkthrough should emphasize your current expertise and how it prepares you for the next step in your career.

5. **Link to the New Role:** After detailing your professional history, connect your background to the role you are applying for. Explain how your experiences have equipped you with the skills and insights needed for this new opportunity. Demonstrate a clear alignment between your past roles and the requirements of the position, reinforcing your suitability for the job.

6. **Conclude with Future Goals:** Wrap up by discussing your career aspirations and how the new role fits into your long-term goals. This shows that you are not only focused on the present but are also thinking strategically about your future career path. It highlights your commitment to continuous growth and how this position aligns with your professional ambitions.

Key Takeaways

1. **Structure and Clarity:** Follow a clear and logical structure to ensure the interviewer can easily follow your career progression. This helps in presenting a coherent and comprehensive picture of your professional journey.

2. **Relevance:** Focus on experiences and achievements that are most relevant to the job you are applying for. This demonstrates you have carefully considered how your background aligns with the job requirements and shows your suitability for the role.

3. **Use Metrics:** Quantify your achievements with specific metrics to make your contributions more tangible. Numbers and data points help illustrate your successes clearly, making your experience more impactful and credible.

4. **Future Orientation:** Conclude by connecting your past experiences to your future aspirations, showing how the role aligns with your career goals. This demonstrates your forward-thinking mindset and commitment to professional growth.

3. WHAT MADE YOU APPLY FOR THIS POSITION?

Tips

1. **Show Genuine Interest:** When answering this question, it's important to convey your genuine interest in the role and the company. Highlight specific aspects of the job and the organization that attracted you. This shows the interviewer that you have done your homework and are sincerely interested in what the company offers. Avoid generic statements; instead, focus on what makes this opportunity unique and exciting for you.

2. **Align with Career Goals:** Demonstrating how this position aligns with your long-term career goals is essential. This not only shows that you are strategic in your career planning but also that you view this role as a significant step in your professional journey. Discuss how the responsibilities and opportunities offered by the role align with your aspirations and contribute to your overall career trajectory.

3. **Highlight Relevant Skills:** Emphasize the skills and experiences that make you a strong candidate for the position. This helps the interviewer see how you can immediately add value to the team and the company. Focus on the specific competencies that align with the job description, and mention how you've successfully applied these skills in your previous roles.

4. **Be Specific:** Avoid vague or broad statements. Instead, provide specific reasons why this job and company stand out to you. Reference aspects such as the company's culture, values, projects, or recent achievements that resonate with you. Specificity not only demonstrates your interest but also shows that you have a clear understanding of what the company does and how you can contribute.

Response Framework

1. **Express Enthusiasm for the Role:** Start by clearly expressing your genuine interest in the position. Mention what initially attracted you to the role, whether it was the job description, the company's reputation, or specific aspects of the position that align with your passions. This sets a positive tone and demonstrates your excitement about the opportunity.

2. **Highlight Your Alignment with the Company:** Discuss how your values, professional interests, or career aspirations align with the company's mission, culture, or recent achievements. Show that you have done thorough research on the company and explain why it stands out to you as a desirable place to work. This illustrates that your interest is both specific and informed.

3. **Connect the Role to Your Career Goals:** Explain how this position fits into your long-term career goals. Identify specific responsibilities or challenges within the role that align with your professional aspirations. This demonstrates that you are not only looking for a job but are also strategically planning your career path.

4. **Showcase Relevant Skills and Experiences:** Link your past experiences and key skills to the requirements of the position. Highlight how your background has prepared you to excel in this role by drawing parallels between the job responsibilities and your own professional achievements. This reinforces your suitability for the position.

5. **Discuss Your Future Contribution:** Conclude by outlining what you hope to achieve in this role and how you envision contributing to the company's success. Mention any goals or projects you are excited to tackle, showing that you are forward-thinking and eager to make a positive impact. This final piece shows your commitment to both the role and the company's long-term vision.

Key Takeaways

1. **Genuine Interest:** Demonstrate real enthusiasm for the role and the company. Specificity is key—discuss concrete aspects that attracted you to the position and the organization.

2. **Career Alignment:** Clearly explain how the position aligns with your long-term career goals. This shows that you're strategic about your career path and see this role as a key step in your professional development.

3. **Relevant Skills:** Emphasize the skills and experiences that make you a strong candidate. Focus on how your background aligns with the job requirements, and provide examples to illustrate your capabilities.

4. **Specificity:** Be detailed in explaining why this job and company stand out to you. Avoid generic responses by referencing specific aspects of the role and the company that align with your interests and values.

4. WHAT ARE YOUR CAREER GOALS?

<u>**Tips**</u>

1. **Be Specific:** When discussing your career goals, clarity is key. Outline both short-term and long-term objectives, ensuring you provide a detailed picture of your aspirations. Avoid vague statements; instead, focus on specific roles, skills, or achievements you aim to reach. This specificity demonstrates that you have a well-thought-out plan and are actively working towards it. Being specific also makes your goals more believable and achievable in the eyes of the interviewer, showing that you're serious about your career development.

2. **Align with the Job:** It's crucial that your career goals align closely with the position you're applying for. This shows the interviewer that you view this role as a logical step in your career path and that you're genuinely interested in growing with the company. Discuss how the role fits into your broader career plan and how it can help you achieve your professional aspirations. This alignment also reinforces your commitment to the position and the company, making you a more attractive candidate.

3. **Show Progression:** Illustrate how your career goals have evolved over time. Highlight key experiences and learning opportunities that have shaped your professional journey and prepared you for this role. Discuss how previous roles have contributed to your development and how this position can further your growth. This demonstrates your ability to grow and adapt, qualities that are highly valued by employers.

4. **Be Realistic:** While ambition is important, your career goals should be grounded in reality. Setting attainable goals shows that you have a pragmatic approach to your career and understand the necessary steps to reach your objectives. This balance of ambition and realism makes your goals more credible, showing that you are thoughtful about your professional development.

<u>**Response Framework**</u>

1. **Introduce Your Career Vision:** Begin by presenting a clear and concise overview of your career aspirations. Include both short-term and long-term goals to give a comprehensive picture of your professional journey. This sets the stage for the rest of your response and indicates that you have a strategic approach to your career development.

2. **Outline Short-Term Goals:** Discuss your immediate career objectives, focusing on the specific skills, experiences, or milestones you aim to achieve in the near future. Explain how the position you are applying for fits into these goals, highlighting the opportunities it provides for growth and learning. This demonstrates that you are deliberate about your next career step and view this role as integral to your progress.

3. **Articulate Long-Term Goals:** Next, describe your vision for your long-term career trajectory. Identify the areas of expertise you want to develop, the positions you aspire to attain, or the impact you hope to make in your field. This part of the response shows that you have a clear direction and are committed to achieving sustained professional growth over time.

4. **Connect Goals to the Role:** Explain how the role you are applying for aligns with your career goals. Highlight how the responsibilities, challenges, and opportunities presented by the position will help you achieve both your short-term and long-term objectives. This connection underscores your suitability for the role and your enthusiasm for contributing to the organization.

5. **Conclude with Future Aspirations:** Wrap up by discussing how this role serves as a key step in your career journey. Mention the specific skills or experiences you hope to gain and how they will propel you toward your ultimate career goals. This forward-thinking perspective emphasizes your commitment to continuous development and positions you as a candidate who is eager to grow with the company.

Key Takeaways

1. **Specificity:** Clearly articulate your short-term and long-term career goals. Avoid vague language and be precise about what you want to achieve. This clarity helps the interviewer understand your career direction and how you plan to get there.

2. **Alignment:** Ensure your goals align with the position you're applying for. Show that this role is a logical and meaningful step in your career path. Demonstrating this alignment makes you a more compelling candidate.

3. **Progression:** Highlight how your career goals have evolved over time and how previous experiences have shaped them. This illustrates your ability to learn and grow, making you a valuable asset to any team.

4. **Realism:** Set achievable, realistic goals. This balance of ambition and practicality demonstrates that you have a thoughtful and measured approach to your career development. It reassures the interviewer that you're not only driven but also grounded in your expectations.

5. WHY DID YOU CHOOSE YOUR MAJOR?

Tips

1. **Reflect Personal Interests:** When explaining why you chose your major, focus on how your personal interests and passions played a role in your decision. Discuss the aspects of the field that naturally drew your attention and how they align with your inherent abilities and curiosities. This shows that your choice was made thoughtfully, based on genuine enthusiasm rather than external pressures or convenience. Emphasizing your personal connection to the subject matter can make your explanation more compelling and relatable.

2. **Link to Career Goals:** Clearly articulate how your major ties into your long-term career aspirations. Demonstrating that your choice was part of a strategic plan for your professional future highlights your foresight and commitment. Discuss how the skills and knowledge gained from your major will help you achieve your career objectives. This not only shows that you are goal-oriented but also that you have been deliberate in aligning your education with your professional path.

3. **Highlight Skills and Knowledge:** Focus on the specific skills and knowledge you acquired through your major that are relevant to the job you are applying for. This includes technical abilities, critical thinking, problem-solving, or any other competencies that are pertinent to the role. By connecting your academic experiences to the demands of the job, you make a strong case for your preparedness and suitability for the position.

4. **Use Personal Stories:** Incorporating personal stories or experiences can make your response more engaging and memorable. These anecdotes can illustrate the moment you realized your passion for the subject or how you overcame challenges in your studies. Personal stories add a layer of authenticity to your response, helping the interviewer see the genuine motivation behind your choices.

Response Framework

1. **Introduce Your Major and Motivation:** Begin by clearly stating your major and briefly explaining the key factors that influenced your choice. These might include personal interests, academic strengths, or external influences such as mentors or industry trends. This introduction sets the foundation for your response and provides context for your decision-making process.

2. **Highlight Intellectual and Personal Interests:** Delve into specific aspects of the subject matter that intrigued you and motivated you to pursue this major. Focus on particular topics, theories, or concepts that sparked your interest and kept you engaged throughout your studies. This section should convey your genuine passion and intellectual curiosity, showing that your choice was driven by a deep-seated interest in the field.

3. **Align with Career Goals:** Discuss how your major aligns with your long-term career aspirations. Explain the connection between your academic background and your career plans, demonstrating that your choice was strategic and informed by a clear vision of your future. This shows that you have been thoughtful and purposeful in your educational journey, with a focus on achieving specific career objectives.

4. **Emphasize Relevant Skills and Knowledge:** Identify the key skills and knowledge you gained through your major that are applicable to the job you are applying for. Highlight how these competencies have been developed through coursework, projects, or practical experiences, and explain how they prepare you to succeed in your desired role. This section demonstrates that your academic training is directly relevant and valuable to your professional pursuits.

5. **Connect with a Personal Experience:** Conclude by sharing a personal story or experience that exemplifies your commitment to your major. This could be an academic project, a challenge you faced, or a defining moment that reaffirmed your choice. A personal anecdote adds depth to your response, making it more memorable and relatable to the interviewer.

Key Takeaways

1. **Reflect Personal Interests:** Ensure your explanation emphasizes how your personal interests and passions influenced your decision to pursue your major. This connection adds depth and authenticity to your response.

2. **Link to Career Goals:** Clearly demonstrate how your major aligns with your long-term career aspirations. This alignment shows that you have been strategic and deliberate in your academic choices, which strengthens your overall candidacy.

3. **Highlight Skills and Knowledge:** Focus on the relevant skills and knowledge gained from your major that directly prepare you for the job at hand. This makes your academic background appear highly relevant and valuable to the employer.

4. **Use Personal Stories:** Incorporate personal stories to make your explanation more engaging and memorable. These anecdotes help to personalize your response, making it more impactful and relatable to the interviewer.

6. WHAT DO YOU KNOW ABOUT OUR COMPANY?

Tips

1. **Research Thoroughly:** Before your interview, invest time in learning about the company's history, mission, values, products, and services. Additionally, familiarize yourself with recent news, major achievements, and the company's position within the industry. Demonstrating a deep understanding of the company will show that you are well-prepared and genuinely interested in being part of their team. This level of preparation also allows you to discuss the company with confidence, which can help you stand out from other candidates.

2. **Highlight Key Aspects:** Focus on specific elements of the company that genuinely resonate with you. These could include its mission, corporate culture, recent innovations, or achievements. Highlighting these aspects shows that you have done thorough research and that you share a connection with the company's core values or strategic direction. This targeted approach makes your interest in the company more relevant and personal.

3. **Align with Your Values:** Explain how the company's mission and values align with your own professional goals and personal beliefs. By drawing this connection, you emphasize that you see a strong cultural fit and are enthusiastic about contributing to the company's ongoing success. Employers are often looking for candidates who will not only perform well but also integrate seamlessly into their organizational culture.

4. **Be Specific:** Avoid making generic statements that could apply to any company. Instead, use detailed examples from your research to illustrate why this particular company stands out to you. Mention specific projects, company values, or industry contributions that you admire. This specificity will make your response more credible and tailored to the organization.

Response Framework

1. **Express Genuine Interest:** Begin by articulating your genuine interest in the company. Mention how you became aware of the company and what initially drew your attention, whether it was its industry leadership, innovative products, or strong corporate values. This sets a positive and engaged tone for your response, showing that your interest is both informed and sincere.

2. **Provide a Concise Company Overview:** Offer a brief summary of the company's background, including its history, mission, and core values. Focus on elements that are widely recognized and central to the company's identity. This might include its founding principles, growth trajectory, or its role within the industry. This overview should demonstrate your understanding of the company's position in the market and its core objectives.

3. **Highlight Recent Achievements and Initiatives:** Discuss any recent milestones, accomplishments, or strategic initiatives that the company has undertaken. This could include product launches, market expansions, awards, or significant partnerships. Mentioning recent news or developments shows that you are not only knowledgeable about the company's past but are also keeping up with its current trajectory and future potential.

4. **Align with Company Culture and Values:** Explain how the company's culture and values resonate with your own professional goals and personal values. Identify specific aspects of the company's work environment—such as its focus on innovation, collaboration, or sustainability—that appeal to you. This alignment indicates that you would be a strong cultural fit and could thrive within the company's environment.

5. **Connect Personally, If Relevant:** If applicable, share a personal connection or story that illustrates why you feel particularly drawn to the company. This could be an experience, a mentor's influence, or a passion that aligns with the company's mission. Personalizing your response adds depth and relatability, making your interest in the company more memorable and impactful.

Key Takeaways

1. **Research Thoroughly:** Conduct detailed research into the company's history, mission, values, and recent achievements. This will show that you are well-prepared and genuinely interested in joining their team.

2. **Highlight Key Aspects:** Focus on specific aspects of the company that resonate with you. This demonstrates your understanding and appreciation of what makes the company unique, making your interest more compelling.

3. **Align with Your Values:** Draw connections between the company's values and your own professional goals. This emphasizes that you see a strong cultural fit and are enthusiastic about contributing to the company's success.

4. **Be Specific:** Use detailed examples from your research to avoid generic statements. Specificity in your response shows that your interest in the company is well-founded and based on a deep understanding of its operations and culture.

7. HOW DID YOU HEAR ABOUT THIS JOB?

<u>Tips</u>

1. **Be Honest:** When responding to this question, it's important to be straightforward about how you discovered the job opportunity. Whether you found the position on a job board, the company's website, through a referral, or via social media, transparency is essential. Honest responses help build trust with the interviewer, showing that you are genuine in your interest.

2. **Highlight Your Enthusiasm:** Convey your excitement about the job and the company. Expressing enthusiasm demonstrates that you are not only interested in the position but also eager to contribute to the company. This can set a positive tone for the rest of the interview.

3. **Mention Your Research:** If you took the time to research the company or the role after finding the job posting, mention it. This shows that you are proactive and have a genuine interest in the company. It also indicates that you are serious about the opportunity and have taken steps to ensure it's the right fit for you.

4. **Acknowledge the Source:** If you were referred to the job by someone, mention their name (with their permission) and your relationship to them. This not only adds a personal touch to your application but can also strengthen your candidacy, as referrals often carry weight with hiring managers.

<u>Response Framework</u>

1. **State How You Found the Opportunity:** Start by clearly stating how you discovered the job opening. Whether it was through a job board, the company's website, a professional network, or another source, be specific about the channel that brought the opportunity to your attention. This establishes the context for your interest in the role.

2. **Contextualize Your Interest:** Provide a brief explanation of why this job caught your eye. Highlight any aspects of the role, company, or industry that particularly stood out to you. This could be related to your career goals, the company's reputation, or the alignment of the role with your skills and experiences. This step helps to show that your application is thoughtful and intentional.

3. **Express Enthusiasm:** Convey your excitement about the position and the company. Emphasize what attracts you to this specific opportunity, whether it's the chance to work on innovative projects, be part of a dynamic team, or contribute to a mission you believe in. This demonstrates your genuine interest in the role and your eagerness to contribute to the company's success.

4. **Mention Any Additional Research:** If applicable, discuss any further research you conducted after learning about the job. Mention visiting the company's website, reviewing recent news, or exploring

their products and services. This shows that you've taken the initiative to learn more about the organization and are serious about your application.

5. **Acknowledge Referrals or Connections:** If you were referred to the job by someone, acknowledge that connection. Briefly mention who referred you and your relationship with them, explaining how they know you and why they thought you would be a good fit for the role. This can add credibility to your application and strengthen your candidacy.

Key Takeaways

1. **Be Honest:** Always provide a clear and honest explanation of how you found out about the job. Authenticity is key to building trust with your interviewer and showing that you are genuinely interested in the opportunity.

2. **Highlight Your Enthusiasm:** Demonstrate your excitement about the job and the company. This not only reflects positively on your attitude but also shows that you are motivated and eager to contribute.

3. **Mention Your Research:** If you conducted any research about the company or role after discovering the job, be sure to mention it. This indicates that you are diligent and proactive, qualities that are highly valued by employers.

4. **Acknowledge the Source:** If a referral played a role in your application, be sure to acknowledge it. This adds a personal element to your response and can enhance your credibility, especially if the referral comes from someone respected within the company.

8. WHAT MOTIVATES YOU?

Tips

1. **Be Authentic:** When answering this question, focus on what genuinely drives you in your professional life. Authenticity is crucial because it helps the interviewer understand your core values and work ethic. A sincere response will resonate more effectively and give insight into what keeps you engaged and productive at work.

2. **Align with the Role:** It's important to connect your motivations with the specific role you are applying for. Show how the job's responsibilities and environment align with what drives you. This not only demonstrates that you are a good fit for the position but also that you are likely to stay motivated and perform well in the role.

3. **Highlight Professional and Personal Motivations:** A well-rounded answer includes both professional and personal motivations. Discuss how these motivations influence your approach to work and your drive to succeed. This approach helps paint a complete picture of what inspires you and how it translates into your professional life.

4. **Provide Examples:** Illustrate your motivations with examples from your past experiences. Specific examples make your response more tangible and credible, allowing the interviewer to better understand how your motivations have shaped your career.

Response Framework

1. **Identify Core Motivations:** Begin by clearly identifying the key areas that generally motivate you in your professional life. These could be related to challenges, achieving excellence, contributing to

meaningful work, or personal growth. Establishing these core motivations upfront sets the stage for a focused and cohesive response.

2. **Professional Drivers:** Delve into the specific professional factors that drive you, such as the satisfaction of meeting goals, the excitement of problem-solving, the desire for continuous learning, or the fulfillment from collaborative work. Relate these drivers to your career trajectory, highlighting how they have influenced your success in previous roles. This shows that your motivations are not only theoretical but have practical applications in your work.

3. **Personal Influences:** Incorporate personal motivations that influence your professional life. These could include the pursuit of work-life balance, the desire to make a positive impact, or the importance of personal growth and development. Explain how these personal motivations integrate with your career, providing a more holistic view of what drives you.

4. **Connection to the Role:** Conclude by tying your motivations to the role you are applying for. Discuss specific elements of the job that align with what drives you, such as opportunities for innovation, leadership, or professional development. This demonstrates that you have thoroughly considered how this position will fulfill your personal and professional aspirations, reinforcing your enthusiasm and fit for the role.

Key Takeaways

1. **Be Authentic:** Reflect on what genuinely motivates you in your professional life and express this clearly. Authenticity is key to making your response compelling and believable.

2. **Align with the Role:** Ensure your motivations are connected to the job you are applying for. Show that the role's responsibilities and culture resonate with what drives you, making you an ideal fit for the position.

3. **Highlight Professional and Personal Motivations:** Balance your answer by including both professional and personal sources of motivation. This gives a more complete picture of what inspires you and how it impacts your work.

4. **Provide Examples:** Use specific examples from your past experiences to back up your points. Examples add credibility to your response and help the interviewer understand how your motivations have guided your career decisions.

9. DESCRIBE YOUR IDEAL WORK ENVIRONMENT.

Tips

1. **Be Specific:** When discussing your ideal work environment, it's important to be clear and precise. Address various aspects such as company culture, physical space, management style, and team dynamics. Specificity demonstrates that you've given thoughtful consideration to what conditions enable you to perform your best. This not only shows self-awareness but also helps the interviewer understand how well you might fit into their existing environment.

2. **Align with the Company:** Before the interview, research the company's culture and work environment. Tailor your description to align with what the company offers, highlighting similarities between your ideal environment and the company's actual environment. This approach shows that you've done your homework and are genuinely interested in the role, enhancing your appeal as a candidate.

3. **Highlight Productivity:** Emphasize how your ideal work environment contributes to your productivity and overall job satisfaction. By doing so, you demonstrate an understanding of your work habits and how specific conditions can help you excel. This focus on productivity is likely to resonate with employers, who are interested in candidates who can thrive and contribute positively in their settings.

4. **Reflect Personal and Professional Needs:** Incorporate both personal and professional elements into your response. Discussing how the environment impacts both your work performance and personal well-being offers a holistic view of your motivations and needs. This balanced approach helps the interviewer see you as a candidate who is thoughtful about your work-life integration.

Response Framework

1. **Introduction:** Begin by emphasizing that your ideal work environment is one that supports both your professional growth and personal well-being. Highlight that this balance is crucial for achieving high levels of productivity and job satisfaction. This sets a foundation for discussing specific elements that create this ideal environment for you.

2. **Company Culture:** Outline the type of company culture that aligns with your values and work style. Whether you thrive in a collaborative, innovative, or results-driven environment, explain how these cultural elements help you perform at your best. This demonstrates that you've thoughtfully considered how your ideal work environment matches the company's culture.

3. **Physical Workspace:** Describe the physical aspects of the work environment that help you stay productive and motivated. Discuss elements such as workspace layout, access to quiet areas for focus, open spaces for collaboration, or the importance of natural light and ergonomic design. This shows that you recognize how the physical setting contributes to your overall effectiveness and comfort at work.

4. **Management Style:** Explain the type of management style that enables you to excel. Whether you value autonomy with supportive oversight, regular feedback, or opportunities for professional development, clarify how these leadership qualities help you succeed. This provides insight into the type of leadership you respond to best and sets expectations for how you work with supervisors.

5. **Team Dynamics:** Describe the team dynamics that enhance your work experience. Highlight the importance of mutual respect, diverse perspectives, strong collaboration, and open communication. Explain how these dynamics contribute to a positive and motivating environment, demonstrating your ability to work well within a team and contribute to a constructive workplace culture.

Key Takeaways

1. **Be Specific:** Clearly articulate the elements of your ideal work environment, focusing on company culture, physical space, management style, and team dynamics. Specificity helps paint a clear picture of the conditions that allow you to excel.

2. **Align with the Company:** Align your description with the company's known culture and environment. Demonstrating this alignment not only shows that you're a good fit but also that you've thoroughly researched the company.

3. **Highlight Productivity:** Focus on how your ideal work environment enhances your productivity. This demonstrates your self-awareness and shows that you understand the conditions under which you perform best.

4. **Reflect Personal and Professional Needs:** Incorporate both personal and professional aspects into your description to provide a well-rounded view of what motivates and engages you. This balanced approach can help the interviewer see how you would fit into their team.

10. WHAT ARE YOUR LONG-TERM CAREER ASPIRATIONS?

Tips

1. **Be Honest and Ambitious:** When discussing your long-term career aspirations, honesty is key. Articulate your goals clearly, demonstrating both ambition and practicality. Employers appreciate candidates who are forward-thinking and have a clear vision for their future. Your aspirations should reflect a balance between ambition and realism, showing that you have thought carefully about your career path and are committed to achieving your goals.

2. **Align with the Role:** It's crucial to connect your long-term goals with the position you're applying for. Show the interviewer how this role fits into your broader career plan and how you see yourself growing within the company. This alignment indicates that you view the organization as a place where you can develop and contribute over the long term, which can be very appealing to potential employers.

3. **Highlight Continuous Learning:** Emphasize your commitment to continuous learning and professional development. In today's rapidly changing work environment, showing that you are dedicated to keeping your skills and knowledge up-to-date is important. This also demonstrates that you are proactive in your career development, always seeking to improve and adapt.

4. **Showcase Leadership and Impact:** If your long-term goals include leadership or making a significant impact within your field, make sure to highlight this. Discuss your aspirations to take on greater responsibilities, mentor others, or lead projects that contribute meaningfully to the organization. This not only shows your desire to grow but also your potential to drive positive change within the company.

Response Framework

1. **Introduction:** Start by expressing your passion for your industry or field. Outline a broad vision of where you see yourself in the long term. This sets a positive tone and provides context for the specific goals you will discuss. Your introduction should convey enthusiasm and a clear direction for your career path.

2. **Professional Growth:** Discuss your commitment to continuous learning and professional development. Outline your goals related to acquiring new skills, staying current with industry trends, and advancing your expertise. This shows that you are proactive about your career growth and are dedicated to remaining competitive in your field. Highlight how these efforts will contribute to your long-term success.

3. **Leadership Aspirations:** If applicable, mention your desire to take on leadership roles in the future. Explain how you aim to develop the necessary skills and experience to lead effectively. Discuss your interest in mentoring others, driving team success, and contributing to the company's strategic goals. This helps the interviewer envision you as a future leader who is invested in both personal and organizational growth.

4. **Impact and Contribution:** Talk about the broader impact you hope to have in your career. This could involve making a difference in your industry, advancing innovation, supporting sustainability, or promoting social responsibility. Emphasize your desire to contribute to meaningful change and your commitment to working on initiatives that align with your values. This demonstrates that your aspirations are not solely focused on personal achievement but also on making a positive impact.

Key Takeaways

1. **Be Honest and Ambitious:** Articulate your long-term goals clearly, balancing ambition with realism. Employers want to see that you are driven and have a practical plan for your career.

2. **Align with the Role:** Connect your long-term aspirations to the job you're applying for, showing how this position is a stepping stone in your career journey. This demonstrates that you see a future with the company and are committed to growing within it.

3. **Highlight Continuous Learning:** Emphasize your dedication to continuous learning and professional development. This shows that you are proactive in keeping your skills relevant and are always looking for ways to grow.

4. **Showcase Leadership and Impact:** If your goals include leadership or making a significant impact, highlight this in your response. Demonstrating your desire to take on more responsibility and contribute to the company's success makes you a more attractive candidate.

CHAPTER 2
SKILLS AND STRENGTHS

11. WHAT ARE YOUR STRENGTHS?

Tips

1. **Be Specific:** When discussing your strengths, it's important to select qualities that are directly relevant to the job you're applying for. Tailoring your strengths to match the job requirements helps the interviewer see how you would be a strong fit for the role. Avoid vague statements and instead focus on skills or attributes that will clearly benefit the company in this position.

2. **Provide Examples:** Concrete examples are crucial in making your strengths believable and relatable. When you discuss a strength, back it up with a specific instance where you successfully applied this strength in a professional setting. This approach not only supports your claim but also demonstrates your ability to apply your strengths in real-world situations.

3. **Show Impact:** It's not enough to just mention your strengths; you need to highlight the positive outcomes they have led to in your previous roles. Discuss the tangible results or achievements that your strengths have contributed to. This could include increased efficiency, successful project completions, or improved team dynamics, showing that your strengths have had a meaningful impact on your work.

4. **Be Honest and Humble:** While it's important to be confident in discussing your strengths, it's equally important to maintain a sense of humility. Avoid overstating your abilities, and be sincere about what you bring to the table. This balance will help you come across as both competent and approachable, which is appealing to employers.

Response Framework

1. **Introduction:** Begin by providing a concise overview of your core strengths, particularly those most relevant to the position you're applying for. This introduction should give the interviewer a quick understanding of the key attributes that define your professional capabilities. By highlighting these strengths upfront, you set the stage for a more detailed discussion.

2. **Strength 1 - Identification and Application:** Identify your first strength and explain why it is relevant to the role. Discuss how this strength has been a consistent asset in your career. Highlight how it has enabled you to achieve specific goals or overcome challenges in your previous roles. Focus on the value this strength has added to your past positions and how it can be leveraged in the role you're interviewing for.

3. **Strength 2 - Impact and Contribution:** Introduce your second strength, emphasizing its impact on your professional journey. Describe how you've utilized this strength to contribute positively to your team or organization. This could include improving processes, driving results, or enhancing collaboration. Ensure that your explanation clearly demonstrates how this strength aligns with the requirements of the new role.

4. **Strength 3 - Results and Future Potential:** Discuss your third strength, detailing how it has led to measurable successes in your career. Whether it's a technical skill, a personal trait, or a specific expertise, show how this strength has produced tangible results. Explain how you intend to apply this strength in the new role to contribute to the company's objectives and drive future success.

5. **Future Application:** Conclude by tying all your strengths together, explaining how they collectively equip you to excel in the position you're applying for. Outline your vision for how these strengths will help you achieve success in the role and support the company's goals. This final piece should reinforce your confidence in your ability to make a meaningful impact in the new position.

Key Takeaways

1. **Be Specific:** Choose strengths that align closely with the job you are applying for, making it clear how these qualities will help you succeed in the role.

2. **Provide Examples:** Use specific examples from your past experiences to back up each strength, ensuring that your claims are credible and relatable to the interviewer.

3. **Show Impact:** Highlight the positive impact your strengths have had in previous roles, emphasizing measurable results or significant achievements that demonstrate your effectiveness.

4. **Be Honest and Humble:** Approach the discussion of your strengths with confidence, but avoid exaggeration. Maintaining a balance between confidence and humility will make your response more authentic and compelling.

12. WHAT SKILLS CAN YOU BRING TO THIS ROLE?

Tips

1. **Be Relevant:** When responding to this question, focus on the skills that are most relevant to the job you're applying for. Start by carefully reviewing the job description to identify the key skills the employer is seeking. Tailor your response to highlight these skills, demonstrating that you understand the role's requirements and are well-suited to meet them. This approach shows the interviewer that you have thoughtfully considered how your skill set aligns with the company's needs.

2. **Provide Examples:** To make your response more impactful, support each skill you mention with a concrete example from your past experience. This not only makes your response more credible but also gives the interviewer a clear picture of how you have successfully applied these skills in real-world situations. Discuss the context in which you used the skill, the actions you took, and the results you achieved, making sure these examples are relevant to the role you are seeking.

3. **Show Impact:** Highlighting the positive impact of your skills is crucial. When discussing each skill, mention specific outcomes or achievements that resulted from your application of that skill. This could include quantifiable results like increased efficiency, improved team performance, or successful project outcomes. Demonstrating the tangible benefits of your skills reinforces your value as a candidate.

4. **Be Honest and Confident:** It's important to be honest about your skills while also conveying confidence in your abilities. Avoid exaggeration and focus on the strengths that you genuinely possess. Confidence in your response indicates self-awareness and a solid understanding of how your skills can contribute to the success of the company.

Response Framework

1. **Introduction:** Begin by providing a concise summary of the key skills you possess that are directly relevant to the role you are applying for. This introduction should highlight your core competencies and set the stage for a deeper discussion of how these skills align with the job requirements.

2. **Skill 1 - Identification and Relevance:** Identify your most relevant skill and explain why it is crucial for the role. Detail how this skill has been essential in your previous positions, focusing on the impact it has had on your performance and the value it added to your team or organization. Discuss the context in which you've applied this skill and the positive outcomes that resulted, ensuring that the example clearly illustrates your proficiency.

3. **Skill 2 - Demonstrated Impact:** Present your second key skill, elaborating on its relevance to the role. Explain how this skill has contributed to your success in previous roles, providing a clear example that showcases your ability to apply it effectively. Emphasize any measurable outcomes or significant achievements that highlight your competence and the potential benefits of bringing this skill to the new role.

4. **Skill 3 - Application and Outcomes:** Discuss a third skill that is important for the position, illustrating its application with a specific instance from your professional experience. Describe the situation, your approach, and the positive results achieved. This example should further demonstrate your qualifications and align with the requirements of the job, reinforcing your suitability for the role.

5. **Future Application and Contribution:** Conclude by discussing how you plan to leverage these skills in the new role to contribute to the company's success. Outline how these strengths will help you achieve the goals of the position and support the company's objectives. This final point demonstrates your forward-thinking mindset and eagerness to apply your skills to help the organization thrive.

Key Takeaways

1. **Be Relevant:** Focus on the skills that are directly relevant to the job you're applying for. Tailor your response to the role's requirements to demonstrate your fit for the position.

2. **Provide Examples:** Support each skill with a specific example from your past experience. This makes your response more credible and allows the interviewer to see how you've successfully applied these skills in real situations.

3. **Show Impact:** Highlight the positive impact your skills have had in previous roles. Discuss specific outcomes or achievements to reinforce the value you bring to the role.

4. **Be Honest and Confident:** Be truthful about your skills and present them with confidence. This shows that you are self-aware and genuinely capable of contributing to the company's success.

13. HOW DO YOUR SKILLS ALIGN WITH THE REQUIREMENTS OF THIS JOB?

<u>Tips</u>

1. **Be Relevant:** Tailor your response by focusing on the skills that are most pertinent to the job description. Before the interview, thoroughly review the job requirements to identify the key skills the employer is seeking. Highlight these specific skills in your response to demonstrate that you are well-suited for the role and can meet its demands effectively. This shows that you've done your homework and understand what the company is looking for in a candidate.

2. **Use Examples:** Providing specific examples from your past experiences is crucial. These examples not only make your response more credible but also help the interviewer visualize how you have applied your skills in real-world situations. When you discuss each skill, illustrate it with a concrete example that highlights your ability to use that skill effectively in a professional setting.

3. **Highlight Achievements:** Focus on the achievements that demonstrate your ability to fulfill the job requirements successfully. Mentioning specific results, such as improved performance metrics or completed projects, showcases the impact of your skills. This reinforces your qualifications and gives the interviewer confidence in your potential to contribute to their organization.

4. **Be Confident:** Express confidence in your ability to excel in the role. Confidence, paired with honesty, conveys that you are self-assured and capable of taking on the responsibilities of the position. This positive attitude is attractive to employers who are looking for candidates who believe in their own capabilities and are ready to add value to the team.

<u>Response Framework</u>

1. **Introduction:** Begin with a brief overview that highlights how your key skills are well-suited to the job's specific requirements. This introduction should clearly state your understanding of the role's demands and set the stage for a detailed discussion on how your skills align with these expectations.

2. **Skill 1 - Alignment and Evidence:** Identify your most relevant skill and explain how it directly matches one of the core requirements of the job. Describe a situation from your past experience where you successfully applied this skill, focusing on the actions you took and the positive outcomes achieved. This example should clearly demonstrate your proficiency and relevance to the role.

3. **Skill 2 - Demonstrated Competence:** Present another critical skill that aligns with the job's needs. Detail how this skill has been pivotal in your previous roles, providing a specific example that showcases your ability to excel in this area. Highlight any measurable results or significant contributions that underscore the impact of this skill in a professional setting.

4. **Skill 3 - Further Reinforcement:** Discuss a third key skill that is pertinent to the position. Illustrate its relevance by sharing an example from your experience where this skill was crucial to achieving success. Ensure that this example aligns with the job's requirements, further reinforcing your qualifications and your ability to meet the role's expectations.

5. **Future Application and Contribution:** Conclude by discussing how you intend to apply these skills in the new role to contribute to the company's goals. Emphasize your enthusiasm for using your strengths to support the organization's success and your proactive approach to making a positive impact in the role. This forward-looking statement ties your past experience to the potential contributions you can make in the future.

<u>Key Takeaways</u>

1. **Be Relevant:** Focus on the skills that are directly relevant to the job. Tailoring your response to the role's specific requirements demonstrates that you are a good fit for the position.

2. **Use Examples:** Illustrate each skill with a specific example from your past experiences. This makes your response more credible and helps the interviewer see how you've applied your skills in real-world situations.

3. **Highlight Achievements:** Emphasize the accomplishments that demonstrate your ability to meet the job requirements successfully. Mentioning specific results shows that you can deliver tangible benefits.

4. **Be Confident:** Present your skills with confidence, showing that you believe in your ability to excel in the role. Confidence, coupled with honesty, leaves a positive impression and underscores your readiness for the position.

14. WHAT SETS YOU APART FROM OTHER CANDIDATES?

Tips:

1. **Highlight Unique Skills:** When addressing what sets you apart, focus on specific skills or experiences that make you unique compared to other candidates. Consider what you bring to the table that others may not. This could be a blend of technical expertise, soft skills, or industry knowledge that directly relates to the job. Emphasizing these attributes demonstrates your unique value proposition to the employer.

2. **Use Specific Examples:** To make your claims more credible, back them up with concrete examples from your previous work. Highlight scenarios where your unique skills led to positive outcomes, such as increased efficiency, improved processes, or successful project completions. These examples not only validate your claims but also show how you can replicate that success in the new role.

3. **Demonstrate Cultural Fit:** Understanding the company's culture and values is crucial. Express how your personal values and professional approach align with the company's mission. Showing that you fit into the company's culture indicates that you would not only perform well but also integrate smoothly into their work environment.

4. **Be Confident:** Confidence is key when discussing what sets you apart. Without exaggerating, present your skills and experiences with assurance, making it clear that you believe in your ability to excel in the role. A confident delivery reinforces your suitability for the position and leaves a strong impression on the interviewer.

Response Framework:

1. **Introduction:** Start by briefly summarizing the key attributes that make you distinct from other candidates. Focus on a unique combination of skills, experiences, and qualities that are particularly relevant to the role. This sets the stage for a detailed exploration of what makes you a standout choice.

2. **Unique Skill 1 - Distinctive Expertise:** Identify your most distinctive skill or area of expertise that is crucial for the job. Explain why this skill is particularly valuable in the context of the role you're applying for. Describe how this skill has contributed to your success in the past, highlighting a specific situation where it made a significant impact. This helps demonstrate the practical value you bring to the table.

3. **Unique Skill 2 - Specialized Experience:** Next, discuss another key skill or experience that differentiates you from others. Focus on a specialized area where you have deep experience or have achieved notable success. Provide a clear example of how this experience has led to positive

outcomes in your previous roles, emphasizing how it equips you to excel in the position you are seeking.

4. **Unique Skill 3 - Personal Qualities or Attributes:** Introduce a personal quality or attribute that complements your technical skills and experience. This could be something like a strong work ethic, a collaborative mindset, or an ability to adapt to change. Explain how this quality enhances your professional capabilities and how it aligns with the needs of the role and the company culture.

5. **Cultural Fit and Enthusiasm:** Conclude by discussing how your values and professional ethos align with the company's culture and mission. Highlight your enthusiasm for contributing to the company's goals and your eagerness to bring your unique strengths to the team. This reinforces your fit not just as a candidate with the right skills but also as someone who will thrive within the organization's environment.

Key Takeaways:

1. **Highlight Unique Skills:** Emphasize the specific skills or experiences that set you apart from other candidates. Focus on attributes that make you particularly well-suited for the role.

2. **Use Specific Examples:** Reinforce your claims with concrete examples from your previous work, illustrating how your unique skills have led to successful outcomes. This approach adds credibility to your response.

3. **Demonstrate Cultural Fit:** Show that you understand the company's culture and values, and explain how you embody these traits. This helps to establish that you are a good fit not just professionally, but also culturally.

4. **Be Confident:** Deliver your response with confidence, clearly presenting your strengths and making a compelling case for why you are the best candidate for the role. Confidence, coupled with evidence-based examples, leaves a lasting positive impression.

15. HOW DO YOU HANDLE STRESSFUL SITUATIONS?

Tips:

1. **Stay Calm:** The ability to remain calm under pressure is crucial in stressful situations. Emphasize your approach to managing stress by discussing techniques like mindfulness, deep breathing, or other methods you use to maintain composure. Being able to control your emotions and stay focused when faced with challenges is a quality employers highly value.

2. **Organize and Prioritize:** Effective organization and prioritization are key to managing stress. Highlight how you assess the situation, prioritize tasks based on urgency, and break down complex tasks into manageable steps. This approach shows that you can handle multiple demands without becoming overwhelmed and can maintain productivity under pressure.

3. **Seek Solutions:** A proactive approach to problem-solving is essential when dealing with stress. Instead of focusing on the problem, emphasize how you quickly assess the situation, identify solutions, and take decisive action. This mindset not only helps in managing stress but also demonstrates your ability to think clearly and effectively in challenging situations.

4. **Team Collaboration:** Stressful situations often require effective teamwork and communication. Discuss how you collaborate with your team to manage stress, share workloads, and find solutions.

Leveraging the strengths of your colleagues and maintaining open lines of communication can ease the pressure and lead to more efficient problem-solving.

Response Framework:

1. **Introduction:** Begin by briefly explaining your general approach to handling stress. Emphasize the importance of staying composed and focused, and introduce the idea that managing stress effectively is key to maintaining productivity and achieving positive outcomes in challenging situations.

2. **Staying Calm and Focused:** Describe how you maintain calmness in stressful situations. Discuss specific techniques you use to manage stress, such as mindfulness practices, deep breathing, or taking a step back to assess the situation. This demonstrates your ability to stay composed under pressure, which is critical for clear thinking and effective decision-making.

3. **Prioritizing and Organizing:** Highlight your approach to organizing and prioritizing tasks when under stress. Explain how you evaluate the situation to determine which tasks require immediate attention and how you break down larger projects into smaller, manageable steps. This shows your ability to manage your workload efficiently, even in high-pressure scenarios.

4. **Problem-Solving Approach:** Focus on your proactive problem-solving skills. Discuss how you handle stress by quickly assessing the situation, identifying potential solutions, and taking decisive action. This illustrates your ability to turn challenges into opportunities and your commitment to finding effective solutions in a timely manner.

5. **Collaboration and Communication:** Conclude by discussing how you leverage teamwork and communication during stressful times. Explain how you collaborate with your colleagues, delegate tasks appropriately, and provide support to ensure that the team works together efficiently. This underscores your ability to lead or contribute to a team under pressure, ensuring that everyone is aligned and working towards a common goal.

Key Takeaways:

1. **Stay Calm:** Emphasize the importance of remaining calm under pressure. Discuss the techniques you use to manage stress and maintain your focus during challenging situations. This demonstrates emotional intelligence and resilience.

2. **Organize and Prioritize:** Highlight your organizational skills and your ability to prioritize tasks effectively in stressful situations. This shows that you can handle multiple demands and maintain productivity under pressure, a key quality employers look for.

3. **Seek Solutions:** Focus on your proactive approach to problem-solving. Explain how you assess stressful situations, identify solutions, and take action to resolve issues. This demonstrates your ability to think clearly and act decisively in challenging scenarios.

4. **Team Collaboration:** Discuss the role of teamwork and communication in managing stress. Highlight how you collaborate with colleagues to share workloads and find solutions, demonstrating your ability to work effectively in a team and contribute to collective success.

16. DESCRIBE A SKILL YOU HAVE RECENTLY DEVELOPED.

Tips:

1. **Be Specific:** Start by identifying the skill you have recently developed. Clearly explain why you chose to focus on this particular skill and its relevance to your career. This shows that your development efforts are intentional and aligned with your professional goals.

2. **Learning Process:** Detail the steps you took to acquire this new skill. This could include formal education, online courses, hands-on practice, or seeking mentorship. Highlighting your learning process demonstrates your commitment to continuous improvement and your proactive approach to skill development.

3. **Impact:** Discuss how this new skill has positively impacted your work. Provide specific examples that demonstrate the tangible benefits, such as improved efficiency, enhanced performance, or better decision-making. This not only shows the value of the skill but also your ability to apply it effectively.

4. **Future Application:** Conclude by explaining how you plan to use this skill moving forward. Whether it's to enhance your current role, contribute to future projects, or support your long-term career goals, showing foresight in how you will apply this skill demonstrates your dedication to ongoing growth and adding value to your organization.

Response Framework:

1. **Identify the Skill:** Start by clearly identifying the specific skill you have recently developed. Briefly explain why you chose to focus on this particular skill and how it aligns with your professional goals. This introduction sets the context for the skill's relevance to your career and showcases your commitment to continuous improvement.

2. **Detail the Learning Process:** Next, describe the process you followed to develop this skill. Outline the steps you took, such as enrolling in courses, engaging in self-study, seeking mentorship, or practicing regularly. Highlight any challenges you encountered and how you overcame them. This section emphasizes your proactive approach to learning and your ability to persevere through obstacles.

3. **Demonstrate Impact:** Illustrate how this newly acquired skill has positively impacted your work. Provide specific examples that show how the skill has enhanced your performance, contributed to team success, or added value to projects. This part of your response should highlight the practical application of the skill and the tangible benefits it has brought to your professional environment.

4. **Future Application:** Conclude by discussing how you plan to continue using and refining this skill in the future. Explain how it will help you achieve your long-term career goals and contribute to your organization's success. This forward-looking perspective demonstrates your strategic thinking and commitment to leveraging your skills for ongoing professional development.

Key Takeaways:

1. **Be Specific:** Clearly identify the skill you have developed, focusing on its relevance to your career. This demonstrates intentional and strategic personal development.

2. **Learning Process:** Describe the steps you took to develop the skill, highlighting your commitment to learning and your proactive approach to skill acquisition. This showcases your dedication to continuous improvement.

3. **Impact:** Emphasize the tangible benefits that this new skill has brought to your work. Use specific examples to illustrate the positive outcomes, which underscores your ability to apply new knowledge effectively.

4. **Future Application:** Conclude by explaining how you plan to use this skill moving forward. This demonstrates foresight, a commitment to ongoing development, and the ability to leverage your skills to contribute to your organization's success.

17. HOW DO YOU STAY CURRENT WITH INDUSTRY TRENDS?

Tips:

1. **Be Proactive**: Staying updated with industry trends requires a proactive approach. Regularly engage with various sources of information, such as industry publications, newsletters, and social media. Highlight your commitment to consistently seeking out new knowledge. This shows that you are not only aware of the importance of staying current but also take deliberate actions to remain informed.

2. **Continuous Learning**: Emphasize your dedication to continuous learning through formal and informal education. This can include online courses, webinars, and certifications. Your willingness to invest time and effort into learning demonstrates your commitment to professional growth and staying competitive in your field.

3. **Networking**: Networking is an essential component of staying current with industry trends. Discuss how you actively participate in professional associations, attend conferences, and engage with industry peers. Networking provides opportunities to learn from others, share insights, and stay updated on the latest developments.

4. **Application of Knowledge:** It's not enough to simply stay informed—you must also apply what you learn. Explain how you integrate new trends and knowledge into your work. Demonstrating practical application of industry trends shows that you are not just passively consuming information but actively using it to drive innovation and improve performance.

Response Framework:

1. **Proactive Engagement:** Begin by explaining your proactive approach to staying informed about industry trends. Discuss how you regularly engage with key resources such as industry publications, reputable blogs, newsletters, and relevant social media channels. Emphasize that you prioritize staying updated as an integral part of your professional routine, demonstrating your commitment to remaining knowledgeable in your field.

2. **Continuous Learning:** Highlight your dedication to continuous learning as a means of staying current. Describe the various educational opportunities you pursue, such as enrolling in online courses, attending webinars, or obtaining industry-specific certifications. This section should emphasize your active pursuit of knowledge and your desire to stay at the forefront of industry developments, ensuring you are always prepared to adapt to new trends.

3. **Networking and Collaboration:** Discuss the importance of networking in staying informed about industry trends. Explain how you participate in industry events, conferences, and professional associations to connect with other professionals. Networking allows you to exchange ideas, gain diverse perspectives, and stay aware of emerging trends. Mention how you also collaborate with colleagues and peers to discuss new developments and share insights.

4. **Application of Knowledge:** Conclude by explaining how you integrate the knowledge gained from staying current with industry trends into your work. Provide an overview of how you have successfully applied new ideas, technologies, or best practices to enhance your role or contribute to your organization's success. This demonstrates that your efforts to stay informed are not just theoretical but lead to practical, value-added outcomes.

Key Takeaways:

1. **Be Proactive:** Regularly engage with multiple sources to stay informed about the latest industry trends. This proactive approach ensures you remain up-to-date and ready to apply new knowledge.

2. **Continuous Learning:** Invest in your professional development through continuous learning. Engaging in courses, webinars, and certifications helps you stay competitive and knowledgeable in your field.

3. **Networking**: Actively participate in networking activities and industry events. Building and maintaining relationships with professionals in your field provides valuable insights and helps you stay connected with the latest trends.

4. **Application of Knowledge:** Apply the trends and knowledge you acquire to your work. Demonstrating how you integrate new information into your role shows that you are not only informed but also capable of leveraging your knowledge to drive success.

18. WHAT TECHNICAL SKILLS DO YOU HAVE?

Tips:

1. **Be Specific:** When discussing your technical skills, it's crucial to be specific and relevant to the position you're applying for. Avoid broad statements, and instead, focus on particular tools, software, or technologies in which you are proficient. This precision not only demonstrates your expertise but also shows that you have a clear understanding of the role's technical requirements.

2. **Use Examples:** Illustrating your technical skills with real-life examples is key to showcasing your hands-on experience. Describe specific projects or tasks where you effectively utilized these skills. This approach helps the interviewer visualize how your technical abilities translate into tangible results in a professional setting.

3. **Stay Current:** The technology landscape evolves rapidly, so it's important to highlight how you keep your skills up to date. Mention any recent certifications, courses, or self-directed learning initiatives that demonstrate your commitment to continuous improvement. Staying current not only enhances your expertise but also shows your adaptability to new tools and technologies.

4. **Relevance:** Align the technical skills you discuss with the job description. Make sure the skills you highlight are those that the company specifically values and needs. This alignment shows that you have tailored your response to meet the expectations of the role, making you a more attractive candidate.

Response Framework:

1. **Identify Key Technical Skills:** Start by identifying and clearly outlining the technical skills that are most relevant to the job you are applying for. Focus on specific tools, software, programming languages, or technologies you are proficient in, ensuring these skills align with the requirements mentioned in the job description. This initial summary sets the stage for a more detailed exploration of your technical expertise.

2. **Demonstrate Proficiency:** Discuss how you have successfully applied these technical skills in previous roles. Describe specific projects or tasks where your technical abilities played a crucial role, such as improving operational efficiency, solving complex problems, or driving key outcomes. This

section should demonstrate your practical experience and the value you've brought to past employers through your technical expertise.

3. **Emphasize Continuous Learning:** Highlight any recent training, certifications, or ongoing learning experiences that have contributed to enhancing your technical skills. This could include online courses, workshops, or industry certifications that keep you updated with the latest technologies and trends. Emphasizing your commitment to continuous learning shows that you are proactive about staying current in your field.

4. **Align with Role Requirements:** Conclude by aligning your technical skills with the specific needs of the role you're pursuing. Explain how your expertise directly addresses the technical requirements of the job and how you plan to leverage your skills to contribute effectively to the company's goals. This alignment reinforces your suitability for the role and your readiness to make an immediate impact.

Key Takeaways:

1. **Be Specific:** Clearly articulate your technical skills, focusing on those that are most relevant to the job. This specificity demonstrates your expertise and relevance to the role.

2. **Use Examples:** Support your claims with examples from your past experience. Providing tangible examples of how you've applied your technical skills makes your qualifications more convincing.

3. **Stay Current:** Highlight any recent efforts to stay current with industry advancements. Continuous learning is essential in technical fields, and showcasing your commitment to this adds value to your candidacy.

4. **Relevance:** Ensure that the technical skills you highlight are aligned with the job requirements. Demonstrating this alignment shows that you understand the role and are well-prepared to meet its demands.

19. HOW DO YOU PRIORITIZE YOUR TASKS?

Tips:

1. **Be Specific:** Clearly articulate your method for prioritizing tasks. Whether you use a particular framework, tool, or approach, specificity helps the interviewer understand how you manage your workload. This clarity demonstrates your ability to organize and handle multiple responsibilities effectively.

2. **Use Examples:** Providing real-life examples of how you've prioritized tasks in the past adds credibility to your method. It shows that you can apply your prioritization techniques in real-world scenarios, giving the interviewer confidence in your ability to manage tasks efficiently in the role.

3. **Mention Tools:** If you use specific tools or techniques for prioritizing tasks, be sure to mention them. Whether it's a project management software, a scheduling tool, or a particular methodology, discussing these tools shows that you have a structured and systematic approach to managing your work.

4. **Link to Role:** Ensure that your prioritization method is relevant to the job you're applying for. Tailoring your response to the specific demands of the role demonstrates that you understand the job's requirements and are prepared to manage tasks effectively within that context.

Response Framework:

1. **Describe Your Approach:** Begin by outlining your systematic approach to prioritizing tasks. Explain the criteria you use to determine the urgency and importance of tasks, such as deadlines, project goals, or the potential impact on the team or organization. This sets the foundation for a well-structured response that demonstrates your ability to manage time and resources effectively.

2. **Explain Your Methodology:** Detail the specific steps you take to prioritize tasks. This could involve categorizing tasks by urgency, setting up a task list, or using the Eisenhower Matrix (urgent/important grid) to decide which tasks to address first. Highlight how you break down larger tasks into manageable steps to maintain focus and momentum. This showcases your ability to handle complex workloads efficiently.

3. **Discuss Tools and Techniques:** Mention any tools or techniques you use to support your prioritization process. This might include project management software like Asana or Trello, calendar systems, or productivity apps that help you stay organized. Discuss how these tools assist you in tracking progress, setting reminders, and ensuring that nothing falls through the cracks.

4. **Align with Job Requirements:** Conclude by connecting your prioritization skills to the specific needs of the role you are applying for. Discuss how your method will enable you to meet the job's demands, manage multiple responsibilities, and contribute effectively to the company's objectives. This reinforces your ability to excel in the position by bringing a disciplined approach to task management.

Key Takeaways:

1. **Be Specific:** Describe your prioritization method in detail to show that you have a clear and structured approach to managing tasks.

2. **Use Examples:** Illustrate your method with examples from your past experiences to demonstrate its effectiveness and relevance.

3. **Mention Tools:** Highlight any productivity tools or techniques you use, showing that you are equipped with the right tools to manage your workload efficiently.

4. **Link to Role:** Ensure your approach aligns with the job requirements, demonstrating that you can handle the specific demands of the position effectively.

20. WHAT IS YOUR APPROACH TO PROBLEM-SOLVING?

Tips:

1. **Be Structured:** When discussing your approach to problem-solving, it's important to outline a clear and logical method. This not only demonstrates your ability to think critically but also shows the interviewer that you have a systematic approach to tackling challenges.

2. **Use Examples:** Real-life examples are essential for illustrating your problem-solving skills. They provide concrete evidence of how you apply your approach in practical situations, making your response more relatable and convincing.

3. **Mention Tools:** Highlighting any tools, frameworks, or techniques you use for problem-solving is beneficial. Whether it's a specific methodology like root cause analysis or a tool like SWOT analysis, mentioning these shows that you have a structured approach to resolving issues.

4. **Link to Role:** Make sure to align your problem-solving approach with the specific requirements of the job you're applying for. This demonstrates that you understand the challenges of the role and are equipped to handle them effectively.

Response Framework:

1. **Define the Problem:** Start by explaining how you identify and define the problem. Describe the steps you take to gather relevant information, consult with stakeholders, and ensure a thorough understanding of the issue. Emphasize the importance of accurately defining the problem as the foundation for an effective solution.

2. **Analyze the Problem:** Outline your process for analyzing the problem to uncover its root cause. Discuss the techniques or tools you use to break down the problem into manageable components. Highlight how you seek to understand not just the symptoms but the underlying factors contributing to the issue. This shows your analytical skills and attention to detail.

3. **Generate Possible Solutions:** Describe how you approach generating potential solutions. Focus on your method for brainstorming and evaluating different options, considering their feasibility, risks, and potential impact. Mention the importance of collaboration, if applicable, and how you incorporate diverse perspectives to enhance the solution process. This step demonstrates your ability to think creatively and strategically.

4. **Implement the Solution:** Explain your approach to implementing the chosen solution. Detail how you develop a clear plan, assign responsibilities, and set timelines. Emphasize the importance of communication with stakeholders throughout the process to ensure everyone is aligned. Highlight your ability to adapt the plan as needed based on feedback or changing circumstances.

5. **Evaluate the Outcome:** Conclude by discussing how you evaluate the effectiveness of the solution after implementation. Describe the metrics or methods you use to assess the outcome, gather feedback, and determine if the problem has been fully resolved. Mention how you reflect on the process to identify lessons learned and improve your problem-solving approach in the future.

Key Takeaways:

1. **Be Structured:** Outline a clear, step-by-step approach to problem-solving. This shows that you have a systematic method for tackling challenges and making decisions.

2. **Use Examples:** Provide real-life examples to illustrate your problem-solving skills. This adds credibility to your approach and shows how you apply it in practice.

3. **Mention Tools:** Highlight any specific tools, frameworks, or techniques you use in your problem-solving process. This demonstrates your familiarity with structured methodologies and your ability to apply them effectively.

4. **Link to Role:** Ensure your problem-solving approach is relevant to the job you're applying for. This alignment shows that you are prepared to handle the specific challenges of the role and can contribute effectively to the organization.

CHAPTER 3
EXPERIENCE AND ACHIEVEMENTS

21. DESCRIBE YOUR PREVIOUS JOB EXPERIENCE.

Tips:

1. **Be Relevant:** When discussing your previous job experience, it's essential to tailor your response to the job you're applying for. Highlight the skills and experiences that align most closely with the job description. This shows the interviewer that you have taken the time to understand the role and that your background is well-suited for it.

2. **Be Concise:** While it's important to provide enough detail to be informative, keep your answer concise. Focus on key achievements and major responsibilities that had a significant impact. Avoid going into unnecessary detail or mentioning irrelevant experiences.

3. **Show Progression:** Demonstrate how your career has progressed by explaining how each role has built upon the last. This shows that you are continuously developing your skills and are ready to take on new challenges.

4. **End with the Present:** Conclude your response by explaining why you are interested in the new role and how your past experiences have prepared you for it. This leaves the interviewer with a clear understanding of your career trajectory and enthusiasm for the position.

Response Framework:

1. **High-Level Overview:** Begin by providing a brief summary of your professional background. This should include your overall years of experience, the industries you've worked in, and the key roles you've held. This introduction sets the context for a deeper dive into your specific job experiences.

2. **Focus on Relevant Experience:** Discuss your most recent position in detail, highlighting responsibilities and accomplishments that are most relevant to the job you're applying for. Describe the scope of your role, including key duties, and focus on the impact you made, such as improvements in processes, productivity, or outcomes.

3. **Discuss Career Progression:** Briefly mention previous roles that have contributed to your skill set and professional growth. Emphasize positions that demonstrate your progression in terms of responsibilities, skills acquired, and achievements. This showcases your career development and readiness for the new role.

4. **Highlight Special Projects:** If applicable, mention any significant projects or initiatives you've been involved in that are relevant to the position you're applying for. Discuss your role in these projects, the challenges you faced, and the outcomes you achieved. This highlights your ability to manage complex tasks and deliver results.

5. **Connect Experience to the New Role:** Explain how your past experiences make you a strong candidate for the role. Focus on how your skills, knowledge, and achievements align with the job requirements. Show your enthusiasm for applying your experience to new challenges within the company.

6. **Future Contributions and Aspirations:** Conclude by expressing your eagerness to contribute to the company's goals and how you see this role fitting into your long-term career aspirations. This demonstrates your commitment to growth and how you plan to leverage your experience to add value to the organization.

Key Takeaways:

1. **Relevance is Key:** Focus on the aspects of your experience that are most relevant to the job you're applying for. This demonstrates that you have thoughtfully considered how your background aligns with the job requirements.

2. **Conciseness Matters:** Keep your response clear and focused. Avoid unnecessary details and stick to the most impactful parts of your experience. This helps maintain the interviewer's attention and leaves a strong impression.

3. **Showcase Growth:** Highlight your career progression by discussing how each role has built on the previous one. This shows your commitment to continuous improvement and your readiness for the next step in your career.

4. **Align with the Job:** Make sure your skills and experiences clearly align with the job you're applying for. Articulate how your background makes you a strong candidate and how you can add value to the company.

22. WHAT ACHIEVEMENTS ARE YOU MOST PROUD OF?

Tips:

1. **Be Specific:** When discussing your achievements, it's essential to provide specific details that clearly illustrate the impact of your accomplishments. Use metrics and quantifiable results wherever possible to highlight your success. This level of detail helps the interviewer visualize your contributions and understand the extent of your impact.

2. **Be Relevant:** Focus on achievements that are directly relevant to the job you're applying for. By aligning your past successes with the role's requirements, you demonstrate that you have the experience and skills needed to excel in the position.

3. **Show Impact:** Emphasize the significance of your achievements and how they benefited your previous employers. Whether it's increasing revenue, improving efficiency, or enhancing customer satisfaction, showcasing the positive outcomes of your work helps the interviewer see the value you can bring to their organization.

4. **End with a Takeaway:** Conclude each achievement by connecting it back to the job you're applying for. This reinforces your suitability for the role and shows that your past experiences have prepared you to contribute effectively to the company's goals.

Response Framework:

1. **General Overview:** Begin by briefly introducing the scope of your career achievements. Highlight the areas where you have made the most significant impact, such as leadership, innovation, or performance improvement. This provides context and sets the stage for discussing specific accomplishments.

2. **Highlight Key Achievement #1:** Select a key achievement that exemplifies your ability to drive results. Describe the situation or challenge you faced, the actions you took to address it, and the measurable outcomes that followed. Focus on the impact of your efforts, such as increased revenue, cost savings, or enhanced efficiency, and emphasize how this achievement demonstrates your strengths relevant to the role.

3. **Highlight Key Achievement #2:** Choose another significant accomplishment that showcases your expertise in a different but relevant area. Again, describe the challenge, your approach, and the results.

This could involve leading a successful project, implementing a new strategy, or overcoming a significant obstacle. This achievement should further reinforce your qualifications and consistency in delivering positive outcomes.

4. **Highlight Key Achievement #3:** Discuss a third achievement that adds depth to your experience. This could involve an initiative that improved customer satisfaction, introduced a new product, or expanded market reach. Focus on the skills and knowledge you applied and how this accomplishment is particularly relevant to the position you're applying for.

5. **Connect Achievements to the Role:** Tie your achievements back to the job you're interviewing for. Explain how these past successes have equipped you with the skills, experience, and mindset necessary to excel in the role. Highlight how your proven track record of success aligns with the company's goals and how you plan to contribute to similar achievements in the new position.

6. **Future Aspirations:** Conclude by discussing your commitment to building on these achievements in the new role. Express your enthusiasm for the opportunity to apply your experience to new challenges and your dedication to continuous growth and contribution to the company's long-term success.

Key Takeaways:

1. **Be Specific:** Clearly detail your achievements, using quantifiable results to demonstrate the impact of your work. This makes your accomplishments more tangible and compelling.

2. **Be Relevant:** Focus on achievements that are directly relevant to the job you're applying for. This helps the interviewer see how your experience aligns with the role's requirements and how you can add value.

3. **Show Impact:** Highlight the significance of your achievements and their positive effects on your previous employers. This underscores the value you can bring to the new role.

4. **End with a Takeaway:** Conclude each achievement with a takeaway that ties it back to the job you're applying for. This reinforces your suitability for the position and leaves a strong impression on the interviewer.

23. TELL ME ABOUT A TIME YOU EXCEEDED EXPECTATIONS AT WORK.

Tips:

1. **Be Specific:** When answering this question, it's important to choose a particular instance where you clearly exceeded expectations. Provide enough context so that the interviewer understands the situation, your role, and the challenge you faced. This context will make your story more relatable and impactful.

2. **Highlight Skills:** Emphasize the key skills and competencies you utilized to exceed expectations. This not only showcases your strengths but also helps the interviewer see how your abilities align with the requirements of the job you are applying for.

3. **Quantify Results:** Use numbers, percentages, or other quantifiable data to demonstrate the success of your actions. This makes your accomplishment more concrete and shows the real impact of your efforts.

4. **Relate to the Role:** Make sure to connect your story to the specific role you're interviewing for. Explain how the skills and experience you gained in this instance can be applied to the new position, showing the interviewer that you are well-equipped to add value to their team.

Response Framework:

1. **Brief Introduction:** Start by introducing the situation where you exceeded expectations. Mention your role and the overall context to set the scene for your story. This gives the interviewer a clear understanding of your position and responsibilities at the time.

2. **Set the Context:** Describe the situation or project that required you to go above and beyond your typical duties. Explain the challenges or issues you encountered and why they were significant. This helps the interviewer grasp the stakes involved and why your actions were particularly important.

3. **Outline Your Actions:** Detail the specific actions you took to exceed expectations. Focus on the steps you personally initiated and the strategies you implemented. Highlight how you approached the problem creatively or proactively, showcasing your problem-solving abilities, leadership, and initiative.

4. **Discuss the Results:** Explain the outcomes of your actions, emphasizing the positive impact on the company or team. Use concrete metrics, such as numbers, percentages, or other quantifiable data, to demonstrate the success of your efforts. This evidence is crucial for showing that you can deliver measurable results.

5. **Highlight Relevant Skills:** Identify the key skills that were essential to your success in this situation. Discuss how these skills were applied effectively and how they are relevant to the role you are applying for. This demonstrates that you possess the competencies needed to excel in the new position.

6. **Connect to the Role:** Conclude by linking your experience to the job you're interviewing for. Explain how this situation has prepared you to contribute effectively to the company and why your track record of exceeding expectations makes you a strong candidate for the role. This connection reinforces your suitability and enthusiasm for the position.

Key Takeaways:

1. **Be Specific:** Choose a detailed example that clearly illustrates how you exceeded expectations. Providing context and explaining your actions helps the interviewer understand the significance of your achievement.

2. **Highlight Skills:** Emphasize the skills that were essential to your success. This not only showcases your strengths but also helps the interviewer see how your abilities align with the job you're applying for.

3. **Quantify Results:** Use data and metrics to make your accomplishment more tangible. Quantifying the results of your actions demonstrates the real impact of your work and strengthens your case as a candidate.

4. **Relate to the Role:** Connect your story to the job at hand by explaining how your past experience has equipped you to excel in the new role. This shows the interviewer that you have a proven track record and are ready to contribute to their team.

24. DESCRIBE A PROJECT YOU LED AND ITS OUTCOME.

Tips:

1. **Be Relevant:** Choose a project that directly showcases your skills and experiences relevant to the role you're applying for. Focus on highlighting the aspects of the project that align most closely with the job requirements. This will help the interviewer see how your experience makes you a strong candidate.

2. **Detail Your Role:** Clearly articulate your responsibilities and actions as the project leader. This is your opportunity to demonstrate your leadership, decision-making, and problem-solving abilities. Make sure to emphasize how you managed the project from start to finish, including how you navigated challenges.

3. **Focus on Results:** Use specific metrics or outcomes to illustrate the impact of the project. Quantifiable results are particularly compelling, as they provide concrete evidence of your effectiveness and the value you brought to the organization. Highlighting measurable success helps solidify your contribution.

4. **Relate to the Job:** Draw connections between the project and the role you are applying for. Show how the skills and experiences you gained can be applied to benefit the prospective employer. This will help the interviewer understand how you can bring similar success to their organization.

Response Framework:

1. **Brief Introduction:** Start by giving a concise overview of the project you led. Mention your role and the primary objective or goal of the project. This sets the context and provides the interviewer with a clear understanding of your leadership responsibility.

2. **Set the Context:** Explain the situation that necessitated the project. Discuss the challenges, problems, or opportunities that prompted the project, and why it was important to the organization. This background information helps the interviewer understand the significance of the project and the stakes involved.

3. **Outline Your Actions:** Detail the specific actions you took to lead the project. Describe how you managed the team, allocated resources, and navigated any obstacles that arose. Focus on your leadership approach, including how you motivated your team, made decisions, and kept the project on track. This section should highlight your problem-solving abilities and your capacity to manage a complex initiative.

4. **Discuss the Results:** Share the outcomes of the project, emphasizing measurable results where possible. Discuss the impact your leadership had on achieving the project's goals, such as increased efficiency, cost savings, or enhanced customer satisfaction. This is a crucial part of your answer as it demonstrates the tangible benefits of your efforts.

5. **Highlight Relevant Skills:** Identify the key skills that were critical to the success of the project. These might include project management, strategic planning, communication, or team leadership. Emphasize how these skills are relevant to the role you are applying for, showing that you possess the competencies needed to excel in similar challenges.

6. **Connect to the Role:** Conclude by linking your experience from the project to the position you're applying for. Explain how the skills, knowledge, and insights you gained from leading this project will help you contribute effectively in the new role. This connection reinforces your suitability for the job and your readiness to take on new challenges.

Key Takeaways:

1. **Be Relevant:** Select a project that best highlights the skills and experiences needed for the job. This ensures that your example is directly applicable and strengthens your candidacy.

2. **Detail Your Role:** Clearly describe your specific responsibilities and actions in the project. This showcases your leadership capabilities and problem-solving skills, helping the interviewer understand your approach to managing complex tasks.

3. **Focus on Results:** Use quantifiable outcomes to demonstrate the impact of your work. This adds credibility to your story and shows the value you bring to the organization.

4. **Relate to the Job:** Connect your project experience to the role you're applying for, illustrating how you can deliver similar results for the prospective employer. This shows that you are not only qualified but also ready to contribute meaningfully to their team.

25. HOW HAVE YOU CONTRIBUTED TO YOUR PREVIOUS TEAMS?

Tips:

1. **Be Specific:** When discussing your contributions to previous teams, provide specific examples that highlight your impact. Use quantifiable data wherever possible to demonstrate the tangible results of your efforts. This helps the interviewer understand the real value you added to your team.

2. **Highlight Teamwork:** Emphasize your ability to collaborate effectively with team members. Focus on how you communicated, cooperated, and contributed to the team's collective success. This demonstrates your ability to work well within a team environment, which is a key quality employers look for.

3. **Show Initiative:** Highlight instances where you took the initiative or went beyond your regular responsibilities to benefit the team. This shows your proactive nature and willingness to lead or support others when necessary, qualities that are highly valued in any workplace.

4. **Relate to the Role:** Make sure to connect your past contributions to the skills and experiences relevant to the job you are applying for. This will help the interviewer see how your past successes can translate to future success in their organization.

Response Framework:

1. **Brief Introduction:** Begin by summarizing your role within the team and highlighting the core skills or expertise you brought to the table. This sets the context for discussing your contributions and demonstrates your understanding of your role's importance within the team dynamic.

2. **Teamwork and Collaboration:** Discuss how you actively contributed to fostering collaboration and teamwork. Detail specific actions you took to enhance team cohesion, communication, or cooperation. Highlight how your collaborative efforts helped to achieve team goals or improve overall team performance.

3. **Leadership and Initiative:** Describe instances where you took on a leadership role or went beyond your usual responsibilities to support the team. This could involve mentoring colleagues, leading a project, or addressing a challenge that required innovative thinking. Emphasize the positive impact your leadership or initiative had on the team's success, showcasing your ability to lead by example.

4. **Problem-Solving and Innovation:** Provide examples of how you identified and addressed challenges or opportunities for improvement within the team. Discuss the steps you took to solve problems,

implement innovative solutions, or streamline processes. Focus on the outcomes, demonstrating how your problem-solving skills led to tangible benefits for the team.

5. **Results and Impact:** Summarize the measurable results of your contributions. Whether it's through improved efficiency, higher team morale, or successful project outcomes, use specific metrics or outcomes to showcase the value you added to the team. This reinforces the effectiveness of your contributions.

6. **Connection to the Role:** Conclude by linking your past contributions to the role you're applying for. Highlight how your experience in driving team success through collaboration, leadership, and problem-solving aligns with the expectations of the new role. This demonstrates that you are well-prepared to bring similar value to the prospective team.

Key Takeaways:

1. **Be Specific:** Provide concrete examples and metrics to illustrate your contributions. This makes your impact more tangible and impressive to the interviewer.

2. **Highlight Teamwork:** Emphasize your ability to collaborate and contribute to a team's success. Show how your communication and cooperation skills played a role in achieving team goals.

3. **Show Initiative:** Highlight instances where you took proactive steps to lead or support your team. This demonstrates your ability to go beyond your regular duties to ensure the team's success.

4. **Relate to the Role:** Connect your past contributions to the job you're applying for. This helps the interviewer see how your previous experience can bring value to their organization and makes you a strong candidate for the position.

26. TELL ME ABOUT A TIME YOU IMPROVED A PROCESS.

Tips:

1. **Be Specific:** When discussing how you improved a process, focus on providing clear, detailed examples. Quantify the results of your efforts wherever possible to demonstrate the impact. Specificity helps the interviewer understand the tangible benefits of your actions.

2. **Highlight Problem-Solving:** Emphasize your ability to identify inefficiencies and devise practical solutions. Show how your analytical skills allowed you to pinpoint areas for improvement and how your problem-solving skills helped implement effective changes.

3. **Show Initiative:** Make sure to highlight the proactive steps you took to improve the process. This not only demonstrates your leadership and initiative but also your willingness to go beyond your regular duties to make improvements.

4. **Relate to the Role:** Tie your experience in process improvement to the job you are applying for. Demonstrating that your skills and experiences are directly applicable to the new role makes your case stronger as a candidate.

Response Framework:

1. **Brief Introduction:** Start by briefly introducing the situation where you recognized the need for process improvement. Mention your role at the time and the context in which the process was

identified as needing improvement. This sets the stage for the interviewer to understand the background and your involvement.

2. **Identifying the Problem:** Explain how you identified the inefficiencies or challenges within the existing process. Discuss the specific issues that were causing problems, such as bottlenecks, errors, or delays, and the negative impact these issues were having on productivity, quality, or overall outcomes. This shows your analytical skills and your ability to recognize areas for improvement.

3. **Taking Initiative:** Describe the steps you took to address the identified problem. This might involve conducting research, gathering data, consulting with colleagues, or brainstorming potential solutions. Emphasize your proactive approach in leading or contributing to the development of a new or improved process, including your rationale for choosing the particular solution.

4. **4Implementation:** Detail how you implemented the new process or changes. Explain the actions you took to ensure the new process was smoothly integrated, such as organizing training sessions, providing clear communication, and setting up feedback mechanisms. Highlight your role in managing the change and how you supported your team or colleagues throughout the transition.

5. **Results and Impact:** Conclude by discussing the results of your process improvement efforts. Provide quantifiable outcomes, such as increased efficiency, reduced errors, cost savings, or improved customer satisfaction. Emphasize how your initiative positively impacted the team or organization and how it contributed to achieving broader goals.

6. **Connection to the Role:** Finally, tie your experience with process improvement to the role you're applying for. Explain how your skills in identifying inefficiencies, taking initiative, and implementing effective solutions are relevant to the job. Demonstrate your readiness to apply these abilities to help the company achieve its objectives.

Key Takeaways:

1. **Be Specific:** Use clear, detailed examples and metrics to illustrate the impact of your process improvement efforts. Specific examples make your contribution more tangible and impressive.

2. **Highlight Problem-Solving:** Emphasize your analytical and problem-solving skills by explaining how you identified inefficiencies and developed effective solutions. This showcases your ability to think critically and improve operations.

3. **Show Initiative:** Demonstrate your leadership and proactive nature by highlighting the steps you took to improve the process. This shows that you are willing to take the initiative and drive positive change.

4. **Relate to the Role:** Tie your experience to the job you are applying for, showing the interviewer how your skills in process improvement can benefit their organization. This helps reinforce your suitability for the role.

27. WHAT HAS BEEN YOUR MOST CHALLENGING PROJECT?

Tips:

1. **Be Specific:** When describing your most challenging project, provide clear and detailed information about the nature of the project, the specific challenges you encountered, and your role in overcoming them. This specificity helps the interviewer understand the complexity of the situation and your contributions.

2. **Highlight Problem-Solving Skills:** Focus on how you navigated and resolved complex issues throughout the project. Emphasize your critical thinking and problem-solving abilities, demonstrating your capacity to manage obstacles effectively.

3. **Show Leadership and Initiative:** Illustrate your leadership skills by detailing how you took charge of the project, motivated your team, and drove the initiative forward. Highlight instances where you proactively addressed challenges or made key decisions that influenced the project's success.

4. **Demonstrate Impact:** Showcase the positive outcomes of the project, emphasizing the measurable results achieved through your efforts. This could include improvements in efficiency, cost savings, customer satisfaction, or any other relevant metrics.

Response Framework:

1. **Brief Introduction:** Start by providing a concise overview of the project, including your role and the primary objective of the project. Clearly state why this particular project was challenging, offering context that helps the interviewer understand the scope and significance of the project.

2. **Identifying the Challenge:** Describe the specific challenges or obstacles that made the project difficult. These could include resource constraints, tight deadlines, technical difficulties, or coordination issues among team members. Explain how these challenges impacted the project's progress and the potential risks they posed to the overall success of the initiative.

3. **Taking Initiative:** Discuss the proactive steps you took to address these challenges. Detail your role in leading or contributing to the project, focusing on how you organized your team, developed strategies, and made critical decisions to overcome the difficulties. Emphasize your problem-solving abilities and leadership skills, highlighting how you kept the project aligned with its goals.

4. **Overcoming Obstacles:** Explain the specific actions you took to navigate and overcome the obstacles. This could include adjusting the project plan, reallocating resources, or implementing new processes. Discuss how you managed risks and maintained team morale despite the challenges, ensuring the project stayed on track.

5. **Results and Impact:** Conclude by outlining the results of the project. Highlight the positive outcomes and the impact your efforts had on the organization. Quantify these results if possible, such as by mentioning improvements in efficiency, cost savings, or other measurable benefits, to demonstrate the effectiveness of your approach.

6. **Connection to the Role:** Finally, connect your experience with this challenging project to the role you are applying for. Explain how the skills and knowledge you gained are directly relevant to the new position, and how your ability to successfully manage challenging projects makes you a strong candidate for the job.

Key Takeaways:

1. **Be Specific:** Provide detailed descriptions of the project, the challenges faced, and your role in overcoming them. Specificity adds depth and clarity to your response.

2. **Highlight Problem-Solving Skills:** Focus on the problem-solving strategies you used to tackle the project's challenges. Demonstrating your ability to navigate and resolve issues is crucial.

3. **Show Leadership and Initiative:** Emphasize your leadership qualities by explaining how you took charge of the project and motivated your team. Leadership and initiative are key traits that employers value.

4. **Demonstrate Impact:** Highlight the positive outcomes and measurable results of your efforts. Showing the tangible benefits of your work reinforces your capability and effectiveness in managing challenging projects.

28. DESCRIBE A TYPICAL WORKDAY AT YOUR LAST JOB.

Tips:

1. **Be Detailed:** When describing a typical workday, offer a structured overview of your tasks and responsibilities. This gives the interviewer a clear picture of your daily activities and how you manage your time. Avoid being overly general; specificity helps convey the scope and complexity of your role.

2. **Highlight Key Activities:** Focus on the most significant parts of your work that showcase your skills and contributions. Emphasize activities that align with the job you are applying for. This helps the interviewer see how your past experiences prepare you for their role.

3. **Show Time Management:** Demonstrate your ability to manage time effectively and prioritize tasks. Explain how you balance multiple responsibilities and stay organized throughout the day. This is crucial for roles that require strong time management and multitasking abilities.

4. **Relate to the Job:** Tailor your response to the job you are applying for by highlighting how your typical day's activities are relevant to the new role. This helps the interviewer see how your experience aligns with their expectations.

Response Framework:

1. **Brief Introduction:** Start by briefly introducing your role and the context of your typical workday. Mention your job title, key responsibilities, and the overall work environment, whether it's a fast-paced corporate setting, a collaborative team-based atmosphere, or a more independent role. This sets the stage for describing your daily activities.

2. **Morning Routine:** Outline how you typically begin your day. This could include reviewing your schedule, checking emails, prioritizing tasks, or attending morning meetings. Highlight how these activities help you set the tone for the rest of the day, ensuring you are organized and focused on your key responsibilities.

3. **Mid-Morning Tasks:** Describe the core tasks you typically handle during the mid-morning. This could involve attending important meetings, collaborating with colleagues, or engaging in strategic planning. Emphasize how these activities contribute to your overall objectives and how they align with your role's expectations.

4. **Afternoon Responsibilities:** Discuss the tasks you usually tackle in the afternoon, such as project execution, analysis, or client interactions. Mention any specific tools or techniques you use to manage these responsibilities effectively. Explain how these tasks are central to your role and how they impact your team or organization.

5. **Late Afternoon Routine:** Detail how you wind down your day, including activities like wrapping up ongoing projects, completing administrative tasks, or preparing for the next day. Highlight how you ensure that your day ends on a productive note, leaving you well-prepared for the following day.

6. **End of Day Wrap-Up:** Explain how you conclude your workday, whether by reviewing progress, setting goals for the next day, or aligning with your team on key objectives. This shows your commitment to maintaining consistency and staying aligned with broader company goals.

7. **Connection to the Role:** Finally, tie your typical workday back to the position you are applying for. Highlight how the skills, habits, and experiences from your daily routine make you well-suited for the new role. Demonstrate that your structured approach to work will help you excel in the job you're pursuing.

Key Takeaways:

1. **Be Detailed:** Provide a clear and structured overview of your daily tasks, offering a glimpse into your work habits and responsibilities.

2. **Highlight Key Activities:** Focus on significant tasks that showcase your skills and how they align with the role you are applying for.

3. **Show Time Management:** Demonstrate your ability to effectively manage time, prioritize tasks, and stay organized throughout the day.

4. **Relate to the Job:** Connect your daily activities to the requirements of the new role, showing how your experience makes you a strong candidate.

29. WHAT ROLE DO YOU USUALLY TAKE IN A TEAM SETTING?

Tips:

1. **Be Specific:** Clearly identify the role you usually take in team settings, such as a leader, coordinator, or contributor. Use specific examples to illustrate how you fulfill this role and the impact you have on the team's success. Specificity helps the interviewer understand how you function within a group.

2. **Highlight Skills:** Emphasize the key skills that make you effective in your preferred role, such as leadership, communication, organization, or problem-solving. Highlighting these skills shows your strengths and how they contribute to team dynamics.

3. **Show Flexibility:** While you may prefer a certain role, it's important to demonstrate your flexibility and ability to adapt to different roles when needed. This shows that you are a versatile team player who can adjust to the team's needs.

4. **Relate to the Job:** Tailor your response to the specific job you're applying for by connecting your team role to the responsibilities of the position. This alignment shows that your experience and skills are a good fit for the role.

Response Framework:

1. **Brief Introduction:** Begin by identifying the role you typically assume in a team setting. Clearly state the role, such as leader, facilitator, strategist, or supporter, and explain why this role suits your strengths and working style. This helps set the stage for discussing your contributions and effectiveness in a team environment.

2. **Main Responsibilities:** Outline the key responsibilities you usually undertake in this role. Discuss how you contribute to the team's objectives, manage tasks, and support your colleagues. Highlight the actions you consistently take that drive team success, such as coordinating efforts, providing direction, or fostering collaboration.

3. **Skills and Contributions:** Focus on the skills that make you particularly effective in your chosen role. Discuss how your skills, such as communication, organization, or problem-solving, contribute to the

overall success of the team. Emphasize any tools or strategies you use to enhance your contributions, demonstrating your proactive approach to teamwork.

4. **Adaptability and Flexibility:** Describe your ability to adapt to different roles within a team as needed. Explain how you can step into various roles depending on the situation, showcasing your versatility and willingness to collaborate. Provide a brief example of a time when you adapted your role to meet the team's needs, reinforcing your flexibility.

5. **Connection to the Role:** Conclude by tying your experience in team settings to the job you are applying for. Explain how the role you typically take and the skills you bring align with the responsibilities of the position. This final connection helps the interviewer understand how you will integrate into their team and contribute to the organization's success.

Key Takeaways:

1. **Be Specific:** Clearly define the role you typically take in a team and provide examples to illustrate your experience.

2. **Highlight Skills:** Emphasize the skills that support your effectiveness in your preferred role, such as leadership, communication, or problem-solving.

3. **Show Flexibility:** Demonstrate your ability to adapt to different roles as needed, showing that you are a versatile and collaborative team player.

4. **Relate to the Job:** Connect your experience in team settings to the job you're applying for, showing how your role and skills align with the position's requirements.

30. HOW DO YOU MEASURE SUCCESS IN YOUR ROLE?

Tips:

1. **Be Specific:** When discussing how you measure success, clearly define the key metrics and benchmarks you rely on. These could include quantitative goals like revenue targets or project completion rates, as well as qualitative measures such as client satisfaction or team collaboration. Specificity helps the interviewer understand the concrete ways you evaluate your performance.

2. **Highlight Impact:** Emphasize how your chosen metrics demonstrate the impact of your work on the organization. Whether it's increasing efficiency, driving sales, or enhancing customer satisfaction, showing the tangible results of your efforts reinforces your value.

3. **Align with Company Goals:** Make sure that the metrics you use to measure success are in alignment with the broader goals of the company. This demonstrates that you understand the organization's priorities and are focused on contributing to its overall success.

4. **Show Continuous Improvement:** Mention how you utilize feedback and data to identify areas for improvement. Demonstrating a commitment to continuous learning and adaptation shows that you are proactive in enhancing your performance over time.

Response Framework:

1. **Brief Introduction:** Start by explaining that you measure success in your role through a combination of metrics and outcomes that align with both your responsibilities and the organization's goals. This provides a foundation for discussing specific ways you evaluate your performance.

2. **Quantitative Metrics:** Discuss the importance of quantitative metrics in measuring success. These might include achieving key performance indicators (KPIs), hitting sales targets, meeting deadlines, or increasing efficiency. Explain how you set clear, measurable goals and track progress against them. Emphasize your commitment to exceeding these benchmarks to drive performance and contribute to the organization's success.

3. **Qualitative Metrics:** Explain that you also measure success using qualitative factors. This could involve client satisfaction, team collaboration, or the quality of your work. Mention that you regularly seek feedback from clients, peers, or supervisors to assess your effectiveness in these areas. Highlight that this approach ensures a well-rounded evaluation of your performance, focusing on the impact you have on relationships and team dynamics.

4. **Aligning with Company Goals:** Describe how you align your personal success metrics with the broader strategic objectives of the company. Discuss how you work with leadership to ensure your KPIs support key business goals, such as enhancing customer satisfaction, driving innovation, or improving operational efficiency. This shows that you understand the importance of your role within the larger organizational framework.

5. **Continuous Improvement:** Conclude by explaining how you use the data and feedback you gather to continuously improve your performance. Discuss your commitment to regularly reviewing your progress, learning from challenges, and adapting your strategies to ensure ongoing success. This forward-thinking approach demonstrates your dedication to personal and professional growth within the role.

Key Takeaways:

1. **Be Specific:** Define the metrics and benchmarks you use to measure success, using clear examples to illustrate your approach.

2. **Highlight Impact:** Focus on how these metrics demonstrate your impact on achieving organizational goals.

3. **Align with Company Goals:** Show that your measures of success are aligned with the company's broader objectives, reinforcing your commitment to the organization's success.

4. **Show Continuous Improvement:** Discuss how you use feedback and data to continuously improve your performance, emphasizing a proactive and adaptive mindset.

CHAPTER 4
BEHAVIORAL QUESTIONS

31. TELL ME ABOUT A TIME YOU FAILED. HOW DID YOU DEAL WITH THAT SITUATION?

Tips:

1. **Be Honest:** When discussing a failure, it's important to acknowledge the mistake without deflecting blame onto others. Owning up to your role in the failure shows maturity and accountability, which are key traits that employers value.

2. **Highlight Learning:** Focus on what you learned from the experience. Employers are less concerned about the failure itself and more interested in how it helped you grow and improve. Discuss the insights gained and how they have positively impacted your approach to work since then.

3. **Show Resilience:** Emphasize your ability to recover from the setback. Talk about how you applied the lessons learned to prevent similar issues in the future and how this experience has made you more resilient and resourceful.

4. **Be Specific:** Provide concrete details about the situation. Describe what went wrong, the steps you took to address the problem, and the outcomes of your actions. Specific examples help to paint a clear picture of how you handle adversity.

Response Framework:

1. **Brief Introduction:** Start by introducing the situation where you encountered a failure. Provide a brief overview of the context, including your role and the specific circumstances that led to the challenge. This sets the stage for discussing the failure and how you managed it.

2. **Acknowledging the Failure:** Explain the failure clearly, taking responsibility for your role in the situation. Discuss what went wrong and why it was significant. Acknowledging your failure openly demonstrates self-awareness and the ability to reflect on your actions.

3. **Steps Taken to Address the Issue:** Describe the specific steps you took to address the failure once it became apparent. This could involve analyzing the situation, identifying the root cause, and implementing corrective actions. Highlight your problem-solving skills and how you took initiative to mitigate the impact of the failure.

4. **Lessons Learned:** Discuss the key lessons you learned from this experience. Focus on how the failure provided valuable insights and how you applied these learnings to improve your approach in future situations. Emphasize the importance of growth and resilience, showing that you view failures as opportunities for development.

5. **Applying the Lessons:** Conclude by explaining how you have applied the lessons learned from this failure to subsequent projects or roles. Describe how these changes have positively impacted your work and how they have contributed to your success in overcoming similar challenges in the future. This demonstrates your commitment to continuous improvement and your ability to turn setbacks into stepping stones for growth.

Key Takeaways:

1. **Be Honest:** Acknowledge your role in the failure without making excuses, demonstrating accountability and maturity.

2. **Highlight Learning:** Focus on the lessons learned and how they have contributed to your professional development and improved your approach to work.

3. **Show Resilience:** Illustrate your ability to bounce back from setbacks, showing that you can apply the lessons learned to prevent similar issues in the future.

4. **Be Specific:** Provide detailed examples of the situation, your actions, and the results to give a clear understanding of how you handle failure and use it as a stepping stone for growth.

32. DESCRIBE A TIME YOU MOTIVATED OTHERS. HOW DID YOU ACCOMPLISH IT?

Tips:

1. **Be Specific:** When discussing how you motivated others, focus on a particular situation. Detail the context, the challenges the team faced, and the specific actions you took to inspire and drive the team forward. This specificity provides a clear narrative and demonstrates your leadership abilities.

2. **Highlight Impact:** Emphasize the tangible results of your motivational efforts. Whether it's improved team morale, meeting a tight deadline, or achieving a significant project milestone, showcasing the positive outcomes helps underline the effectiveness of your approach.

3. **Show Empathy:** Understanding what motivates individuals is crucial. Tailor your motivational techniques to the unique needs and personalities of your team members. This shows that you are not only a leader but also someone who genuinely cares about the well-being and growth of your team.

4. **Reflect on Skills:** Highlight the leadership and communication skills that were instrumental in motivating others. This reflection not only shows your self-awareness but also illustrates how you can apply these skills in the role you're applying for.

Response Framework:

1. **Brief Introduction:** Begin by setting the context for the situation where you needed to motivate others. Mention your role, the team's dynamics, and the challenges faced that required a boost in motivation. This provides the background necessary to understand the significance of your actions.

2. **Understanding the Team:** Discuss how you took the time to understand the individual motivations and concerns of your team members. Explain the methods you used, such as one-on-one meetings or informal check-ins, to gather insights into what would drive each person. This step emphasizes the importance of empathy and personalized leadership.

3. **Setting Clear Goals:** Describe how you established clear, achievable goals to provide direction and focus for the team. Explain how you aligned these goals with the strengths and capabilities of each team member, breaking down the larger objective into manageable tasks. This shows your ability to create structure and clarity in a challenging situation.

4. **Providing Support and Recognition:** Detail the ways you offered support to the team, ensuring that they had the resources and encouragement needed to succeed. Discuss how you maintained open lines of communication, addressed obstacles promptly, and provided regular recognition for progress. This demonstrates your commitment to fostering a positive and motivating environment.

5. **Encouraging Collaboration:** Explain how you promoted collaboration and teamwork, such as organizing regular meetings or brainstorming sessions. Highlight how you encouraged open communication and knowledge-sharing, reinforcing a sense of unity and collective effort within the team. This step underscores the importance of a collaborative work culture.

6. **Outcome and Reflection:** Conclude by discussing the positive outcomes of your motivational efforts. Mention the specific achievements of the team, such as meeting deadlines or exceeding expectations. Reflect on how this experience reinforced your belief in the value of empathetic leadership, clear communication, and team support in achieving success.

Key Takeaways:

1. **Be Specific:** Focus on a particular situation, detailing the challenges faced and the specific actions you took to motivate your team.

2. **Highlight Impact:** Emphasize the positive outcomes, such as improved team morale or successful project completion, to demonstrate the effectiveness of your approach.

3. **Show Empathy:** Tailor your motivational techniques to the individual needs of your team members, showing that you understand and value each person's unique contributions.

4. **Reflect on Skills:** Highlight the leadership and communication skills you used, demonstrating your ability to inspire and guide others effectively.

33. TELL ME ABOUT A TIME YOU HAD TO HANDLE MULTIPLE PROJECTS AT ONCE. HOW DID YOU PRIORITIZE?

Tips:

1. **Be Specific:** When discussing a situation where you had to manage multiple projects, focus on a concrete example that illustrates your ability to juggle various responsibilities effectively. This specificity helps the interviewer understand how you handle complex, high-pressure situations.

2. **Highlight Techniques:** Emphasize the methods and tools you used to prioritize tasks. Whether it's project management software, time-blocking techniques, or frameworks like the Eisenhower Matrix, explaining your approach demonstrates your strategic thinking and organizational skills.

3. **Show Results:** Discuss the outcomes of your efforts to manage and prioritize the projects. This could include meeting deadlines, achieving project goals, or improving team efficiency. Highlighting these results shows that your approach was not only well-organized but also effective.

4. **Reflect on Skills:** Use this opportunity to showcase your organizational, time management, and communication skills. These are critical competencies in any role that requires handling multiple tasks or projects simultaneously.

Response Framework:

1. **Brief Introduction:** Start by briefly introducing the scenario where you were required to manage multiple projects simultaneously. Provide context about the nature of the projects and the competing demands you faced. This sets the stage for discussing how you approached the challenge of prioritization.

2. **Assessing Priorities:** Explain how you assessed the importance and urgency of each project. Discuss your approach to evaluating deadlines, stakeholder expectations, and potential impact on the organization. This shows your ability to analyze and determine which tasks needed immediate attention versus those that could be scheduled later.

3. **Planning and Organization:** Describe the steps you took to organize the workload. Mention the planning techniques or frameworks you used, such as creating a project plan, breaking tasks into manageable pieces, and establishing clear timelines. Highlight how this organization helped you to maintain focus and ensure that each project received the necessary attention.

4. **Utilizing Tools and Techniques:** Discuss any tools or methods you employed to manage and track your projects effectively. This might include project management software, prioritization matrices, or

time-blocking techniques. Explain how these tools helped you stay organized, keep track of progress, and adjust priorities as needed.

5. **Communication and Delegation:** Emphasize the importance of communication in managing multiple projects. Detail how you coordinated with your team, set expectations, and delegated tasks based on team members' strengths. Highlight your ability to maintain clarity and ensure alignment among all stakeholders throughout the process.

6. **Outcome and Reflection:** Conclude by discussing the outcomes of your efforts. Explain how your prioritization and time management strategies led to successful project completion. Reflect on what you learned from the experience and how it reinforced your ability to manage multiple high-priority tasks effectively.

Key Takeaways:

1. **Be Specific:** Provide a detailed account of a situation where you managed multiple projects, focusing on the actions you took to handle the workload.

2. **Highlight Techniques:** Discuss the tools and methods you used to prioritize and manage tasks, demonstrating your strategic approach to project management.

3. **Show Results:** Emphasize the successful outcomes of your efforts, showing that your prioritization and management strategies were effective.

4. **Reflect on Skills:** Highlight the organizational, time management, and communication skills that were essential to successfully managing multiple projects. These skills are critical in roles that require handling complex tasks under pressure.

34. DESCRIBE A TIME YOU WENT THROUGH A MAJOR CHANGE AT WORK. HOW DID YOU ADAPT?

Tips:

1. **Be Specific:** When discussing a significant change at work, provide a clear example that illustrates the context and impact of the change. This could involve organizational restructuring, a shift in job responsibilities, or a change in leadership. The more detailed your example, the better it will demonstrate your ability to handle change.

2. **Highlight Adaptability:** Emphasize the specific steps you took to adapt to the change. Whether you sought additional training, adjusted your workflow, or proactively communicated with new team members, showcasing your adaptability is key. This not only highlights your flexibility but also your ability to maintain productivity in the face of change.

3. **Show Results:** Discuss the positive outcomes that resulted from your ability to adapt. This could include improved team efficiency, successful project completions, or enhanced relationships with colleagues. Demonstrating tangible results reinforces the effectiveness of your approach.

4. **Reflect on Skills:** Use this opportunity to highlight the skills that helped you navigate the change successfully. This might include problem-solving, communication, time management, or leadership abilities. Reflecting on these skills shows self-awareness and a proactive mindset, both of which are highly valued by employers.

Response Framework:

1. **Brief Introduction:** Begin by briefly describing the context of the major change at work. Specify the nature of the change, such as a restructuring, new leadership, or a shift in company strategy. This sets the stage for explaining how you adapted to the situation.

2. **Understanding the Change:** Explain how you took steps to fully understand the change. Discuss your approach to gathering information, such as attending meetings, reviewing relevant documents, or seeking clarification from leadership. Emphasize the importance of understanding the reasons behind the change and how it impacted your role and the organization.

3. **Adapting to New Responsibilities:** Describe how you adjusted to any new responsibilities or changes in your role. This might include learning new skills, collaborating with new team members, or adopting new processes. Highlight your proactive approach to adapting, such as seeking additional training, mentoring, or taking the initiative to learn new tools or techniques.

4. **Effective Communication:** Discuss the role of communication in navigating the change. Explain how you maintained open lines of communication with your manager, colleagues, and any other stakeholders involved. Emphasize the importance of regular check-ins, feedback, and collaboration to ensure everyone was aligned and addressing challenges effectively.

5. **Maintaining Productivity:** Detail the strategies you employed to stay productive during the transition. This could involve prioritizing tasks, using project management tools, or implementing time management techniques to handle the increased workload or shifting priorities. Explain how you ensured that your work continued to meet high standards despite the changes.

6. **Outcome and Reflection:** Conclude by describing the outcomes of your adaptation efforts. Highlight any positive results, such as improved team cohesion, successful project completions, or enhanced efficiency. Reflect on what you learned from the experience and how it strengthened your ability to handle future changes.

Key Takeaways:

1. **Be Specific:** Clearly detail a significant workplace change and the context surrounding it to provide a compelling example.

2. **Highlight Adaptability:** Focus on the specific steps you took to adapt to the change, demonstrating your flexibility and ability to maintain productivity.

3. **Show Results:** Discuss the positive outcomes that resulted from your adaptability, reinforcing the effectiveness of your approach.

4. **Reflect on Skills:** Highlight the key skills, such as communication, problem-solving, and time management, that enabled you to successfully navigate the change. This shows self-awareness and a proactive approach to challenges.

35. TELL ME ABOUT A TIME YOU SET A GOAL FOR YOURSELF. HOW DID YOU ENSURE YOU ACHIEVED IT?

Tips:

1. **Be Specific:** When discussing a goal you've set, it's important to be clear and specific. Choose a goal that is concrete and measurable, allowing the interviewer to understand its significance. Avoid vague or general goals, as they may not effectively demonstrate your ability to plan and achieve objectives.

2. **Highlight Planning:** Explain how you planned to achieve the goal. This could include breaking down the goal into smaller, manageable tasks, setting deadlines, and identifying resources you needed. Show that you approached the goal methodically and thoughtfully, rather than impulsively.

3. **Show Determination:** Emphasize your commitment to achieving the goal. Discuss any obstacles you encountered along the way and how you overcame them. This demonstrates your resilience and ability to stay focused even when faced with challenges.

4. **Reflect on Success:** Conclude by discussing the outcome of your efforts. Reflect on what you learned from the experience and how achieving this goal has contributed to your personal or professional growth. This helps the interviewer see the broader impact of your goal-setting behavior.

Response Framework:

1. **Brief Introduction:** Begin by introducing the goal you set for yourself, providing context for why this goal was significant. This could involve personal or professional aspirations, or a specific need to develop skills or achieve a milestone in your career. This sets the stage for the rest of your response.

2. **Setting the Goal:** Explain the rationale behind choosing this goal. Discuss how it aligned with your long-term objectives or responded to a particular challenge or opportunity. This demonstrates strategic thinking and self-awareness in your career development.

3. **Planning and Preparation:** Detail the steps you took to plan and prepare for achieving your goal. Outline how you broke down the goal into manageable tasks, created a timeline, and identified resources or support systems you would need. This shows your ability to approach goals methodically and systematically.

4. **Overcoming Obstacles:** Discuss any challenges or obstacles you encountered along the way. Explain how you identified these challenges and the strategies you used to overcome them. This could involve time management, adjusting your plans, seeking support, or staying motivated despite setbacks. Highlighting this shows your resilience and problem-solving skills.

5. **Achieving the Goal:** Describe the actions you took to stay on track and ensure the successful completion of your goal. Discuss the results of your efforts and how achieving this goal impacted your career or personal development. This underscores your ability to follow through on commitments and achieve meaningful outcomes.

6. **Reflecting on the Experience:** Conclude by reflecting on what you learned from the experience. Discuss how the process of setting and achieving this goal has influenced your approach to future challenges and goals. This demonstrates your commitment to continuous improvement and your ability to apply lessons learned to future endeavors.

Key Takeaways:

1. **Be Specific:** Clearly describe a concrete and relevant goal to provide a strong example of your goal-setting abilities.

2. **Highlight Planning:** Detail the planning and preparation involved in reaching the goal, emphasizing a methodical approach.

3. **Show Determination:** Demonstrate your commitment by discussing the obstacles you overcame and the strategies you used to stay focused.

4. **Reflect on Success:** Discuss the positive outcome of achieving your goal and what you learned from the experience, showing how it contributed to your growth and success.

36. WHAT'S AN EXAMPLE OF A TIME YOU DISAGREED WITH A BOSS OR COLLEAGUE? HOW DID IT GO?

Tips:

1. **Be Professional:** When discussing a disagreement, it's crucial to maintain professionalism. Focus on the issue at hand rather than personal conflicts. Avoid negative language and emphasize a constructive approach to resolving the disagreement. This shows maturity and the ability to handle workplace conflicts diplomatically.

2. **Highlight Communication:** Emphasize how you used communication skills to address and resolve the disagreement. Discuss how you listened to the other person's perspective, articulated your own views clearly, and worked towards a mutual understanding. This highlights your ability to navigate challenging conversations effectively.

3. **Show Collaboration:** Demonstrate that you were willing to collaborate to find a solution. Highlight how you sought common ground and worked with the other party to achieve a successful outcome. This shows your ability to work well with others, even when opinions differ.

4. **Reflect on the Outcome:** Discuss the positive results of the disagreement and what you learned from the experience. Whether it led to a better outcome for the project or improved your working relationship, reflecting on the benefits shows that you can turn challenges into opportunities for growth.

Response Framework:

1. **Brief Introduction:** Begin by introducing the context of the disagreement. Clearly state who the disagreement was with (a boss or colleague) and the general nature of the conflict. This sets the stage for the rest of your response by providing context and showing that the situation was significant.

2. **Setting the Scene:** Explain the importance of the situation, detailing why the issue was critical to the project or the team's objectives. Mention the differing perspectives that led to the disagreement and how it began to impact progress or team dynamics. This helps the interviewer understand the stakes involved.

3. **Approach to Resolution:** Describe the steps you took to address the disagreement. Focus on your approach to communication, such as arranging a meeting to discuss the issue openly, bringing data or evidence to support your viewpoint, and encouraging the other party to share their perspective. Highlight your commitment to a respectful and constructive dialogue.

4. **Finding Common Ground:** Discuss how you worked with the other party to find a mutually agreeable solution. Emphasize the importance of listening, understanding each other's perspectives, and integrating the best aspects of both viewpoints. This shows your ability to collaborate and focus on the collective goal rather than personal preferences.

5. **Outcome:** Detail the positive results that emerged from resolving the disagreement. Explain how the final solution benefited the project, team, or organization, and how it exceeded expectations. This reinforces the value of effective conflict resolution and collaborative problem-solving.

6. **Reflecting on the Experience:** Conclude by reflecting on what you learned from the experience. Highlight how the situation strengthened your ability to handle disagreements in a professional manner, improved your communication skills, and reinforced the importance of collaboration in achieving successful outcomes.

Key Takeaways:

1. **Be Professional:** Maintain professionalism by focusing on the issue rather than personal conflicts, ensuring a constructive approach.

2. **Highlight Communication:** Emphasize the role of clear and respectful communication in resolving the disagreement.

3. **Show Collaboration:** Demonstrate how collaboration and finding common ground led to a successful resolution.

4. **Reflect on the Outcome:** Discuss the positive results and lessons learned, showcasing your ability to turn challenges into opportunities for growth.

37. DESCRIBE A DIFFICULT WORK SITUATION AND HOW YOU OVERCAME IT.

Tips:

1. **Be Specific:** When describing a difficult work situation, ensure that you provide a clear and detailed account of what happened. Avoid vague descriptions and focus on the specific challenges you faced. This helps the interviewer understand the context and the gravity of the situation.

2. **Highlight Your Role:** Emphasize your personal involvement in overcoming the challenge. Focus on what you specifically did to address the situation. This showcases your ability to take initiative and contribute meaningfully to problem-solving efforts.

3. **Show Problem-Solving Skills:** Demonstrate your ability to think critically and act decisively under pressure. Highlight the steps you took to analyze the situation, identify solutions, and implement them effectively. This illustrates your problem-solving capabilities and your ability to handle difficult situations.

4. **Focus on the Outcome:** Conclude by discussing the positive results of your actions and any lessons you learned from the experience. This reinforces your ability to not only overcome challenges but also to grow from them.

Response Framework:

1. **Brief Introduction:** Start by providing a concise overview of the difficult situation you faced at work. Set the context by mentioning your role, the nature of the challenge, and its significance to your team or organization. This helps the interviewer understand the gravity of the situation and your position within it.

2. **Setting the Scene:** Describe the specific details that made the situation difficult. This could include challenges like tight deadlines, resource constraints, technical issues, or team conflicts. Emphasize the impact these challenges had on the project, team morale, or client relationships. This section should highlight the stakes involved and why it was crucial to address the problem.

3. **Approach to Resolution:** Discuss the steps you took to resolve the situation. Focus on your problem-solving process, including how you identified the root cause of the issue, the strategies you developed to address it, and how you communicated with stakeholders. Highlight your initiative, leadership, and ability to collaborate with others to find a solution.

4. **Implementing the Plan:** Explain how you executed your plan to overcome the challenge. Detail the specific actions you took, such as reallocating resources, adjusting timelines, or improving

communication channels. Mention any changes you made to team dynamics or processes to ensure the situation was resolved effectively.

5. **Outcome:** Describe the results of your efforts. Highlight the positive impact your actions had on the project, team, or organization, such as meeting revised deadlines, improving client satisfaction, or enhancing team performance. Use quantifiable data where possible to demonstrate the effectiveness of your solution.

6. **Reflecting on the Experience:** Conclude by reflecting on what you learned from the experience. Discuss how it improved your problem-solving skills, leadership abilities, or adaptability. Emphasize how this situation prepared you to handle similar challenges in the future, making you a more effective and resilient professional.

Key Takeaways:

1. **Be Specific:** Provide a detailed account of the situation to give the interviewer a clear understanding of the challenges you faced.

2. **Highlight Your Role:** Emphasize your personal involvement and leadership in overcoming the challenge, showcasing your ability to take charge in difficult situations.

3. **Show Problem-Solving Skills:** Demonstrate your ability to analyze problems, develop solutions, and implement them effectively under pressure.

4. **Focus on the Outcome:** Highlight the positive results of your actions and the lessons you learned, showing your ability to turn challenges into opportunities for growth.

38. GIVE AN EXAMPLE OF HOW YOU HANDLED A CONFLICT AT WORK.

Tips:

1. **Be Specific:** When discussing a conflict at work, clearly describe the situation, providing enough context so that the interviewer can fully understand the background and the stakes involved. This helps to frame the scenario and emphasizes the importance of resolving the issue effectively.

2. **Highlight Your Role:** Focus on your personal contributions to resolving the conflict. This allows you to showcase your leadership and conflict-resolution skills. Make it clear what actions you took to address the situation.

3. **Show Emotional Intelligence:** Demonstrate your ability to manage emotions, both your own and those of others, during the conflict. This is a key aspect of professionalism and is crucial in maintaining a positive work environment.

4. **Focus on Resolution:** Emphasize the steps you took to resolve the conflict and the positive outcomes that resulted. This shows that you can not only handle difficult situations but also turn them into opportunities for collaboration and improvement.

Response Framework:

1. **Brief Introduction:** Start by briefly introducing the conflict you encountered at work. Set the context by explaining your role and the nature of the conflict. This could involve a disagreement with a colleague, a clash of ideas, or differing opinions on how to approach a project. This introduction provides a clear understanding of the situation and its relevance to your job.

2. **Setting the Scene:** Describe the specific circumstances that led to the conflict. Explain the key points of disagreement and why the issue was significant for the team or project. Highlight any potential impacts the conflict could have had if it wasn't addressed, such as delays, reduced productivity, or strained working relationships. This section sets up the importance of resolving the conflict.

3. **Approach to Resolution:** Detail the steps you took to address the conflict. Focus on your problem-solving and communication skills. Explain how you approached the other party involved, how you facilitated a constructive conversation, and how you ensured that both sides were heard. Emphasize your use of active listening, empathy, and diplomacy to reach a mutually agreeable solution.

4. **Implementing the Solution:** Discuss how you and the other party agreed on a resolution. Describe the actions taken to implement the solution, whether it involved compromising, testing different approaches, or redefining goals. Highlight how you maintained open communication and monitored progress to ensure the conflict was fully resolved.

5. **Outcome:** Describe the positive results that came from resolving the conflict. Focus on the benefits to the project, team morale, or working relationships. Use quantifiable outcomes if possible, such as improved performance metrics or successful project completion. This demonstrates the effectiveness of your conflict resolution skills.

6. **Reflecting on the Experience:** Conclude by reflecting on what you learned from the experience. Discuss how handling the conflict improved your communication, negotiation, and leadership skills. Emphasize how this experience has prepared you to manage future conflicts more effectively, making you a more adaptable and collaborative team member.

Key Takeaways:

1. **Be Specific:** Clearly describe the conflict and the context to provide a comprehensive understanding of the situation.

2. **Highlight Your Role:** Emphasize your personal actions in resolving the conflict, showcasing your leadership and problem-solving abilities.

3. **Show Emotional Intelligence:** Demonstrate your ability to manage emotions, maintain professionalism, and foster a positive work environment.

4. **Focus on Resolution:** Highlight the steps you took to resolve the conflict and the successful outcome that followed, illustrating your ability to turn challenges into opportunities for growth.

39. DESCRIBE A TIME WHEN YOU HAD TO LEARN SOMETHING QUICKLY.

Tips:

1. **Be Relevant:** Select an example that is directly relevant to the job you are applying for. Ensure the scenario you choose highlights skills or knowledge areas that align with the role's requirements.

2. **Highlight Your Approach:** Focus on the methods and strategies you employed to learn quickly. This could include self-study, seeking out resources, or collaborating with others. Emphasize your ability to be proactive and resourceful.

3. **Show Results:** Clearly outline the positive outcomes that resulted from your quick learning. Whether it's improved efficiency, successful project completion, or enhanced team performance, make sure the impact of your learning is evident.

4. **Reflect on the Experience:** Discuss what you learned from the experience and how it has prepared you for similar challenges in the future. This reflection shows your ability to grow and adapt from every experience.

Response Framework:

1. **Brief Introduction:** Start by introducing the situation where you needed to learn something quickly. Set the context by explaining the importance of the knowledge or skill and why it was critical to the task or project at hand. This establishes the urgency and relevance of the learning process.

2. **Setting the Scene:** Describe the specific circumstances that necessitated quick learning. Explain the challenge you faced, such as a new tool, process, or subject matter that you had to master rapidly. Highlight any external pressures, like tight deadlines or high stakes, that added to the challenge.

3. **Approach to Learning:** Detail the strategies you employed to learn quickly and effectively. Discuss how you prioritized the most critical information or skills needed for the task. Mention any resources you used, such as online courses, manuals, expert consultations, or peer support. This section should emphasize your ability to focus, organize, and adapt to new information under pressure.

4. **Implementing the Learning:** Explain how you applied the knowledge or skills you acquired in a real-world setting. Discuss the steps you took to ensure that your learning translated into effective action. If applicable, mention how you supported others in adapting to the new knowledge or process, such as by leading training sessions or providing guidance.

5. **Outcome:** Describe the results of your quick learning and implementation. Highlight the positive impact on the project or task, using quantifiable outcomes if possible, such as meeting deadlines, improving efficiency, or achieving specific goals. This demonstrates the effectiveness of your learning and adaptability.

6. **Reflecting on the Experience:** Conclude by reflecting on the lessons learned from the experience. Discuss how this situation enhanced your ability to learn quickly and adapt to new challenges. Emphasize how this skill is relevant to the role you are applying for, showing that you are prepared to handle similar situations in the future.

Key Takeaways:

1. **Be Relevant:** Choose an example that highlights skills pertinent to the job, ensuring the story is directly applicable to the role you are seeking.

2. **Highlight Your Approach:** Focus on the methods and strategies you used to quickly learn something new, demonstrating your proactive and resourceful nature.

3. **Show Results:** Clearly show the positive outcomes that resulted from your quick learning, whether through improved efficiency, successful project completion, or other measurable impacts.

4. **Reflect on the Experience:** Discuss what you learned from the experience and how it prepares you for future challenges, showing your commitment to growth and adaptability.

40. TELL ME ABOUT A TIME WHEN YOU DEMONSTRATED LEADERSHIP.

Tips:

1. **Be Relevant:** Select an example that demonstrates leadership skills pertinent to the job you're applying for. Whether it's leading a team through a challenging project or guiding a group towards a common goal, ensure the situation is directly related to the role you're seeking.

2. **Highlight Your Approach:** Focus on the specific strategies and actions you took to lead effectively. Detail how you managed the team, addressed challenges, and facilitated collaboration. Emphasize your role in decision-making and problem-solving.

3. **Show Results:** Clearly outline the positive outcomes resulting from your leadership. Whether it's meeting a deadline, exceeding performance goals, or improving team dynamics, make sure the impact of your leadership is evident.

4. **Reflect on the Experience:** Discuss what you learned from this leadership experience and how it has prepared you for future roles. This reflection shows your ability to grow and adapt as a leader.

Response Framework:

1. **Brief Introduction:** Begin by introducing the situation where you had the opportunity to demonstrate leadership. Clearly state your role and the context in which your leadership was required. This sets the stage for discussing the specific actions you took.

2. **Setting the Scene:** Describe the circumstances that necessitated your leadership. Highlight the challenges or obstacles that were present, such as a lack of direction, team misalignment, or a critical deadline. This context helps the interviewer understand why strong leadership was essential in this situation.

3. **Leadership Approach:** Outline the approach you took to address the challenges. Discuss the strategies you implemented to lead effectively, such as organizing meetings, setting clear goals, or improving communication. This section should emphasize your proactive steps and your ability to bring order and focus to the situation.

4. **Implementing Leadership:** Detail how you put your leadership plan into action. Explain how you communicated with your team, provided guidance, and motivated team members. Mention any specific actions you took to support and develop your team, such as mentoring, offering feedback, or recognizing achievements. This showcases your hands-on leadership style and your ability to drive the team forward.

5. **Outcome:** Describe the results of your leadership efforts. Highlight the positive impact on the project or team, using concrete metrics or outcomes where possible, such as meeting deadlines, improving team cohesion, or achieving project goals. This demonstrates the effectiveness of your leadership in delivering successful results.

6. **Reflecting on the Experience:** Conclude by reflecting on what you learned from the experience. Discuss how this leadership opportunity reinforced your understanding of effective leadership principles, such as communication, empathy, and adaptability. Emphasize how these lessons continue to influence your leadership style and how they align with the role you are applying for.

Key Takeaways:

1. **Be Relevant:** Choose an example that highlights leadership skills directly related to the job. This demonstrates that you have the necessary expertise for the role.

2. **Highlight Your Approach:** Focus on the strategies and actions you took to lead effectively, showcasing your problem-solving and decision-making abilities.

3. **Show Results:** Emphasize the positive outcomes of your leadership, illustrating the tangible impact you made on the project or team.

4. **Reflect on the Experience:** Discuss what you learned and how it has prepared you for future leadership roles, showing your commitment to continuous improvement and growth as a leader.

CHAPTER 5
SITUATIONAL QUESTIONS

41. WHAT WOULD YOU DO IF YOU WERE ASSIGNED A PROJECT WITH A TIGHT DEADLINE?

Tips:

1. **Assess the Situation:** Start by gaining a clear understanding of the project's scope, requirements, and timeline. This initial assessment is crucial for determining the steps you need to take and identifying any potential challenges.

2. **Prioritize Tasks:** Break down the project into smaller tasks and prioritize them based on their importance and urgency. Identifying the critical path allows you to focus on tasks that are vital to the project's success.

3. **Create a Plan:** Develop a structured plan that outlines each step needed to complete the project. Include clear milestones and deadlines to ensure that you stay on track and can monitor progress effectively.

4. **Communicate Effectively:** Regular communication with stakeholders is essential to manage expectations and keep everyone informed of progress. Address any issues or potential delays as soon as they arise to find collaborative solutions.

5. **Stay Focused:** Maintain a high level of concentration by managing your time efficiently. Limit distractions and allocate specific time slots to each task, ensuring that you can work uninterrupted.

6. **Seek Support:** If the project is too large to manage alone, don't hesitate to delegate tasks to team members or seek assistance from colleagues. Effective teamwork can help ensure that the project is completed on time without sacrificing quality.

Response Framework:

1. **Assess the Situation:** Start by thoroughly assessing the project's scope, objectives, and requirements. Ensure you have a clear understanding of the goals and any constraints by reviewing all documentation and clarifying any ambiguities with relevant stakeholders. This initial step is crucial to accurately gauge the workload and the urgency of the deadline.

2. **Prioritize Tasks:** Next, prioritize the tasks based on their importance and impact on the overall project. Identify the critical path—the sequence of essential tasks that determine the project's completion time—and focus on these high-priority items first. Breaking down the project into manageable tasks allows for efficient time allocation and resource management.

3. **Create a Detailed Plan:** Develop a detailed project plan that outlines each task, with specific milestones and deadlines. Utilize project management tools to map out each step required to complete the project, ensuring that the timeline is realistic and achievable. This plan will serve as a roadmap to keep the project on track and ensure that all aspects are covered.

4. **Communicate Effectively:** Maintain clear and consistent communication with all stakeholders throughout the project. Regularly update them on progress through meetings, reports, or briefings. If any challenges or delays arise, address them promptly by collaborating with the team to find solutions. Effective communication ensures that everyone is aligned and that expectations are managed.

5. **Stay Focused and Manage Time Efficiently:** To meet the deadline, implement strict time management strategies. Allocate specific time slots for each task, minimize distractions, and stay focused on the most critical activities. This disciplined approach helps maintain momentum and ensures that the project progresses according to the plan.

6. **Seek Support and Delegate:** If the project's scope is too large to handle alone, consider delegating tasks to team members or seeking assistance from colleagues. Leveraging the strengths of the team can help distribute the workload more effectively, ensuring that the project is completed on time without compromising on quality.

7. **Monitor and Adjust:** Continuously monitor the progress of the project against the plan. Be prepared to make adjustments if necessary, whether that means reallocating resources, adjusting timelines, or revisiting the priorities. Flexibility in response to unforeseen challenges is key to successfully managing tight deadlines.

Key Takeaways:

1. **Assess the Situation:** Start by understanding the project's scope and requirements thoroughly. This step is critical for setting the foundation for a successful outcome.

2. **Prioritize Tasks:** Focus on the most critical tasks first, ensuring that you allocate your time and resources where they are needed most.

3. **Create a Plan:** Develop a structured plan with clear milestones and deadlines. This will help you stay organized and monitor your progress.

4. **Communicate Effectively:** Keep stakeholders informed of your progress and address any potential issues early to prevent delays.

5. **Stay Focused:** Manage your time efficiently and maintain a high level of focus by minimizing distractions.

6. **Seek Support:** Don't hesitate to delegate tasks or seek help if necessary. Effective teamwork can ensure that the project is completed on time and to a high standard

42. HOW WOULD YOU HANDLE A SITUATION WHERE YOU HAD TO MANAGE A DIFFICULT TEAM MEMBER?

Tips:

1. **Understand the Issue:** Begin by identifying the underlying cause of the team member's challenging behavior. This might involve observing their interactions, reviewing their work, and speaking with other

team members to gather different perspectives. Understanding the root cause is crucial before taking any action.

2. **Communicate Clearly:** Schedule a one-on-one conversation with the team member to discuss the situation. Approach the discussion with empathy, listening to their side of the story while also expressing your observations. Clear communication is key to finding out what might be driving their behavior and determining how best to address it.

3. **Set Expectations:** Once you've had an open conversation, set clear expectations for behavior and performance going forward. This includes defining roles and responsibilities, as well as outlining the specific changes that need to be made. Establishing clear expectations helps create a mutual understanding of what's required to move forward positively.

4. **Provide Support:** Offer the team member resources or guidance to help them improve. This could include additional training, mentoring, or even just regular check-ins. Demonstrating that you're invested in their success shows that you're willing to work with them to overcome their challenges, fostering a more supportive work environment.

5. **Monitor Progress:** Regular follow-ups are essential. Check in with the team member periodically to monitor their progress and provide constructive feedback. Acknowledge improvements, address any ongoing issues, and adjust your approach as necessary. Continuous monitoring reinforces positive behavior changes and keeps the momentum going.

6. **Escalate if Necessary:** If, despite your efforts, the situation does not improve, it may be necessary to escalate the issue to higher management or HR. Escalation should be a last resort, used when all other attempts to resolve the issue have been exhausted. Document your actions and communications throughout the process to ensure there's a clear record of your efforts.

Response Framework:

1. **Understand the Issue:** Start by thoroughly understanding the root cause of the team member's difficult behavior. Observe their interactions and performance, and gather feedback from other colleagues if necessary. Identifying specific issues or patterns is essential for accurately addressing the problem.

2. **Communicate Clearly:** Schedule a private, one-on-one meeting with the team member to discuss the situation. Approach the conversation with empathy, allowing them to share their perspective while you express your concerns. Clear and open communication is crucial for understanding their viewpoint and building a foundation for resolving the issue.

3. **Set Expectations:** During the discussion, clearly outline the roles, responsibilities, and expected behaviors moving forward. Explain how their actions are impacting the team and project outcomes, and set specific, measurable expectations for improvement. Establishing these guidelines creates accountability and sets a clear path for positive change.

4. **Provide Support:** Offer support to help the team member improve, such as additional training, resources, or mentoring. Demonstrating a willingness to invest in their success can be motivating and encourages them to take constructive steps towards better performance. This support is key to facilitating their development and fostering a positive working relationship.

5. **Monitor Progress:** Regularly check in with the team member to monitor their progress and provide ongoing feedback. Use these meetings to acknowledge improvements, address any new concerns, and adjust your approach as necessary. Consistent monitoring helps ensure that the positive changes are sustained and that the team member is staying on track.

6. **Escalate if Necessary:** If the situation does not improve despite your efforts, consider escalating the issue to higher management or HR as a last resort. Document all steps taken, including meetings, feedback provided, and support offered, to maintain a clear record. This documentation is essential for ensuring that the escalation is handled appropriately and fairly.

Key Takeaways:

1. **Understand the Issue:** Identify the root cause of the difficulty by observing and gathering feedback.

2. **Communicate Clearly:** Have an open, honest conversation to discuss the issue and understand the team member's perspective.

3. **Set Expectations:** Clearly define roles, responsibilities, and the expected changes.

4. **Provide Support:** Offer resources and guidance to help the team member improve, showing your investment in their success.

5. **Monitor Progress:** Regularly check in and provide feedback to reinforce positive changes.

6. **Escalate if Necessary:** If improvement doesn't occur, involve higher management or HR, documenting all steps taken to resolve the issue.

43. WHAT WOULD YOU DO IF YOU DISAGREED WITH A DECISION MADE BY YOUR MANAGER?

Tips:

1. **Stay Professional:** It's crucial to maintain respect and professionalism when addressing disagreements with your manager. Keep the focus on the issue, not the individuals involved. Avoid letting emotions or personal feelings dictate your approach, and ensure that your primary goal is to contribute positively to the team and the organization.

2. **Understand the Rationale:** Before raising your concerns, take the time to fully understand your manager's reasoning behind the decision. This may involve asking clarifying questions and listening carefully to their explanations. Gaining insight into their perspective is key to having a constructive discussion and might even reveal factors you hadn't initially considered.

3. **Gather Facts:** Support your viewpoint with relevant data and information. Whether it's performance metrics, industry best practices, or feedback from colleagues, having concrete evidence makes your argument more persuasive and demonstrates that your concerns are based on facts rather than opinions.

4. **Choose the Right Time:** Timing is essential when addressing a disagreement. Choose an appropriate time and setting, ideally a private meeting, where you can discuss the issue without distractions. Addressing the matter at the right moment can make the conversation more productive and less likely to be confrontational.

5. **Communicate Clearly:** When discussing the issue with your manager, be clear and constructive in presenting your viewpoint. Focus on explaining why you believe the decision might not be the best course of action and how it could impact the team or project. It's important to stay calm and objective, keeping the discussion centered on the issue rather than getting personal.

6. **Be Open to Compromise:** Be prepared to find a middle ground or, if necessary, accept the decision. Understand that your manager may have access to information or considerations that you might not be

aware of. Flexibility and a willingness to compromise demonstrate that you are a team player and that you respect your manager's authority.

Response Framework:

1. **Stay Professional:** Begin by emphasizing the importance of maintaining professionalism and respect when addressing any disagreement with your manager. Your focus should be on preserving a positive working relationship and contributing to the overall success of the team and organization.

2. **Understand the Rationale:** Before expressing your disagreement, take the time to fully understand the reasoning behind your manager's decision. This involves asking clarifying questions and actively listening to their explanation. By gaining insight into their perspective, you can approach the discussion with a well-informed and constructive mindset.

3. **Gather Facts:** Support your viewpoint with relevant data and information. Whether it's performance metrics, industry best practices, or feedback from team members, presenting well-researched evidence strengthens your argument and demonstrates that your concerns are grounded in facts rather than personal opinions.

4. **Choose the Right Time:** Select an appropriate time and setting for the discussion, ideally in a private meeting where distractions are minimized. Timing is crucial—addressing the issue when both parties are calm and focused increases the likelihood of a productive conversation aimed at resolving the disagreement.

5. **Communicate Clearly:** During the discussion, present your perspective clearly and constructively. Explain why you believe the decision might have potential drawbacks and discuss the possible impacts on the team or project. Maintaining a calm, issue-focused approach is key to ensuring a successful and respectful dialogue.

6. **Be Open to Compromise:** Finally, demonstrate your willingness to compromise or accept the decision if necessary. Recognize that managers may have access to broader information that influences their choices. Showing flexibility and a readiness to align with the final decision underscores your commitment to the team's success and respect for your manager's authority.

Key Takeaways:

1. **Stay Professional:** Maintain respect and professionalism in all interactions.

2. **Understand the Rationale:** Seek to fully understand the reasoning behind the decision before raising concerns.

3. **Gather Facts:** Support your viewpoint with relevant data and evidence.

4. **Choose the Right Time:** Select an appropriate time and setting for the discussion.

5. **Communicate Clearly:** Present your viewpoint constructively and remain focused on the issue.

6. **Be Open to Compromise:** Be willing to find a middle ground or accept the decision if necessary.

44. HOW WOULD YOU HANDLE AN UPSET CUSTOMER OR CLIENT?

Tips:

1. **Listen Actively:** When dealing with an upset customer, the first and most important step is to listen actively. Allow the customer to express their concerns fully without interruption. This not only helps you understand the issue better but also shows empathy and respect, which can help to diffuse their frustration. Make sure your body language and verbal cues demonstrate that you are attentive and genuinely concerned about their experience.

2. **Stay Calm:** It's vital to maintain your composure, no matter how challenging the situation becomes. By staying calm and professional, you set a positive tone for the conversation and help prevent the situation from escalating. Your calm demeanor can also reassure the customer that you are in control and capable of resolving the issue.

3. **Apologize Sincerely:** Offering a sincere apology is crucial in acknowledging the customer's frustration. Apologize not just for the specific issue they're facing but for the inconvenience it has caused them. A genuine apology demonstrates that you take their concerns seriously and are committed to making things right.

4. **Find a Solution:** After understanding the problem, shift your focus to finding an effective solution. Work within company policies to offer a resolution that meets the customer's needs. If necessary, involve other team members or departments to ensure that the solution is both quick and effective. The goal is to leave the customer feeling that their issue has been addressed adequately.

5. **Follow Up:** After resolving the issue, following up with the customer is key. This could be a phone call, email, or another form of communication, depending on the situation. Following up shows that you care about their overall experience and are committed to ensuring their satisfaction. It also helps to reinforce positive relations and can turn a negative experience into a loyal customer relationship.

Response Framework:

1. **Listen Actively:** Begin by actively listening to the customer or client's concerns without interruption. Allow them to fully express their frustration, showing empathy through your tone and body language. This initial step is crucial for diffusing tension and demonstrating that you genuinely care about their experience.

2. **Stay Calm and Composed:** Maintain a calm and composed demeanor throughout the interaction. Regardless of the customer's emotional state, it's important to remain professional and focused on resolving the issue. Your calmness can help de-escalate the situation and provide reassurance to the customer that their concerns are being taken seriously.

3. **Acknowledge and Apologize:** After understanding the issue, offer a sincere apology for the inconvenience or frustration the customer has experienced. Acknowledging their feelings and apologizing shows that you are taking responsibility and are committed to making things right. This step is vital in rebuilding trust and diffusing any lingering anger.

4. **Identify and Offer a Solution:** Once you've gathered all the necessary information, focus on finding a practical and effective solution. Consider the customer's needs and expectations while working within company policies to provide a satisfactory resolution. If the solution requires collaboration with other departments, ensure that you take the initiative to coordinate these efforts promptly.

5. **Follow Up to Ensure Satisfaction:** After the issue has been resolved, follow up with the customer to confirm their satisfaction. This could be through a phone call or email, depending on the situation. Following up reinforces your commitment to customer satisfaction and helps in maintaining a positive relationship, even after a challenging interaction.

Key Takeaways:

1. **Listen Actively:** Prioritize understanding the customer's concerns by letting them speak without interruption.

2. **Stay Calm:** Maintain professionalism and composure to help de-escalate the situation.

3. **Apologize Sincerely:** A genuine apology can go a long way in rebuilding trust and showing that you take their concerns seriously.

4. **Find a Solution:** Focus on resolving the issue quickly and effectively, working within company policies.

5. **Follow Up:** Ensure the customer is satisfied with the resolution by following up, reinforcing a commitment to excellent service.

45. WHAT STEPS WOULD YOU TAKE IF YOU FOUND A MISTAKE IN YOUR WORK?

Tips:

1. **Acknowledge the Mistake:** The first step in handling a mistake is to promptly acknowledge it. Ignoring or delaying recognition can exacerbate the issue. Acknowledging the mistake not only reflects your integrity but also helps in maintaining the trust of your colleagues and supervisors.

2. **Analyze the Cause:** After recognizing the mistake, it's essential to analyze the root cause. Understanding how and why the error occurred allows you to learn from the situation and prevent similar mistakes in the future. This step is crucial for personal development and improving work processes.

3. **Inform Relevant Parties:** Communication is key in managing mistakes. Once the error has been identified and analyzed, promptly inform those who are affected or involved. This transparency allows everyone to understand the situation and collaborate on finding a solution. It also demonstrates your responsibility and accountability.

4. **Correct the Error:** After communicating the mistake, the next step is to correct it as quickly and efficiently as possible. Whether it involves redoing a task or providing additional information, the focus should be on minimizing any negative impact and ensuring that the solution is implemented effectively.

5. **Implement Preventive Measures:** Finally, to avoid repeating the same mistake, implement preventive measures. This could involve revising your workflow, enhancing quality checks, or seeking feedback from others. Preventive actions not only help in reducing future errors but also contribute to continuous improvement in your work.

Response Framework:

1. **Acknowledge the Mistake:** Begin by immediately recognizing and acknowledging the mistake. It's important to address the issue directly to demonstrate accountability and maintain trust. This step is crucial in preventing the mistake from escalating or causing further complications.

2. **Analyze the Cause:** Next, take the time to investigate and understand the root cause of the mistake. Consider whether it was due to a misunderstanding, a lack of resources, a process gap, or another factor. This analysis is essential for identifying the underlying issue and ensuring that similar mistakes can be avoided in the future.

3. **Inform Relevant Parties:** After understanding the cause, promptly inform all relevant parties about the mistake. Transparency is key here; clearly communicate what the mistake was, the potential impact,

and the steps you are taking to correct it. Keeping everyone informed helps in managing the situation effectively and maintains trust within the team.

4. **Correct the Error:** Once you have informed the necessary parties, take immediate action to correct the mistake. Depending on the nature of the error, this could involve redoing work, correcting data, or updating stakeholders. The focus should be on minimizing any negative impact and resolving the issue as efficiently as possible.

5. **Implement Preventive Measures:** Finally, put measures in place to prevent the mistake from happening again. This might involve revising workflows, introducing additional quality checks, or undergoing further training. By implementing these preventive steps, you demonstrate a commitment to continuous improvement and to delivering high-quality work.

Key Takeaways:

1. **Acknowledge the Mistake:** Prompt recognition of an error is crucial for maintaining trust and preventing further issues.

2. **Analyze the Cause:** Understanding the root cause of the mistake helps in preventing it from happening again and contributes to personal and professional growth.

3. **Inform Relevant Parties:** Clear and transparent communication with those involved is essential for effective problem resolution.

4. **Correct the Error:** Taking swift action to correct the mistake is vital in minimizing its impact and maintaining work quality.

5. **Implement Preventive Measures:** Putting in place procedures to avoid similar mistakes in the future ensures continuous improvement and reliability in your work.

46. DESCRIBE HOW YOU WOULD MANAGE MULTIPLE COMPETING DEADLINES.

Tips:

1. **Prioritize Tasks:** The first step in managing multiple deadlines is to prioritize your tasks. Evaluate each task's urgency and importance, considering factors such as business impact, client expectations, and dependencies. This helps you determine which tasks need immediate attention and which can be scheduled for later.

2. **Create a Schedule:** Once priorities are set, develop a detailed schedule that breaks down each task into smaller, manageable components. Assign specific time slots to these tasks, ensuring that you have a clear plan for completing everything on time. Tools like Gantt charts or project management software can be helpful in visualizing timelines and keeping track of progress.

3. **Communicate Effectively:** Communication is key when juggling multiple deadlines. Keep stakeholders informed about your progress, anticipated completion times, and any potential issues. Regular updates help manage expectations and can provide an opportunity to negotiate deadlines if necessary.

4. **Stay Organized:** Organization is critical to ensure that no task is overlooked. Use project management tools to track deadlines, monitor progress, and stay on top of changes. Staying organized allows you to maintain a clear overview of your workload and ensures that you can quickly adapt to any unexpected developments.

5. **Remain Flexible:** Flexibility is essential when managing competing deadlines. Be prepared to adjust your schedule if unforeseen challenges arise. This might involve re-prioritizing tasks, delegating work, or seeking additional resources. By staying adaptable, you can ensure that all tasks are completed to a high standard, even under pressure.

Response Framework:

1. **Prioritize Tasks:** Begin by assessing the urgency and importance of each task. Evaluate the deadlines, the potential impact on the business, and any task interdependencies. This helps create a clear priority list, ensuring that the most critical tasks receive attention first. Prioritization is key to managing your time effectively and ensuring that high-impact tasks are completed on schedule.

2. **Develop a Structured Schedule:** Once priorities are established, create a detailed schedule that outlines each task's steps and deadlines. Use tools like Gantt charts or project management software to visualize the timeline and allocate specific time blocks for each task. This structured approach allows you to manage your time efficiently, ensuring steady progress across all tasks.

3. **Communicate Regularly:** Effective communication is essential when handling multiple deadlines. Keep all relevant stakeholders informed of your progress with regular updates. This transparency helps manage expectations and enables early detection of potential issues. If challenges arise that could impact deadlines, communicate them promptly to collaborate on adjustments or solutions.

4. **Stay Organized:** Utilize project management tools such as Trello, Asana, or similar platforms to keep track of deadlines, monitor progress, and ensure that no task is overlooked. Staying organized is critical to maintaining a clear overview of all tasks and being able to respond quickly to any changes or urgent needs that may arise.

5. **Maintain Flexibility:** Flexibility is crucial when managing competing deadlines. Be prepared to adjust your plans if unexpected challenges occur, such as shifting priorities or resource constraints. This might involve re-prioritizing tasks, delegating responsibilities, or seeking additional resources. By staying adaptable, you can ensure that all deadlines are met without compromising the quality of your work.

Key Takeaways:

1. **Prioritize Tasks:** Start by evaluating the urgency and importance of each task to determine which ones need immediate attention.

2. **Create a Schedule:** Develop a structured plan that allocates time for each task, ensuring consistent progress across all projects.

3. **Communicate Effectively:** Keep stakeholders informed about your progress and any potential delays to manage expectations and facilitate collaboration.

4. **Stay Organized:** Use project management tools to track deadlines and monitor progress, ensuring that nothing is overlooked.

5. **Remain Flexible:** Be prepared to adjust your plans if unexpected issues arise, allowing you to maintain quality and meet deadlines despite challenges.

47. WHAT WOULD YOU DO IF YOU WERE ASKED TO PERFORM A TASK YOU HAVE NEVER DONE BEFORE?

Tips:

1. **Acknowledge the Challenge:** It's important to admit that the task is new to you. Demonstrating honesty and humility shows that you are open to learning and are not afraid to tackle new challenges. This attitude will help you maintain a positive mindset as you navigate the unfamiliar territory.

2. **Research and Learn:** Take the initiative to research and understand the task thoroughly. Use available resources such as online materials, manuals, and industry best practices. This step helps you build a strong foundation and equips you with the knowledge needed to approach the task with confidence.

3. **Seek Guidance:** Don't hesitate to seek advice from colleagues or experts who have experience with the task. Their insights can provide you with practical tips and shortcuts that might not be immediately obvious. Collaboration also fosters a supportive work environment and helps you build relationships with your team.

4. **Practice and Implement:** Once you've gathered the necessary information, it's time to apply what you've learned. Break the task down into manageable steps and approach it methodically. Practicing and iterating on your approach will help you refine your skills and ensure a higher quality outcome.

5. **Review and Reflect:** After completing the task, take the time to review your work and reflect on the experience. Identifying what went well and what could be improved is crucial for your growth. Seek feedback from others to gain different perspectives and apply these lessons to future tasks.

Response Framework:

1. **Acknowledge the Challenge:** Start by acknowledging that the task is new and outside your current experience. Demonstrating honesty about your unfamiliarity with the task shows humility and a willingness to learn. This approach sets the tone for a proactive and positive mindset, essential for tackling new challenges effectively.

2. **Research and Prepare:** Take the initiative to thoroughly research the task at hand. Utilize available resources such as online tutorials, industry publications, or internal documentation to gain a solid understanding of what is required. Building a foundational knowledge base prepares you to approach the task with greater confidence and reduces the likelihood of mistakes.

3. **Seek Guidance and Collaborate:** Don't hesitate to reach out to colleagues, supervisors, or industry experts who may have experience with the task. Their insights and advice can offer practical tips and best practices that may not be immediately apparent through self-research alone. This step also fosters collaboration and reinforces the idea that teamwork is valuable in navigating new challenges.

4. **Plan, Practice, and Execute:** Once you have gathered the necessary information, create a clear plan of action. Break the task down into manageable steps and approach it methodically. Begin by practicing any new skills required and then proceed to execute the task with careful attention to detail. This structured approach ensures that you manage the task effectively and deliver quality results.

5. **Review and Reflect:** After completing the task, take the time to review your work critically. Reflect on what went well and identify areas for improvement. Gathering feedback from colleagues or supervisors can provide valuable insights that you can apply to future tasks. This reflection helps you learn from the experience and enhances your ability to handle similar challenges in the future.

Key Takeaways:

1. **Acknowledge the Challenge:** Recognize when a task is new to you and approach it as an opportunity to learn.

2. **Research and Learn:** Conduct thorough research and gather all necessary information before starting the task.

3. **Seek Guidance:** Don't hesitate to ask for help or advice from more experienced colleagues or experts.

4. **Practice and Implement:** Break the task into smaller steps, apply what you've learned, and adjust as necessary.

5. **Review and Reflect:** Evaluate your performance and seek feedback to enhance your skills for future tasks.

48. HOW WOULD YOU PRIORITIZE YOUR WORK IF YOUR MANAGER GAVE YOU MULTIPLE TASKS WITH THE SAME DEADLINE?

Tips:

1. **Assess Urgency and Importance:** Begin by evaluating each task to determine its urgency and importance. Understanding which tasks have the most significant impact on the organization's goals or are most time-sensitive can help you prioritize effectively. Using a prioritization matrix or similar tool can be helpful in categorizing tasks into those that are urgent and important versus those that are less critical.

2. **Communicate with Your Manager:** It's essential to have a conversation with your manager to clarify expectations and priorities. Discussing the tasks and understanding their relative importance from your manager's perspective ensures that you're aligned with their vision. This conversation can also provide an opportunity to ask for guidance or additional resources if necessary.

3. **Break Down Tasks:** After determining the priority of each task, break them down into smaller, more manageable steps. This approach not only makes the tasks seem less daunting but also allows you to track your progress more effectively. By setting specific milestones, you can maintain a clear focus and stay on schedule.

4. **Create a Schedule:** Developing a detailed plan or schedule is crucial for managing your time effectively. Allocate specific time blocks to each task, keeping in mind their priority and the effort required. Including buffer times can help accommodate any unforeseen delays or additional tasks that may arise, ensuring that you stay on track.

5. **Stay Flexible:** While it's important to stick to your plan, flexibility is key to handling unexpected changes or new priorities. Regularly reviewing your progress and being ready to adjust your plan as needed allows you to manage your workload effectively, ensuring that you can deliver quality work on time, even under pressure.

Response Framework:

1. **Assess Urgency and Importance:** Start by evaluating the urgency and importance of each task. Use a prioritization framework, such as the Eisenhower Matrix, to categorize tasks based on their impact and time sensitivity. This approach helps you identify which tasks are most critical to the organization's objectives and require immediate attention. By clearly understanding the importance of each task, you can allocate your time and resources more effectively.

2. **Communicate with Your Manager:** Next, engage in a discussion with your manager to clarify their expectations and priorities. This conversation is essential for aligning your efforts with their strategic vision and understanding which tasks they deem most critical. Additionally, this dialogue provides an opportunity to request any necessary resources or support, ensuring you are fully equipped to handle the workload efficiently.

3. **Break Down Tasks:** Once priorities are established, break down each task into smaller, manageable components. This approach makes the workload more digestible and allows for better monitoring of progress. By setting clear milestones for each sub-task, you can keep track of your advancement and identify potential issues early, minimizing risks and ensuring that you remain on schedule.

4. **Create a Schedule:** Develop a detailed schedule that assigns specific time slots to each task based on its priority and the effort required. Incorporate buffer times to accommodate unexpected changes or additional tasks that may arise. Adhering to this structured plan helps maintain organization and focus, ensuring that you make consistent progress on all tasks without missing any deadlines.

5. **Stay Flexible:** Finally, maintain flexibility in your approach. While following the schedule is important, adaptability is key to responding effectively to any new priorities or unforeseen challenges. Regularly review your progress and be prepared to make adjustments as needed to stay aligned with the overall goals. This flexibility ensures that you can meet deadlines while delivering high-quality work across all tasks.

Key Takeaways:

1. **Assess Urgency and Importance:** Evaluate each task based on urgency and impact to prioritize your workload effectively.

2. **Communicate with Your Manager:** Engage in discussions with your manager to align on priorities and expectations.

3. **Break Down Tasks:** Decompose larger tasks into smaller steps to make them more manageable and easier to track.

4. **Create a Schedule:** Develop a detailed plan that allocates time effectively and includes buffer periods for potential disruptions.

5. **Stay Flexible:** Be adaptable and ready to adjust your plan as circumstances change, ensuring you meet all deadlines with high-quality work.

49. WHAT WOULD YOU DO IF A TEAM MEMBER WASN'T CONTRIBUTING TO A PROJECT?

Tips:

1. **Assess the Situation:** Start by carefully observing the team member's behavior and work output. Gather feedback from other team members to get a comprehensive view of the situation. Determine whether the lack of contribution stems from personal issues, skill gaps, or unclear expectations. Understanding the root cause is essential for addressing the issue effectively.

2. **Communicate Directly:** Engage in a private, one-on-one conversation with the team member. Approach the discussion with empathy, showing a genuine interest in understanding their perspective. Use open-ended questions to encourage them to share any difficulties they might be facing. This approach fosters trust and helps to uncover underlying issues that might not be immediately apparent.

3. **Offer Support:** Based on the insights gained from your conversation, offer appropriate support to help the team member improve. This could involve providing additional training, resources, or adjusting their workload to better align with their capabilities. Demonstrating a commitment to their success can motivate the team member to engage more fully with the project.

4. **Set Clear Expectations:** Ensure that the team member clearly understands their role, responsibilities, and the expectations for their contribution. Clarify how their work impacts the overall success of the project. Setting clear expectations can help prevent misunderstandings and align their efforts with the team's goals.

5. **Monitor Progress:** Regularly check in on the team member's progress through scheduled feedback sessions. Offer constructive feedback where necessary and acknowledge improvements. Consistent monitoring helps maintain accountability and ensures that any issues are addressed promptly, keeping the project on track.

Response Framework:

1. **Assess the Situation:** Begin by evaluating the situation to understand why the team member isn't contributing effectively. Observe their behavior and work output to identify any noticeable issues. Engage with other team members to gather their perspectives on the situation. This initial assessment helps determine whether the problem is related to personal challenges, skill gaps, or unclear expectations, allowing you to tailor your approach accordingly.

2. **Communicate Directly:** Initiate a private and direct conversation with the team member to discuss the observed issues. Approach this discussion with empathy, focusing on understanding their viewpoint without making them feel defensive. Use open-ended questions to uncover any underlying challenges they may be facing, whether they are related to personal circumstances or professional difficulties. This step is essential in building trust and ensuring that the team member feels heard and supported.

3. **Offer Support:** Based on the insights gained from your conversation, offer appropriate support to help the team member improve their contribution. This could involve providing additional training, adjusting their workload to better match their strengths, or offering resources that could assist them in overcoming any obstacles. The goal is to empower them to succeed and reinforce the importance of their role within the team.

4. **4. Set Clear Expectations:** Clarify the specific expectations for the team member's role and contribution to the project. Ensure they understand how their work fits into the larger project goals and emphasize the importance of their input. Clear expectations help align their efforts with the team's objectives and provide them with a clear understanding of what is required to meet project standards.

5. **Monitor Progress:** Establish a system of regular check-ins and feedback sessions to monitor the team member's progress. Provide positive reinforcement for any improvements and constructive feedback where further attention is needed. This ongoing support ensures they remain on track and maintains their motivation and commitment to the project. Continuous monitoring allows for timely adjustments and helps sustain their engagement throughout the project.

Key Takeaways:

1. **Assess the Situation:** Begin by understanding the root cause of the team member's lack of contribution through careful observation and feedback.

2. **Communicate Directly:** Engage in empathetic and open communication to understand their perspective and challenges.

3. **Offer Support:** Provide the necessary resources and support to help them overcome obstacles and improve their contribution.

4. **Set Clear Expectations:** Clearly define roles, responsibilities, and expectations to align their efforts with the team's goals.

5. **Monitor Progress:** Regularly check in on their progress and provide feedback to ensure continuous improvement and motivation.

50. HOW WOULD YOU APPROACH A TASK YOU FIND BORING?

<u>Tips:</u>

1. **Understand the Purpose:** It's essential to see the bigger picture when tackling a task you find boring. Recognize how this task contributes to the overall project or organizational goals. Understanding its significance can help you stay motivated, knowing that your work, even on mundane tasks, plays a crucial role in achieving success.

2. **Set Personal Goals:** Establishing clear, personal goals for completing the task can transform a boring activity into a more engaging one. Set deadlines for each segment or create milestones to track your progress. These goals can provide a sense of achievement, making the task feel more meaningful and rewarding.

3. **Break It Down:** Dividing the task into smaller, manageable parts can make it less daunting and easier to handle. Tackling one piece at a time allows you to maintain momentum and stay productive, as each completed step brings a sense of progress.

4. **Stay Organized:** Use tools such as checklists, time management apps, or project management software to keep yourself organized. These tools help you track your progress and ensure you stay on schedule. Staying organized can also prevent frustration, keeping you focused and efficient throughout the task.

5. **Maintain a Positive Attitude:** A positive mindset can make a significant difference when dealing with boring tasks. Viewing the task as an opportunity to demonstrate your reliability and thoroughness can help you stay motivated. Additionally, finding ways to make the task more enjoyable, such as listening to music or rewarding yourself after completing sections, can help maintain a positive outlook.

<u>Response Framework:</u>

1. **Understand the Purpose:** Begin by identifying the task's purpose within the broader context of the project or organization. Understanding how this task contributes to the overall goals can shift your perspective and increase your motivation. Recognizing its importance reinforces your role in the success of the project and makes even mundane tasks feel meaningful.

2. **Set Personal Goals:** Establish specific, personal goals for completing the task. These might include deadlines, quality benchmarks, or efficiency targets. Setting these goals not only helps you stay focused but also creates a sense of accomplishment as you reach each milestone. By transforming the task into a series of smaller challenges, you can stay engaged and work towards clear, tangible outcomes.

3. **Break It Down:** Divide the task into smaller, more manageable steps. This approach makes the task less overwhelming and allows you to see continuous progress. By focusing on completing one step at a time, you maintain momentum and stay motivated. This method also helps ensure that you maintain

high standards of work by concentrating on one aspect at a time, rather than feeling daunted by the task as a whole.

4. **Stay Organized:** Utilize organizational tools such as checklists, task management apps, or calendars to keep track of your progress. Staying organized helps you manage your time effectively and keeps you on schedule. By maintaining a clear structure, you reduce stress and enhance your ability to complete the task efficiently. Organization is key to managing tasks that may not be inherently interesting but are necessary for overall success.

5. **Maintain a Positive Attitude:** Adopt a positive mindset by reminding yourself of the value in completing every task, regardless of how tedious it may seem. Consider the task as an opportunity to demonstrate your reliability and diligence. Find small ways to make the task more enjoyable—perhaps by incorporating short breaks, listening to music, or rewarding yourself after completing sections. A positive attitude keeps you motivated and focused on delivering high-quality results, even in tasks you find less engaging.

Key Takeaways:

1. **Understand the Purpose:** Recognize the task's role within the broader project to increase motivation and see its significance.

2. **Set Personal Goals:** Establish clear goals to create a sense of achievement and maintain your focus on the task.

3. **Break It Down:** Divide the task into smaller, manageable steps to make it less overwhelming and easier to handle.

4. **Stay Organized:** Use tools to keep track of your progress and stay on schedule, which helps in maintaining efficiency.

5. **Maintain a Positive Attitude:** Approach the task with positivity, seeing it as an opportunity to demonstrate your reliability and diligence.

CHAPTER 6

COMPANY FIT AND CULTURE

51. WHY DO YOU WANT TO WORK HERE?

Tips:

1. **Research the Company:** Before the interview, thoroughly research the company's mission, values, culture, and recent accomplishments. This knowledge will allow you to tailor your answer to show how your goals and values align with those of the company. Emphasize aspects of the company that genuinely resonate with you.

2. **Align with Personal Goals:** Clearly articulate how the company's goals and values align with your own professional aspirations. Demonstrating that you see a long-term future with the company and that you're excited about contributing to its success shows that your interest is sincere and well-considered.

3. **Highlight Specific Attractions:** Identify specific aspects of the company that attracted you to apply, such as its innovative projects, leadership in the industry, company culture, or growth opportunities. Mentioning these factors shows that you've done your homework and are genuinely interested in what the company offers.

4. **Show Enthusiasm:** Convey genuine enthusiasm for the role and the company. A positive attitude and excitement about the opportunity can make a strong impression, showing that you're eager to contribute and be part of the company's future.

Response Framework:

1. **Research the Company:** Start by demonstrating that you've done thorough research on the company. Highlight specific aspects of the company's mission, values, or achievements that resonate with you. This shows that your interest is genuine and well-informed. For example, you might mention the company's commitment to innovation, sustainability, industry leadership, or any recent projects or initiatives that caught your attention.

2. **Align with Personal Goals:** Connect the company's mission and goals with your personal career aspirations. Explain how the role aligns with your long-term objectives and why it represents a meaningful next step in your career. By showing that the company's vision is in sync with your personal and professional goals, you make a strong case for why you are an ideal fit for the organization.

3. **Highlight Specific Attractions:** Identify what specifically attracts you to this company over others. This could be the company's culture, reputation, opportunities for growth, or the chance to work on high-impact projects. Emphasize how these factors align with what you are looking for in your next role and how they will help you thrive professionally. This part of the response demonstrates that you are not only interested in the job but also in being part of the company's broader journey.

4. **Show Enthusiasm:** Convey genuine excitement about the opportunity to work at the company. Use this part of your response to express how enthusiastic you are about contributing to the company's success and being part of their team. Mention the specific role you're applying for and how it matches your skills and passions. Enthusiasm is key to showing that you are not only capable but also highly motivated to join the company.

Key Takeaways:

1. **Research the Company:** Show that you understand the company's mission, values, and achievements, and explain how these resonate with your own goals.

2. **Align with Personal Goals:** Demonstrate that your professional aspirations align with the company's objectives and that you see a future for yourself there.

3. **Highlight Specific Attractions:** Mention particular aspects of the company that attracted you, such as its culture, opportunities for growth, or industry leadership.

4. **Show Enthusiasm:** Express genuine excitement about the role and the opportunity to contribute to the company's success, emphasizing how you can add value.

52. HOW DO YOU SEE YOURSELF CONTRIBUTING TO OUR COMPANY?

Tips:

1. **Understand the Role:** Demonstrate a clear understanding of the position and its responsibilities. It's crucial to show that you have thoroughly researched the job and understand what will be expected of you. This helps to convey that you are ready to meet the challenges of the role head-on.

2. **Highlight Key Skills:** Focus on the most relevant skills and experiences that align with the job requirements. Discuss how these skills have helped you succeed in similar roles and how they will enable you to contribute effectively to the company's objectives. Emphasize the direct impact your skills can have on the company's success.

3. **Showcase Unique Contributions:** Identify what sets you apart from other candidates. Whether it's a unique skill set, an innovative approach, or a particular experience, make sure to highlight what makes you uniquely qualified for the role. This could be your ability to think creatively, your track record of successful project management, or your expertise in a specific area.

4. **Align with Company Goals:** Show that your contributions will help the company achieve its long-term goals. Demonstrate that you are thinking beyond just the day-to-day tasks and are committed to contributing to the company's broader mission and vision.

Response Framework:

1. **Understand the Role:** Start by demonstrating a clear understanding of the role you're applying for and how it fits within the company's broader goals. Highlight the key responsibilities of the position and explain how your experience has prepared you to handle these duties effectively. Emphasize your readiness to quickly integrate into the team and begin contributing to the company's success.

2. **Highlight Key Skills:** Identify the key skills that are most relevant to the role and explain how they will enable you to excel. Discuss your experience in applying these skills to achieve measurable results in previous positions. Whether it's expertise in a specific field, proficiency with certain tools, or a proven ability to meet targets, make it clear how these skills will benefit the company. This shows that you have the capabilities required to make a positive impact from day one.

3. **Showcase Unique Contributions:** Go beyond the basic requirements of the job by highlighting what makes you uniquely suited to contribute to the company. Discuss your ability to bring innovative solutions to challenges and share an example of how you've done so in the past. Whether it's improving processes, enhancing team performance, or driving growth, illustrate how your unique contributions can add value to the company.

4. **Align with Company Goals:** Express your alignment with the company's mission, values, or strategic goals. Show that you've researched the company and understand what drives its success. Explain how your personal and professional values align with the company's vision and how you plan to contribute to its strategic objectives. This connection demonstrates that you are not only a good fit for the role but also deeply committed to helping the company achieve its long-term goals.

Key Takeaways:

1. **Understand the Role:** Demonstrate that you have a clear understanding of the job's demands and how you can fulfill them effectively.

2. **Highlight Key Skills:** Focus on the most relevant skills and experiences that directly align with the company's needs.

3. **Showcase Unique Contributions:** Identify and emphasize what makes you a standout candidate, whether it's a unique approach, skill set, or experience.

4. **Align with Company Goals:** Show that you are not just focused on the immediate job tasks but also on contributing to the company's broader goals and mission.

53. WHAT DO YOU KNOW ABOUT OUR COMPANY'S CULTURE?

Tips:

1. **Research Thoroughly:** Before the interview, invest time in understanding the company's culture by exploring their website, social media channels, and employee reviews. Focus on the company's mission, values, and workplace environment. This knowledge allows you to tailor your response effectively and demonstrate that you are genuinely interested in the company.

2. **Align Values:** Identify how your personal and professional values align with those of the company. This alignment is crucial for demonstrating that you would be a good cultural fit. Highlight specific aspects of the culture that resonate with you and explain why they are important to you.

3. **Use Examples:** If possible, reference specific initiatives, programs, or aspects of the company's culture that you admire. This not only shows that you've done your homework but also reinforces your interest in being part of the company.

4. **Be Honest:** While it's essential to align with the company's culture, it's equally important to be honest about your values. Authenticity in your response will resonate more with interviewers and show that you're genuinely considering how you can thrive within their culture.

Response Framework:

1. **Research Thoroughly:** Begin by highlighting the research you've conducted on the company's culture. Mention specific aspects of the culture that stood out to you, such as a commitment to innovation, collaboration, or employee well-being. This demonstrates that you've taken the time to understand the company's environment and values, showing your genuine interest in becoming part of the team.

2. **Align Values:** Next, draw a connection between the company's cultural values and your own professional values. Explain how the company's focus on certain aspects, like innovation or continuous improvement, aligns with your personal work philosophy. This alignment is crucial because it shows that you would not only fit in well but also thrive in the company's environment, contributing effectively to its success.

3. **Use Examples:** Provide specific examples of the company's culture that resonate with you. For instance, mention any well-known initiatives, programs, or practices that the company is known for, such as sustainability efforts or employee development programs. Explain why these initiatives appeal to you and how they align with your own professional goals and values. This reinforces your enthusiasm for the role and the company.

4. **Be Honest:** Finally, express your appreciation for the aspects of the company's culture that encourage collaboration, inclusivity, and open communication. Mention how you thrive in environments where diverse perspectives are valued and ideas are shared freely. By being honest about why these cultural elements are important to you, you demonstrate your readiness to contribute positively to the company's culture and work environment.

Key Takeaways:

1. **Research Thoroughly:** Demonstrate that you have a deep understanding of the company's culture by referencing specific initiatives and values.

2. **Align Values:** Show how your personal and professional values align with the company's culture, and explain why this alignment is important to you.

3. **Use Examples:** Highlight specific programs or aspects of the company's culture that you admire, reinforcing your genuine interest in being part of the company.

4. **Be Honest:** Be authentic in expressing how your values match the company's culture, as this sincerity will resonate more with interviewers.

54. DESCRIBE A TIME WHEN YOU ALIGNED WITH YOUR COMPANY'S CULTURE.

Tips:

1. **Identify Key Values:** Begin by identifying the core values of your company's culture, such as innovation, collaboration, customer focus, or community involvement. Highlighting these values sets the stage for your response and demonstrates that you understand what is important to the organization.

2. **Use a Specific Example:** Choose a specific instance where your actions or decisions clearly reflected these values. Focus on how your behavior aligned with the company's culture in a practical, tangible way. Specific examples are crucial for illustrating your alignment and making your response more impactful.

3. **Highlight Impact:** Discuss the positive outcomes that resulted from your actions, both for the company and for your own professional growth. This not only shows your commitment to the company's culture but also how it has benefited your work and the organization as a whole.

4. **Reflect on Learning:** Conclude by reflecting on what you learned from the experience and how it reinforced your alignment with the company's culture. This demonstrates that you are not only aligned with the culture but also actively learning and growing within it.

Response Framework:

1. **Identify Key Values:** Start by identifying the key cultural values of the company where you had this experience. Highlight the specific value or values that were central to the company's culture, such as collaboration, innovation, customer focus, or integrity. Make sure to choose a value that you strongly align with and that played a significant role in your work.

2. **Describe the Situation:** Provide a brief overview of the situation or project where you demonstrated alignment with this cultural value. Set the context by explaining your role, the objectives of the project, and how the company's cultural value was relevant to the task at hand. This sets the stage for the more detailed discussion that follows.

3. **Highlight Your Actions:** Detail the specific actions you took to align with the company's culture during this situation. Explain how you incorporated the company's value into your approach to the project or task. For example, if the company valued collaboration, describe how you facilitated teamwork, encouraged open communication, or leveraged diverse perspectives to achieve the project's goals.

4. **Emphasize the Impact:** Discuss the results of your actions and how they contributed to the success of the project or the company as a whole. Focus on measurable outcomes, such as meeting or

exceeding goals, improving efficiency, or delivering a successful product. Highlight how your alignment with the company's culture directly influenced these positive outcomes.

5. **Reflect on the Experience:** Conclude by reflecting on what you learned from this experience and how it reinforced your commitment to the company's cultural values. Explain how this alignment not only benefited the company but also helped you grow professionally. This reflection shows your ability to integrate the company's culture into your work and underscores your potential to continue contributing to the company's success in a meaningful way.

Key Takeaways:

1. **Identify Key Values:** Clearly identify the cultural values that your company prioritizes and how they resonate with you. This demonstrates your understanding of and commitment to the company's ethos.

2. **Use a Specific Example:** Provide a concrete example that illustrates how you embodied these values through your actions. Specific examples make your response more credible and relatable.

3. **Highlight Impact:** Discuss the positive outcomes of your actions for both the company and your professional development. This shows the tangible benefits of aligning with the company's culture.

4. **Reflect on Learning:** Conclude with what you learned from the experience and how it reinforced your alignment with the company's culture, showcasing your willingness to grow and adapt.

55. HOW DO YOU HANDLE FEEDBACK AND CRITICISM?

Tips:

1. **Be Open:** When responding to questions about handling feedback and criticism, emphasize your openness to receiving input from others. This shows that you view feedback as a valuable tool for growth rather than something to be defensive about. Highlight your willingness to listen carefully, consider others' perspectives, and learn from their insights.

2. **Stay Professional:** It's important to demonstrate that you handle criticism with professionalism. Make it clear that you don't take feedback personally and that you maintain a calm and composed demeanor when receiving it. This shows your maturity and emotional intelligence in handling potentially challenging situations.

3. **Take Action:** After receiving feedback, it's crucial to take actionable steps toward improvement. Explain how you create a plan to address the areas highlighted and what specific actions you take to enhance your performance. This demonstrates your commitment to using feedback constructively.

4. **Reflect and Grow:** Show that feedback leads to self-reflection and growth for you. Discuss how you regularly evaluate the feedback you receive, track your progress, and adjust your strategies to ensure continuous improvement. This indicates your dedication to personal and professional development.

Response Framework:

1. **Embrace Feedback as a Learning Opportunity:** Begin by expressing your belief that feedback is essential for personal and professional growth. Highlight that you view feedback and criticism as valuable tools that provide insights for improvement. This mindset demonstrates your willingness to learn and your commitment to continuous development.

2. **Approach Feedback with an Open Mind:** Explain how you maintain an open mind when receiving feedback. Emphasize the importance of listening carefully and fully understanding the perspective of the person providing the feedback. This shows that you respect the feedback process and are receptive to different viewpoints, even when they may be critical.

3. **Stay Professional and Respectful:** Discuss how you handle criticism with professionalism. Describe your approach to receiving feedback calmly and respectfully, without becoming defensive. Highlight the importance of acknowledging the feedback and expressing gratitude to the person providing it, as this reflects your maturity and focus on growth.

4. **Take Constructive Action:** Outline the steps you take after receiving feedback. This could include setting specific goals for improvement, seeking additional training, or applying the feedback directly to your work. Emphasize your proactive approach to turning feedback into actionable steps that lead to measurable progress, demonstrating your commitment to self-improvement.

5. **Reflect and Continuously Improve:** Conclude by discussing how you regularly reflect on the feedback you receive and the progress you make. Explain how this reflection allows you to assess your growth, identify further areas for improvement, and build on your strengths. This ongoing process of reflection and adjustment ensures that you are always advancing in your career and contributing effectively to your team and organization.

Key Takeaways:

1. **Be Open:** Show that you are receptive to feedback and see it as a vital tool for growth. This highlights your willingness to adapt and improve based on others' input.

2. **Stay Professional:** Emphasize your ability to handle criticism with grace and professionalism, maintaining a composed and respectful attitude. This reflects your maturity and emotional intelligence.

3. **Take Action:** Discuss the practical steps you take after receiving feedback, demonstrating your proactive approach to personal development and commitment to continuous improvement.

4. **Reflect and Grow:** Illustrate how you use feedback as a catalyst for self-reflection and ongoing growth, underscoring your dedication to evolving and enhancing your skills over time.

56. HOW DO YOU ADAPT TO CHANGE?

Tips:

1. **Embrace Flexibility:** When discussing how you adapt to change, it's important to emphasize your ability to stay flexible and open-minded. Highlight how you view change as an opportunity for growth and learning, which demonstrates your resilience and adaptability in dynamic environments.

2. **Stay Positive:** Show that you maintain a positive attitude towards change, viewing it as an opportunity to innovate and improve. Emphasize that your enthusiasm for new challenges helps you stay motivated and inspires others to embrace change as well.

3. **Continuous Learning:** Explain how you actively seek new knowledge and skills to remain adaptable. Highlight your commitment to continuous learning by mentioning instances where you proactively upskilled yourself to meet changing demands or technologies.

4. **Collaboration and Communication:** Discuss the importance of collaboration and effective communication in navigating change. Demonstrate how you work with others to ensure smooth transitions and align on new objectives, which highlights your teamwork and leadership abilities.

Response Framework:

1. **Embrace Change Proactively:** Begin by emphasizing your proactive approach to change. Highlight that you view change as an inherent part of any dynamic work environment and that you actively prepare for it. This mindset demonstrates your willingness to stay ahead of the curve and adapt smoothly to new situations, making you a valuable and forward-thinking employee.

2. **Stay Positive and Open-Minded:** Discuss how you maintain a positive attitude towards change. Explain that you see change as an opportunity for growth and innovation rather than a disruption. By keeping an open mind, you can easily adapt to new circumstances, find creative solutions, and inspire others to embrace change as well. This approach helps in transforming challenges into opportunities for success.

3. **Prioritize Continuous Learning:** Outline your commitment to continuous learning as a key strategy for adapting to change. Explain how you actively seek out new knowledge and skills, whether through formal training, online courses, or self-directed learning. By staying current with industry trends and technologies, you ensure that you are always prepared to handle changes effectively and contribute valuable insights to your team.

4. **Communicate and Collaborate Effectively:** Highlight the importance of communication and collaboration in managing change. Describe how you engage with colleagues to share information, gather feedback, and develop collective strategies for navigating new challenges. By fostering open communication and a collaborative environment, you help ensure that everyone is aligned and working together towards a successful transition.

5. **Implement and Reflect:** Conclude by discussing how you implement changes and reflect on the outcomes. Explain that after adapting to a new situation, you evaluate the effectiveness of your approach and consider any lessons learned. This reflection helps you continuously improve your adaptability and prepares you for future changes. By doing so, you contribute to ongoing organizational success and demonstrate your resilience in the face of change.

Key Takeaways:

1. **Embrace Flexibility:** Demonstrate your ability to remain flexible and open-minded in the face of change, showcasing your adaptability and willingness to innovate.

2. **Stay Positive:** Emphasize your positive attitude towards change, illustrating how your enthusiasm helps you and your team navigate new situations successfully.

3. **Continuous Learning:** Highlight your commitment to continuous learning as a way to stay adaptable, showing your proactive approach to personal and professional development.

4. **Collaboration and Communication:** Discuss how you leverage collaboration and communication to navigate changes smoothly, underscoring your teamwork and leadership skills in managing transitions effectively.

57. WHAT IS YOUR APPROACH TO WORK-LIFE BALANCE?

Tips:

1. **Set Clear Boundaries:** Establishing clear boundaries between work and personal life is crucial for maintaining balance. Emphasize how setting specific working hours helps you fully focus on work during designated times and relax when off the clock. This approach not only prevents burnout but also enhances productivity by ensuring that both work and personal time are respected.

2. **Prioritize Tasks:** Effective prioritization of tasks allows you to manage your workload efficiently. Discuss how you use tools like to-do lists or project management software to organize tasks and meet deadlines. Prioritizing helps you complete important work on time and reduces stress, allowing for a more balanced life.

3. **Self-Care:** Self-care is vital for sustaining long-term productivity and happiness. Highlight how engaging in activities such as exercise, hobbies, or spending time with loved ones helps you recharge. Self-care practices provide a mental and physical break from work, enabling you to return with renewed energy and focus.

4. **Open Communication:** Maintaining open communication with your team and managers is key to managing expectations and workloads. Explain how you proactively discuss workload concerns and availability with your manager to find solutions. This transparency helps ensure that work demands do not encroach on personal time and fosters a supportive work environment.

Response Framework:

1. **Set Clear Boundaries:** Begin by discussing the importance of setting clear boundaries between work and personal life. Explain that you establish specific working hours and adhere to them as much as possible. This practice allows you to remain fully focused and productive during work hours while ensuring you have dedicated time for relaxation and personal activities. Maintaining these boundaries helps you prevent burnout and stay motivated, ultimately leading to sustained efficiency and job satisfaction.

2. **Prioritize Tasks and Manage Time Effectively:** Outline your strategy for prioritizing tasks to achieve work-life balance. You can emphasize the use of effective time management techniques, such as creating to-do lists, using project management tools, or implementing the Eisenhower Matrix to prioritize tasks based on urgency and importance. By focusing on the most critical tasks first, you can ensure that essential work is completed on time, which reduces stress and allows you to dedicate time to personal activities without compromising your work responsibilities.

3. **Emphasize the Importance of Self-Care:** Highlight the role of self-care in maintaining work-life balance. Discuss how you regularly engage in activities that help you recharge, such as exercising, spending time with loved ones, or pursuing hobbies. These activities are vital for maintaining both physical and mental well-being, enabling you to return to work with renewed energy and focus. Stress that self-care is not just a personal priority but a crucial aspect of sustaining long-term productivity and overall happiness.

4. **Foster Open Communication:** Explain how open communication plays a key role in managing work-life balance. You should regularly discuss your workload and availability with your team and managers to ensure that expectations are aligned. If you ever find your workload overwhelming, you proactively communicate with your manager to explore solutions, such as delegating tasks or adjusting deadlines. This approach helps manage expectations, prevents potential burnout, and fosters a supportive work environment where everyone feels comfortable discussing their needs.

5. **Reflect and Adjust:** Conclude by mentioning that you periodically reflect on your work-life balance and adjust your strategies as needed. Recognize that achieving balance is an ongoing process that requires regular assessment. By being mindful of how your work and personal life are intertwined, you can make necessary adjustments to maintain harmony between the two, ensuring sustained well-being and professional success.

Key Takeaways:

1. **Set Clear Boundaries:** Establishing and adhering to clear boundaries between work and personal life is essential for maintaining focus and preventing burnout.

2. **Prioritize Tasks:** Effective task prioritization and time management are key to handling workloads efficiently while making time for personal activities.

3. **Self-Care:** Engaging in self-care activities is crucial for maintaining physical and mental well-being, which supports long-term productivity.

4. **Open Communication:** Transparent communication with team members and managers helps manage expectations, workloads, and maintain a healthy work-life balance.

58. WHAT VALUES ARE MOST IMPORTANT TO YOU IN A WORKPLACE?

Tips:

1. **Alignment with Personal Values:** When discussing important workplace values, it's essential to focus on those that resonate with your personal beliefs. This approach ensures your response is authentic and demonstrates a strong cultural fit with the company. Your values should naturally align with the role and the company's ethos, reinforcing your commitment to the position.

2. **Examples and Impact:** Providing concrete examples of how these values have influenced your work is key to illustrating your point. This not only shows that you value these principles but also highlights how you actively integrate them into your professional life, leading to successful outcomes.

3. **Relevance to Role and Company:** Tailor your response to align with the company's core values and the specific role you are applying for. This demonstrates that you have done your research and understand what the company stands for, which will strengthen your case as a candidate.

4. **Future Growth:** Discuss how these values will guide your future growth and contribute positively to the company. This shows that you are forward-thinking and committed to long-term development, both personally and within the organization.

Response Framework:

1. **Integrity and Honesty:** Start by explaining that integrity and honesty are foundational values you prioritize in a workplace. Highlight the importance of transparency in fostering trust and effective collaboration. Emphasize that when integrity is upheld as a core value, it creates an environment where open communication thrives, and everyone feels respected and valued. This atmosphere encourages the free exchange of ideas and feedback, leading to more informed decision-making and successful outcomes.

2. **Collaboration and Teamwork:** Next, discuss the significance of collaboration and teamwork in your ideal workplace. Stress that the best results often come from collective effort and the sharing of diverse ideas. Describe how working in an environment that promotes teamwork not only leads to innovative solutions but also fosters a supportive network where each team member's strengths are recognized and leveraged. Mention that you thrive in such collaborative settings and are motivated by the synergy that comes from working closely with others.

3. **Continuous Learning and Development:** Highlight your commitment to continuous learning and development as a critical value. Explain that staying current with industry trends and continually

expanding your skill set is essential for both personal and professional growth. You value workplaces that encourage ongoing learning because they create an environment where both individuals and the organization can thrive. This dedication to self-improvement not only enhances your performance but also enables you to contribute more effectively to your team.

4. **Respect and Inclusivity:** Conclude by discussing the importance of respect and inclusivity. Emphasize that a diverse and inclusive workplace fosters creativity and ensures that all voices are heard, leading to richer discussions and better outcomes. Explain that you are particularly drawn to companies that prioritize inclusivity because you believe that respecting different perspectives and backgrounds is crucial for innovation and team cohesion. This value aligns with your belief in the power of diverse teams to drive success.

Key Takeaways:

1. **Alignment with Personal Values:** Focus on values that resonate with your own beliefs, showing authenticity and cultural alignment with the company.

2. **Examples and Impact:** Use concrete examples to demonstrate how these values have positively influenced your work, showcasing their importance in your professional life.

3. **Relevance to Role and Company:** Tailor your discussion to align with the company's values and the role, highlighting your understanding of the company's culture and how you fit within it.

4. **Future Growth:** Emphasize how these values will guide your future growth and contribute positively to the company, demonstrating your commitment to long-term success.

59. DESCRIBE YOUR IDEAL COMPANY CULTURE.

Tips:

1. **Be Specific:** When describing your ideal company culture, focus on the specific elements that are most important to you. This level of detail demonstrates that you've carefully considered the type of environment in which you thrive. It's essential to articulate these aspects clearly to give a strong sense of what you're looking for.

2. **Relate to Personal Experience:** Use examples from your past experiences to illustrate how these cultural aspects have positively impacted your work. This not only makes your response more relatable but also shows that you have practical experience in environments where these cultural values were present.

3. **Align with the Company:** Tailor your response to highlight aspects of company culture that align with the values of the organization you're applying to. This demonstrates that you've researched the company and understand its ethos, making it clear that you see yourself fitting in well.

4. **Show Flexibility:** While it's important to describe your ideal culture, it's also crucial to convey your adaptability. Employers value candidates who can thrive in various settings, so showing that you are flexible and can adjust to different environments can strengthen your response.

Response Framework:

1. **Collaborative and Supportive Environment:** Begin by outlining that your ideal company culture prioritizes collaboration and mutual support. Emphasize that you thrive in environments where teamwork is encouraged, and team members work together toward shared goals. Mention that you

value regular opportunities for team discussions and brainstorming sessions, as these not only foster innovation but also strengthen team camaraderie. Highlight that a culture of support enhances both productivity and personal growth, aligning with your preference for a workplace that values collective success.

2. **Commitment to Continuous Learning:** Next, discuss the importance of continuous learning and development in your ideal company culture. Explain that you are passionate about staying current with industry trends and continually expanding your skill set. An ideal workplace for you would offer opportunities for ongoing education, such as workshops, training programs, and access to learning resources. Stress that a company that invests in the development of its employees reflects a commitment to both individual and organizational success, which aligns with your professional goals.

3. **Inclusivity and Diversity:** Highlight that inclusivity and diversity are fundamental to the culture you seek. Explain that a workplace that values diverse perspectives and backgrounds fosters creativity and innovation, leading to a more dynamic and effective environment. Mention that inclusivity not only creates a respectful and supportive workplace but also contributes to better business outcomes. A culture that embraces diversity aligns with your belief that a varied workforce is essential for long-term success.

4. **Transparency and Open Communication:** Conclude by emphasizing the importance of transparency and open communication in your ideal company culture. Explain that you thrive in environments where there is clear and open communication across all levels of the organization. Highlight that a culture that encourages feedback and where leadership is transparent about company goals and decisions fosters trust and alignment. This type of environment ensures that everyone is working towards common objectives, which is crucial for maintaining a positive and effective workplace.

Key Takeaways:

1. **Be Specific:** Focus on the specific cultural aspects that are most important to you. This clarity shows that you've given thoughtful consideration to what you need in a work environment to be successful.

2. **Relate to Personal Experience:** Use past experiences to illustrate how these cultural values have positively impacted your work, making your response more relatable and credible.

3. **Align with the Company:** Tailor your response to align with the company's values, demonstrating that you've done your research and understand the company's culture.

4. **Show Flexibility:** While describing your ideal culture, also convey that you are adaptable and can thrive in various environments, which is a valued trait by employers.

60. HOW DO YOU STAY MOTIVATED IN YOUR WORK?

Tips:

1. **Be Authentic:** When discussing how you stay motivated, it's important to share real strategies and experiences that have worked for you. Authenticity in your response helps build trust with interviewers and shows that you have a deep understanding of yourself.

2. **Highlight Positive Habits:** Talk about specific habits or practices that keep you motivated, such as setting goals, taking regular breaks, or seeking feedback. This demonstrates that you take a proactive approach to maintaining your motivation and productivity.

3. **Show Adaptability:** Explain how you adjust your strategies when your motivation wanes. Highlight your resilience and adaptability, showing that you can maintain productivity even when faced with challenges.

4. **Connect to Passion:** Link your motivation to your passion for your work or the specific role you are applying for. This demonstrates your commitment and enthusiasm, which can be particularly compelling to interviewers.

Response Framework:

1. **Setting Clear Goals:** Start by explaining that setting clear and achievable goals is central to maintaining your motivation. Break down larger projects into smaller, manageable tasks, which helps keep you focused and allows you to track progress. By establishing daily or weekly objectives, you create a sense of accomplishment as you complete each milestone. This approach not only keeps you organized but also provides continuous motivation as you see tangible progress toward your overall goals. Regularly reviewing and adjusting these goals ensures they remain relevant and challenging, which is essential for sustaining long-term motivation.

2. **Seeking Feedback and Continuous Improvement:** Emphasize the importance of feedback in maintaining your motivation. Constructive criticism helps you identify areas for improvement, while positive feedback reinforces your strengths. Actively seeking feedback after completing significant tasks or projects keeps you engaged and motivated by highlighting opportunities for growth. Your commitment to continuous learning and improvement ensures that your work remains challenging and rewarding. This focus on development keeps you motivated by driving you to enhance your skills and contribute more effectively to your team and organization.

3. **Staying Connected to the Bigger Picture:** Discuss how understanding the broader impact of your work on the organization's goals is a key motivator. When you see the direct effects of your efforts on the company's success, it fuels your commitment and enthusiasm. Regularly connecting your daily tasks to the larger mission of the organization helps you stay focused and motivated. Knowing that your contributions are valued and make a difference encourages you to work hard and strive for excellence.

4. **Maintaining a Healthy Work-Life Balance:** Highlight the importance of maintaining a healthy work-life balance to sustain your motivation. Ensuring that you have time to recharge through activities you enjoy outside of work, such as exercising or spending time with family, helps prevent burnout. This balance keeps you energized and allows you to approach your work with a fresh perspective. Emphasize that a supportive work environment that values well-being is crucial for long-term motivation and success, enabling you to remain productive and engaged in your work.

Key Takeaways:

1. **Be Authentic:** Discuss genuine strategies that help you stay motivated, demonstrating your self-awareness and authenticity.

2. **Highlight Positive Habits:** Emphasize specific habits or practices that keep you motivated, showing your proactive approach to maintaining productivity.

3. **Show Adaptability:** Describe how you adjust your strategies when motivation dips, highlighting your resilience and ability to adapt to challenges.

4. **Connect to Passion:** Link your motivation to your passion for your field or the specific job, demonstrating your commitment and enthusiasm for your work.

CHAPTER 7
TEAMWORK AND COLLABORATION

61. DESCRIBE YOUR EXPERIENCE WORKING IN A TEAM.

Tips:

1. **Be Specific:** Provide clear and concrete examples of your teamwork experiences. Discuss particular projects, your role within the team, and the outcomes to effectively demonstrate your collaborative abilities.

2. **Highlight Communication:** Emphasize the importance of communication in teamwork. Explain how you ensured clear and open communication among team members to achieve common goals.

3. **Showcase Problem-Solving:** Describe how you and your team addressed challenges. Highlight your involvement in identifying issues and collaborating to find solutions.

4. **Demonstrate Leadership and Support:** If applicable, mention instances where you took on a leadership role or supported team members. This showcases your ability to adapt to different roles within a team, highlighting both leadership and teamwork skills.

Response Framework:

1. **Highlight Your Role in Team Projects:** Begin by outlining your experience working on team-based projects. Describe the context in which you worked as part of a team, such as a major project or initiative that required cross-functional collaboration. Mention your specific role within the team and how your responsibilities contributed to the overall project. This sets the stage for demonstrating your ability to work effectively in a team environment.

2. **Emphasize Effective Communication:** Discuss the importance of clear and effective communication in team settings. Highlight how you facilitated communication within the team, ensuring that all members were aligned and informed. Mention any tools or strategies you used to keep everyone on the same page, such as regular meetings, collaborative platforms, or status updates. This section should underscore your commitment to maintaining transparency and preventing miscommunication, which are crucial for team success.

3. **Showcase Problem-Solving and Adaptability:** Explain how you contributed to problem-solving within the team, particularly when challenges or unexpected issues arose. Detail your approach to identifying problems, brainstorming solutions, and implementing changes. Emphasize your adaptability and willingness to collaborate with others to find the best course of action. This demonstrates your ability to remain flexible and resourceful in a team setting, leading to successful project outcomes.

4. **Discuss Leadership and Support:** If applicable, mention any leadership roles you have taken on within a team. Describe how you balanced leading the team with providing support to ensure that all members could contribute effectively. Highlight how you delegated tasks, fostered an inclusive environment, and motivated the team to achieve collective goals. This section should convey your ability to lead with empathy and support, ultimately strengthening team cohesion and driving success.

5. **Reflect on the Impact of Teamwork:** Conclude by reflecting on the impact that teamwork has had on your professional growth and the success of the projects you've been involved in. Discuss how working collaboratively has enhanced your skills and contributed to achieving significant results. This

reflection reinforces the value you place on teamwork and your commitment to contributing positively to any team you join.

Key Takeaways:

1. **Be Specific:** Use detailed examples to illustrate your teamwork experiences, making your response both credible and relatable.

2. **Highlight Communication:** Focus on how clear and open communication played a role in achieving team goals, showcasing your ability to facilitate effective collaboration.

3. **Showcase Problem-Solving:** Discuss how you and your team tackled challenges, emphasizing your proactive approach to finding solutions together.

4. **Demonstrate Leadership and Support:** Mention instances where you took on leadership roles or supported team members, showing your versatility and collaborative spirit in team environments.

62. HOW DO YOU HANDLE WORKING WITH A TEAM MEMBER WHO HAS A DIFFERENT WORKING STYLE?

Tips:

1. **Understand Differences:** Recognize that everyone has a unique approach to work. Take the time to learn about your team member's working style and preferences. This understanding is the first step towards finding common ground and developing strategies that accommodate both styles.

2. **Communicate Openly:** Ensure that you maintain open lines of communication with your colleague. Regular and clear communication helps prevent misunderstandings and keeps both parties aligned on goals and expectations. This is crucial in working effectively with someone whose style differs from yours.

3. **Be Flexible:** Flexibility is key when working with others, especially those who have different working styles. Show your willingness to adapt by making adjustments to your own style where necessary. This demonstrates your ability to collaborate and find solutions that work for everyone involved.

4. **Focus on Strengths:** Every working style has its strengths. Identify the strengths of your team member and leverage them to improve team performance. By focusing on what each person does best, you can complement each other's skills, leading to more successful outcomes.

Response Framework:

1. **Understand Differences:** Begin by acknowledging the importance of understanding the differences in working styles. Emphasize the value of taking the time to learn about your colleague's approach, including their preferences, motivations, and reasons behind their methods. By gaining this understanding, you can appreciate their perspective and find common ground. This understanding lays the foundation for effective collaboration, ensuring that both working styles can coexist productively.

2. **Communicate Openly:** Highlight the necessity of open and ongoing communication when working with someone who has a different style. Discuss how regular check-ins and transparent discussions can help address potential challenges early on. By keeping communication channels open, you can ensure alignment on goals, expectations, and project milestones. Effective communication also helps to clarify misunderstandings and foster mutual respect, which is crucial for maintaining a positive working relationship.

3. **Be Flexible:** Stress the importance of flexibility in adapting to different working styles. Explain how you are willing to adjust your own approach to better align with your colleague's methods when necessary. For instance, if your colleague prefers a more structured approach, you might incorporate more planning and organization into your workflow. Demonstrating flexibility shows your commitment to the team's success and your ability to adapt to varying circumstances for the benefit of the project.

4. **Focus on Strengths:** Discuss the strategy of focusing on each other's strengths to enhance team performance. By identifying and leveraging the unique strengths that each team member brings to the table, you can create a more balanced and effective team dynamic. For example, if one person excels in analytical tasks while the other is more creative, you can divide responsibilities accordingly to maximize efficiency and results. This approach ensures that each team member can contribute their best, leading to a more successful collaboration.

5. **Maintain a Positive Attitude:** Conclude by emphasizing the importance of maintaining a p5ositive and collaborative attitude throughout the process. By focusing on the shared goals and the value that diverse working styles bring to the team, you can turn potential challenges into opportunities for growth and innovation. A positive attitude helps to keep the team motivated and fosters a culture of mutual respect and cooperation.

Key Takeaways:

1. **Understand Differences:** Taking the time to understand and appreciate different working styles is crucial for finding common ground and fostering effective collaboration.

2. **Communicate Openly:** Clear and open communication is essential for addressing concerns and ensuring that all team members remain aligned on objectives and processes.

3. **Be Flexible:** Flexibility in your working style demonstrates your willingness to adapt and collaborate effectively with others, which is key to successful teamwork.

4. **Focus on Strengths:** Leveraging each other's strengths can significantly enhance team performance and lead to more successful project outcomes.

63. HOW DO YOU ENSURE EFFECTIVE COMMUNICATION WITHIN A TEAM?

Tips:

1. **Establish Clear Goals:** Begin by setting clear and achievable goals that everyone understands. This clarity ensures that all team members are aligned and working towards the same objectives. Clearly defined goals help to minimize misunderstandings and keep the team focused.

2. **Regular Check-ins:** Hold regular meetings to discuss progress, address challenges, and make any necessary adjustments. These check-ins promote transparency, keep everyone informed, and provide opportunities to resolve issues before they escalate.

3. **Active Listening:** Foster a culture of active listening within the team. Encourage team members to listen attentively, avoid interrupting, and ask clarifying questions. This practice ensures that everyone feels heard and valued, which is essential for collaboration.

4. **Use of Tools:** Utilize communication tools that suit the team's needs, such as Slack, Trello, or Microsoft Teams. These tools can enhance communication, facilitate real-time updates, and keep everyone connected, regardless of location.

Response Framework:

1. **Establish Clear Objectives:** Begin by emphasizing the importance of setting clear objectives for the team. Define specific goals and expectations at the outset to ensure that everyone understands the direction and purpose of the project. Clearly communicating these objectives helps to align the team's efforts and minimizes the potential for misunderstandings. When all team members are aware of their roles and how they contribute to the larger goals, communication becomes more focused and effective.

2. **Facilitate Regular Updates:** Regular updates or check-ins are crucial for maintaining open lines of communication. These meetings provide an opportunity for team members to share their progress, discuss any challenges they are facing, and seek input from the group. Regular updates help to ensure that everyone stays informed about the project's status and any changes that may arise. This practice promotes transparency and keeps the team aligned, allowing for quick resolution of any issues that may impede progress.

3. **Practice Active Listening:** Active listening is a fundamental component of effective communication. Encourage team members to practice active listening by giving their full attention during discussions, avoiding interruptions, and asking clarifying questions when necessary. Active listening ensures that everyone's viewpoints are heard and understood, which fosters a collaborative and respectful team environment. It also helps to prevent miscommunication and ensures that all team members feel valued and engaged in the project.

4. **Leverage Communication Tools:** Utilize appropriate communication tools to facilitate efficient and effective communication, especially in remote or dispersed teams. Tools like project management software, instant messaging platforms, and shared documents can streamline communication by providing a centralized space for information sharing and collaboration. Selecting the right tools ensures that the team can easily access necessary information, track progress, and communicate in real-time, leading to more efficient teamwork and successful project outcomes.

5. **Encourage Feedback and Continuous Improvement:** Promote an environment where feedback is encouraged and viewed as a positive tool for improvement. Regularly solicit feedback from team members on communication processes and make adjustments as needed. This ongoing dialogue helps to refine communication strategies and ensures that the team continues to function effectively. By fostering a culture of continuous improvement, you can enhance communication and, ultimately, the team's overall performance.

Key Takeaways:

1. **Establish Clear Goals:** Clear goals are essential for aligning the team and ensuring that everyone is working towards the same objectives. This minimizes misunderstandings and enhances focus.

2. **Regular Check-ins:** Consistent check-ins foster transparency, keep everyone informed, and provide a platform for resolving issues early, which is critical for maintaining momentum in projects.

3. **Active Listening:** Encouraging active listening within the team helps to build a collaborative environment where everyone's input is valued, reducing misunderstandings and fostering a culture of respect.

4. **Use of Tools:** Leveraging appropriate communication tools enhances connectivity, improves task management, and ensures that the team remains organized and efficient, regardless of location or team size.

64. WHAT ROLE DO YOU TYPICALLY TAKE ON A TEAM PROJECT?

Tips:

1. **Understand Your Strengths:** Identify your key skills and understand how they can best benefit the team. By knowing your strengths, you can effectively contribute to the team in a role that maximizes your abilities.

2. **Be Flexible:** While it's important to know your strengths, it's equally crucial to be flexible. The needs of the team or project may change, and being open to taking on different roles demonstrates your adaptability and willingness to support the team in whatever way is needed.

3. **Communicate Clearly:** Clearly communicate your role and responsibilities to the team to avoid confusion. This ensures that everyone knows what to expect from you and how your work fits into the broader project.

4. **Seek Feedback:** Regularly seek feedback from your team members to ensure that you are contributing effectively. Feedback helps you adjust your approach as needed and continue to support the team's success.

Response Framework:

1. **Identify Your Preferred Role:** Begin by discussing the roles you naturally gravitate towards in team projects. Reflect on your strengths and how they align with specific responsibilities within a team. Whether you excel in leadership, coordination, or supporting roles, clearly articulate the position you typically take and explain why it suits your skill set. For instance, you might focus on roles that leverage your organizational skills, strategic thinking, or ability to motivate and align team members with the project's goals.

2. **Emphasize Flexibility:** While you may have a preferred role, it's important to demonstrate your adaptability in team settings. Discuss your willingness to step into different roles based on the project's needs. Explain how you assess the team dynamics and adjust your contributions accordingly to ensure the project's success. This could involve taking on leadership when necessary, or providing support in areas where the team requires additional expertise. Highlight your ability to shift focus and responsibilities as the project evolves, showing that you are a versatile and collaborative team player.

3. **Prioritize Clear Communication:** Effective communication is key to any successful team project. Emphasize your commitment to maintaining open and clear communication with your team members. Discuss how you ensure that everyone understands their roles, responsibilities, and the overall project objectives. Mention specific strategies you use, such as regular check-ins, progress updates, or the use of collaborative tools to track tasks and deadlines. By prioritizing clear communication, you help to prevent misunderstandings and keep the project on track.

4. **Value Collaboration and Feedback:** Collaboration is at the heart of any team project, and seeking feedback is crucial for continuous improvement. Talk about how you actively engage with your team members, soliciting their input and ideas throughout the project. Explain how you use feedback to refine your approach and improve the team's overall performance. Regularly reviewing the project's progress and making necessary adjustments based on team discussions not only enhances the quality of the work but also fosters a culture of trust and mutual respect within the team.

5. **Focus on Contribution to Team Success:** Conclude by highlighting your commitment to the team's success as a whole. Whether you're leading a project or supporting others, emphasize that your primary goal is to contribute effectively to the team's objectives. Discuss how your role, communication skills, flexibility, and commitment to collaboration all serve the greater purpose of achieving the

project's goals. This holistic approach demonstrates that you prioritize the collective success of the team over individual achievements, which is a key trait in any successful team member.

Key Takeaways:

1. **Understand Your Strengths:** Recognizing your strengths allows you to take on roles where you can contribute most effectively, ensuring you add maximum value to the team.

2. **Be Flexible:** Flexibility is key to adapting to the dynamic needs of a project, demonstrating your ability to support the team in various ways as situations evolve.

3. **Communicate Clearly:** Clear and consistent communication about your role and responsibilities ensures that the team operates efficiently and with aligned expectations.

4. **Seek Feedback:** Regularly seeking feedback helps you improve your performance, better align with team goals, and continuously enhance your contribution to the team's success.

65. HOW DO YOU HANDLE CONFLICTS WITHIN A TEAM?

Tips

1. **Stay Calm and Objective:** When dealing with conflicts within a team, it's crucial to stay calm and maintain objectivity. Avoid letting emotions dictate your response, as this can exacerbate the situation. Instead, focus on understanding the facts and different perspectives involved. This approach allows you to address the issue fairly and work towards a resolution that benefits the entire team.

2. **Communicate Openly:** Open communication is key to resolving conflicts effectively. Encourage team members to voice their concerns and viewpoints in a respectful and constructive manner. By facilitating an open dialogue, you can uncover the root causes of the conflict and work collaboratively towards a solution.

3. **Seek Common Ground:** Aim to find common ground where all parties involved can agree. Compromise and flexibility are often necessary to resolve conflicts in a way that satisfies everyone. Identifying shared goals and interests helps to align the team and fosters a cooperative environment.

4. **Follow Up:** After the conflict has been resolved, it's important to follow up with the team to ensure that the solution is working and that no residual issues remain. This helps to reinforce a positive team dynamic and prevents similar conflicts from arising in the future.

Response Framework

1. **Stay Calm and Objective:** Begin by emphasizing the importance of maintaining composure and objectivity when addressing conflicts within a team. Describe how staying calm allows you to assess the situation clearly, without letting emotions influence your judgment. By focusing on the facts and the core issues at hand, you can approach the conflict with a level-headed perspective, which is crucial for facilitating a constructive resolution.

2. **Encourage Open Communication:** Effective conflict resolution hinges on open and respectful communication. Discuss your approach to fostering an environment where team members feel comfortable expressing their concerns and viewpoints. Highlight the importance of actively listening to all parties involved and ensuring that each person's perspective is acknowledged. This open dialogue helps to uncover the root causes of the conflict and paves the way for finding a solution that addresses everyone's needs.

3. **Focus on Common Goals:** Finding common ground is key to resolving conflicts and moving the team forward. Explain how you work to identify shared goals and interests that can serve as a basis for compromise. By redirecting the team's focus toward these common objectives, you help shift the discussion from individual differences to collective success. This approach not only resolves the immediate conflict but also strengthens the team's cohesion and commitment to achieving their goals.

4. **Develop Collaborative Solutions:** Once the common ground is established, describe your process for facilitating the development of a collaborative solution. Encourage team members to brainstorm and contribute ideas, ensuring that the final resolution incorporates input from all parties. This collaborative approach not only resolves the conflict but also fosters a sense of ownership and accountability among the team members, leading to more sustainable outcomes.

5. **Follow Up and Reinforce Positive Dynamics:** Finally, emphasize the importance of following up after a conflict has been resolved. Regular check-ins with the team members involved help to ensure that the agreed-upon solutions are being implemented effectively. These follow-ups also provide an opportunity to address any lingering issues and reinforce the positive communication and collaboration practices that were established during the resolution process. By maintaining ongoing support and monitoring, you can help prevent future conflicts and promote a healthy, collaborative team environment.

Key Takeaways

1. **Stay Calm and Objective:** Approach conflicts with a calm and objective mindset to ensure fair and effective resolutions.

2. **Communicate Openly:** Open and respectful communication is essential for understanding different perspectives and addressing the root causes of conflicts.

3. **Seek Common Ground:** Focusing on shared goals and interests helps to find mutually agreeable solutions and strengthen team cohesion.

4. **Follow Up:** Regular follow-ups ensure that the resolution is effective, maintain a positive team environment, and prevent future conflicts.

66. DESCRIBE A TIME WHEN YOU HAD TO COORDINATE WITH TEAM MEMBERS IN DIFFERENT LOCATIONS.

Tips

1. **Be Specific:** When discussing your experience coordinating with team members across different locations, provide specific details about the project, the various locations involved, and the communication tools utilized. This specificity helps the interviewer understand the complexity and scope of your role, giving a clearer picture of your coordination capabilities.

2. **Highlight Communication Skills:** Emphasize your ability to communicate effectively across different time zones and cultures. Discuss strategies you used to ensure clear, consistent communication and how you managed to keep everyone informed and aligned, despite the geographical barriers.

3. **Focus on Problem-Solving:** Identify any challenges that arose during the project, such as time zone differences or cultural misunderstandings, and explain how you addressed these issues. This highlights your problem-solving skills and your ability to manage and lead remote teams successfully.

4. **Show Impact:** Discuss the outcomes of the project, particularly how your coordination efforts contributed to its success. Use specific metrics, such as increases in sales or efficiency improvements, to quantify your impact and demonstrate the effectiveness of your leadership in a remote team environment.

Response Framework

1. **Outline the Situation:** Start by clearly defining the context of the project or task that required coordination across different locations. Provide an overview of the project's goals, the number of team members involved, and their geographic spread. This sets the stage for discussing the specific challenges and strategies you employed.

2. **Emphasize Communication Strategies:** Highlight the communication methods you used to ensure effective collaboration among team members in different locations. Discuss the tools and platforms that facilitated seamless communication, such as video conferencing for meetings, messaging apps for instant updates, and project management software for tracking tasks. Explain how you adapted your communication approach to accommodate different time zones, ensuring that all team members stayed informed and engaged.

3. **Address Problem-Solving Techniques:** Identify the challenges you encountered due to the geographic and cultural differences within the team, such as time zone discrepancies, language barriers, or varying work cultures. Describe the specific problem-solving strategies you implemented to overcome these obstacles. This might include rotating meeting times to be inclusive of all team members, establishing clear communication guidelines to avoid misunderstandings, or creating a process for continuous task handoffs across time zones to maintain project momentum.

4. **Highlight Collaboration and Inclusivity:** Discuss how you fostered an inclusive and collaborative environment, despite the physical distances. Emphasize the importance of encouraging team members to share their ideas and concerns openly. Explain how you ensured that everyone's contributions were valued and that there was a strong sense of team cohesion, even when working remotely.

5. **Demonstrate the Impact:** Conclude by detailing the successful outcome of the project, linking it directly to the effective coordination and communication strategies you employed. Quantify the results if possible, such as meeting deadlines, achieving or exceeding project goals, or receiving positive feedback from stakeholders. This final point reinforces the value of your approach and the positive impact it had on the project's success.

Key Takeaways

1. **Be Specific:** Providing detailed information about the project, including the locations and tools used, helps illustrate the complexity and scale of your coordination efforts.

2. **Highlight Communication Skills:** Clear and consistent communication is crucial in remote teams. Emphasize the strategies you used to maintain effective communication across different time zones and cultures.

3. **Focus on Problem-Solving:** Demonstrating how you overcame challenges, such as time zone differences or cultural misunderstandings, showcases your problem-solving abilities and leadership skills.

4. **Show Impact:** Use specific metrics to quantify the success of the project, highlighting how your coordination and leadership contributed to achieving the project's goals.

67. HOW DO YOU CONTRIBUTE TO A POSITIVE TEAM ENVIRONMENT?

Tips

1. **Be Proactive:** Discuss how you actively work to create a positive team environment. This could include organizing team-building activities, initiating regular check-ins, or simply being a positive presence in daily interactions. The goal is to show that you don't just wait for a positive environment to happen—you take steps to create it.

2. **Promote Open Communication:** Emphasize the importance of transparent communication. Explain how you encourage team members to express their ideas and concerns freely, ensuring that everyone feels included and valued. Effective communication is key to preventing misunderstandings and fostering a collaborative atmosphere.

3. **Show Empathy:** Highlight your ability to understand and consider your team members' feelings and perspectives. Empathy is crucial for supporting colleagues through challenges and building a strong, supportive team. Discuss how you listen to and accommodate others' needs to maintain a healthy team dynamic.

4. **Celebrate Successes:** Talk about the importance of recognizing and celebrating team achievements. Acknowledging both individual and group successes helps to boost morale and motivation. Share how you ensure that accomplishments are noticed and appreciated, contributing to a positive and encouraging team environment.

Response Framework

1. **Encourage Open Communication:** Start by emphasizing the importance of open communication in creating a positive team environment. Explain how you actively foster an atmosphere where all team members feel comfortable sharing their ideas, feedback, and concerns. You can describe how you ensure that everyone has the opportunity to speak during meetings and how you promote transparency by encouraging honest and respectful dialogue. Highlight the use of tools or techniques that facilitate open communication, such as regular team meetings, feedback sessions, or collaborative platforms.

2. **Lead by Example:** Discuss how you lead by example in promoting positivity within the team. This includes maintaining a positive attitude, showing respect for all team members, and being consistent in your actions and decisions. Explain how your behavior sets the tone for the rest of the team, encouraging others to follow suit. Emphasize the importance of being approachable and supportive, making yourself available to help team members when needed, and demonstrating a strong work ethic that others can emulate.

3. **Recognize and Celebrate Achievements:** Describe how you contribute to a positive environment by recognizing and celebrating both individual and team accomplishments. Explain the various ways you acknowledge achievements, such as through public recognition in meetings, personalized messages, or organizing team celebrations. Highlight the impact of these actions on team morale, motivation, and overall productivity. Emphasize that recognizing successes helps reinforce a culture of appreciation and encourages continuous effort and excellence.

4. **Provide Support and Empathy:** Focus on the role of empathy in contributing to a positive team environment. Discuss how you make an effort to understand the challenges your colleagues may face, whether work-related or personal. Describe how you offer support, such as adjusting workloads, providing assistance with tasks, or simply being a listening ear. Emphasize that by showing empathy and understanding, you help build trust and a sense of belonging within the team, which fosters a more collaborative and supportive work environment.

5. **Promote Inclusivity and Team-Building:** Highlight your commitment to creating an inclusive environment where everyone feels valued. Explain how you actively work to involve all team members in discussions and decisions, ensuring that diverse perspectives are considered. Discuss any initiatives or activities you organize to strengthen team cohesion, such as team-building exercises or social events. Emphasize the importance of inclusivity in driving innovation and ensuring that all team members feel like they are an integral part of the group.

Key Takeaways

1. **Be Proactive:** Actively work to create a positive atmosphere by organizing team activities and maintaining regular communication. Proactivity in fostering a supportive environment leads to stronger team dynamics.

2. **Promote Open Communication:** Open communication ensures that all team members feel valued and included. Encourage transparency and inclusivity to build trust and collaboration.

3. **Show Empathy:** Empathy strengthens team cohesion by supporting colleagues through challenges. Understanding and accommodating the needs of team members fosters a healthy and resilient team dynamic.

4. **Celebrate Successes:** Recognizing and celebrating achievements enhances motivation and morale. Regularly acknowledging both individual and team successes reinforces a positive and encouraging work environment.

68. WHAT STRATEGIES DO YOU USE TO MOTIVATE YOUR TEAM?

Tips

1. **Be Inclusive:** When leading a team, involve members in decision-making processes to create a sense of ownership and accountability. Inclusivity fosters a collaborative environment where everyone feels valued and integral to the project's success. This approach not only enhances motivation but also drives innovation by encouraging diverse perspectives.

2. **Recognize Achievements:** Regularly acknowledging and celebrating both individual and team successes is essential for maintaining high morale. Recognition can take many forms, from verbal praise in meetings to personalized notes or team celebrations. This practice reinforces the value of each member's contributions and cultivates a culture of appreciation, which is crucial for sustained motivation.

3. **Set Clear Goals:** Establishing clear, achievable goals provides direction and purpose for the team. When everyone understands their objectives and how their role contributes to the overall success, they are more likely to stay motivated. Additionally, providing the necessary resources and support ensures that team members can meet these goals, helping to maintain focus and momentum.

4. **Provide Opportunities for Growth:** Offering opportunities for professional development and career advancement keeps the team engaged and motivated. By encouraging continuous learning, such as through training programs, certifications, or mentorship opportunities, you show that the organization values its employees' growth. This investment in their development helps to retain top talent and fosters a committed and motivated team.

Response Framework

1. **Foster Inclusivity and Collaboration:** Start by explaining how fostering an inclusive environment is central to your motivation strategy. Emphasize the importance of involving team members in decision-making processes, encouraging collaborative discussions, and seeking input from everyone. Highlight that when team members feel their opinions are valued, they are more likely to take ownership of their work and remain committed to the team's success. This approach builds trust and fosters a strong sense of team unity, which is crucial for maintaining high motivation levels.

2. **Recognize and Celebrate Achievements:** Next, discuss the importance of recognizing and celebrating both individual and team achievements. Explain how you regularly acknowledge successes through verbal praise, written commendations, or team celebrations. Recognition reinforces the value of each team member's contributions and creates a positive work culture where achievements are celebrated. This boosts morale, encourages continued high performance, and keeps the team engaged and motivated over the long term.

3. **Set Clear and Attainable Goals:** Clarify how setting clear, achievable goals is a key part of your strategy. Describe how you ensure that all team members understand their specific objectives and the role they play in achieving the team's overall goals. By providing the necessary resources and support, you help the team stay focused and aligned with these objectives. Regular check-ins and progress reviews allow you to make timely adjustments, ensuring that the team remains on track and motivated.

4. **Offer Growth and Development Opportunities:** Highlight the role of professional growth in motivating your team. Explain how you provide opportunities for team members to enhance their skills through training, certifications, and other learning opportunities. Additionally, discuss the importance of mentorship programs where more experienced team members can guide others, fostering a culture of growth and progression. By investing in the team's development, you not only improve their capabilities but also instill a sense of career advancement, which keeps them motivated and committed to continuous improvement.

Key Takeaways

1. **Be Inclusive:** Involve team members in decision-making to create a sense of ownership and accountability. This inclusivity fosters a motivated and cohesive team.

2. **Recognize Achievements:** Regularly acknowledging and celebrating successes helps to maintain high morale and reinforces the value of each member's contributions.

3. **Set Clear Goals:** Clear, achievable goals provide direction and purpose, which are essential for sustaining motivation. Regular check-ins and support help keep the team focused.

4. **Provide Opportunities for Growth:** Offering professional development and career advancement opportunities demonstrates that the organization values its employees, fostering a motivated and engaged team.

69. HOW DO YOU HANDLE TEAM MEETINGS?

Tips

1. **Be Prepared:** Effective meetings begin with thorough preparation. Ensure that you create a clear agenda and share it with the team ahead of time, ideally at least 24 hours in advance. This allows participants to review the topics, prepare their input, and gather any necessary materials. Preparation minimizes surprises and maximizes productivity, as everyone comes ready to contribute meaningfully.

2. **Facilitate Engagement:** Actively involve all participants to foster a collaborative atmosphere. Use techniques such as round-robin discussions or breakout sessions to ensure everyone has an opportunity to speak and contribute. Encouraging diverse perspectives not only enriches the conversation but also makes team members feel valued and engaged in the process.

3. **Stay on Track:** Keeping the meeting focused on its objectives is essential. Begin by reviewing the agenda and setting clear time limits for each topic. This helps manage the flow of the meeting and prevents digressions. Utilize tools like timers or gentle reminders to keep discussions within the allotted time, ensuring that the meeting remains productive and efficient.

4. **Follow Up:** After the meeting, summarize the key points, decisions, and assigned tasks. Send a follow-up communication, such as an email, detailing these elements to ensure that everyone understands their responsibilities and deadlines. Follow-up ensures accountability and helps maintain momentum as the team progresses towards its goals.

Response Framework

1. **Be Thoroughly Prepared:** Start by explaining that preparation is key to conducting effective team meetings. You emphasize the importance of setting a clear agenda that outlines the key topics, objectives, and any necessary background materials. Mention that you share this agenda with the team well in advance—typically at least 24 hours—so that everyone has time to review and prepare their input. This approach ensures that all participants come to the meeting ready to contribute meaningfully, leading to more focused and productive discussions.

2. **Facilitate Active Engagement:** Next, describe how you prioritize active participation during meetings. Highlight your use of techniques like round-robin discussions or breakout sessions, which ensure that every team member has the opportunity to voice their ideas and opinions. Explain that this inclusive approach not only enriches the discussion by incorporating diverse perspectives but also fosters a sense of ownership and collaboration among the team. By encouraging full engagement, you help create a meeting environment where everyone feels their contributions are valued.

3. **Maintain Focus and Structure:** Discuss the importance of maintaining focus throughout the meeting to ensure that objectives are met efficiently. Explain that you start each meeting by reviewing the agenda and setting clear time limits for each topic. This structure helps keep discussions on track and prevents the meeting from veering off course. You might mention that you use timers or provide gentle reminders to ensure that each topic is addressed within the allotted time, thereby ensuring that all critical issues are covered.

4. **Ensure Effective Follow-Up:** Conclude by emphasizing the significance of follow-up after the meeting to reinforce clarity and accountability. Explain that you take detailed notes during the meeting, capturing key decisions, action items, and deadlines. After the meeting, you send out a summary to the team, reiterating what was discussed and outlining each person's responsibilities moving forward. This follow-up communication helps prevent misunderstandings and keeps the team aligned on their tasks, ensuring that momentum is maintained and objectives are achieved.

Key Takeaways

1. **Be Prepared:** Thorough preparation, including setting and sharing an agenda in advance, is essential for productive meetings. It ensures that all participants come ready to contribute.

2. **Facilitate Engagement:** Encourage active participation using techniques like round-robin discussions and breakout sessions to ensure everyone's voice is heard, fostering a collaborative environment.

3. **Stay on Track:** Keeping meetings focused on objectives through a clear agenda and effective time management strategies is vital for maintaining productivity and efficiency.

4. **Follow Up:** Summarize key points, decisions, and action items after the meeting, providing follow-up communication to ensure clarity, accountability, and continued progress.

70. WHAT DO YOU THINK MAKES A TEAM SUCCESSFUL?

<u>**Tips**</u>

1. **Clear Communication:** Emphasize the importance of open and transparent communication within the team. Clear communication ensures that all team members are on the same page regarding objectives, responsibilities, and timelines. Regular updates, feedback loops, and accessible communication channels are crucial for maintaining transparency and addressing any potential issues early on.

2. **Shared Goals:** Discuss the significance of having common objectives that align with the team's efforts. When a team shares the same goals, it fosters unity and provides a clear direction, motivating everyone to work collaboratively. Clearly defined, measurable goals help in tracking progress and keeping the team focused on achieving its mission.

3. **Diverse Skills:** Highlight the benefits of a team composed of members with varied skills and perspectives. Diversity in skills enhances a team's ability to innovate and solve problems more effectively. A successful team leverages the unique strengths of its members, which not only contributes to a dynamic working environment but also ensures comprehensive coverage of tasks and challenges.

4. **Mutual Respect:** Stress the value of respect and trust among team members for a harmonious work environment. Mutual respect fosters a positive atmosphere where everyone feels valued and encouraged to contribute. Trust reduces conflicts and promotes open communication, which is essential for effective collaboration and overall team success.

<u>**Response Framework**</u>

1. **Clear Communication:** Start by emphasizing that clear communication is the foundation of any successful team. Explain that when communication is open and transparent, every team member understands their role, the team's goals, and the timelines for tasks. Discuss the importance of regular meetings, such as daily stand-ups or weekly check-ins, to maintain this clarity. Highlight the use of communication tools like Slack or project management software, which help organize tasks and facilitate real-time updates. By prioritizing clear communication, the team can quickly address any issues and remain aligned on collective objectives.

2. **Shared Goals:** Next, highlight the importance of shared goals in unifying the team and providing a clear direction. When everyone is working towards the same objectives, it fosters collaboration and a sense of purpose. Explain the value of setting clear, measurable goals, which allow the team to track progress and make necessary adjustments. Mention the effectiveness of breaking larger goals into smaller milestones, as this approach helps maintain momentum and offers opportunities to celebrate successes along the way, keeping the team motivated and focused on the ultimate outcome.

3. **Diverse Skills:** Discuss how a diverse set of skills within the team enhances its ability to innovate and solve problems. Each team member brings unique strengths and perspectives, which leads to more creative solutions and a well-rounded approach to projects. Emphasize the importance of encouraging cross-functional collaboration, as it broadens the team's capabilities and fosters a culture of continuous learning. By leveraging the varied expertise within the team, the group can tackle a wider range of challenges and produce higher-quality results.

4. **Mutual Respect:** Conclude by stressing the critical role of mutual respect in building a positive and productive team environment. When team members respect each other's ideas, skills, and contributions, it builds trust and reduces the likelihood of conflicts. A respectful atmosphere encourages open communication, where everyone feels comfortable sharing their thoughts and feedback. This trust leads to more effective collaboration and a stronger overall performance. Suggest implementing initiatives like peer recognition programs to reinforce a culture of appreciation and respect, which ultimately contributes to the team's long-term success.

Key Takeaways

1. **Clear Communication:** Effective communication is vital for team alignment and problem-solving. Regular updates and accessible communication channels ensure that everyone is informed and engaged.

2. **Shared Goals:** Having common objectives that are clearly defined and measurable provides the team with direction and motivation, ensuring that all efforts are aligned.

3. **Diverse Skills:** A team with varied skills and perspectives is better equipped to innovate and solve problems, leading to more comprehensive and effective outcomes.

4. **Mutual Respect**: Respect and trust among team members are essential for fostering a positive work environment and facilitating open communication, which is crucial for successful collaboration.

CHAPTER 8
LEADERSHIP AND MANAGEMENT

71. DESCRIBE YOUR LEADERSHIP STYLE.

Tips

1. **Be Reflective:** Begin by reflecting on the core principles that define your leadership approach. Think about your experiences, the lessons you've learned, and how they have shaped your unique style. Understanding your leadership philosophy will help you articulate it clearly and confidently.

2. **Highlight Key Traits:** Focus on specific traits and behaviors that characterize your leadership. Whether it's empathy, decisiveness, strategic thinking, or adaptability, choose the qualities that best represent how you lead and manage your team. Highlighting these traits gives insight into what your team can expect from you as a leader.

3. **Provide Examples:** Strengthen your description by using concrete examples from your past experiences. These examples should demonstrate how your leadership style has been effective in real situations. This adds credibility and shows that your approach has practical, successful applications.

4. **Connect to the Role:** Tailor your response to align your leadership style with the needs of the role you are applying for. Explain how your approach will benefit the organization and contribute to its success. This shows that you have thought about how your leadership can make a positive impact in the specific context of the job.

Response Framework

1. **Empathetic Leadership:** Begin by discussing how empathy plays a central role in your leadership style. Emphasize the importance of understanding and addressing the needs and challenges of your team members. Explain that you prioritize active listening, providing tailored guidance, and offering the necessary support to help your team succeed. Highlight how this empathetic approach fosters a supportive work environment, builds trust, and motivates the team to perform at their best. Mention that by ensuring each team member feels valued and understood, you maintain high morale and drive the team toward achieving shared goals.

2. **Decisive and Strategic Decision-Making:** Next, describe how decisiveness and strategic thinking are key components of your leadership style. Explain that in your role as a leader, making timely and informed decisions is essential for maintaining momentum and achieving objectives. Discuss how you rely on data-driven insights to inform your decisions and ensure they are aligned with the organization's strategic goals. This focus on strategy ensures that the team's efforts are not only focused but also effective in driving the organization forward. Mention that your ability to make clear and strategic decisions helps navigate challenges and seize opportunities, contributing to the team's overall success.

3. **Mentorship and Development:** Conclude by highlighting your commitment to mentorship and development. Explain that you believe in investing in your team's growth as it not only enhances individual performance but also strengthens the entire team dynamic. Describe how you actively mentor team members, provide constructive feedback, and create opportunities for continuous learning and development. By fostering an environment where professional growth is prioritized, you empower your team to reach their full potential, which leads to greater contributions to the organization. This focus on development ensures that the team remains competitive, motivated, and capable of adapting to new challenges.

Key Takeaways

1. **Be Reflective:** Start by understanding and articulating the core principles that guide your leadership style. This reflection helps you convey your leadership philosophy with clarity.

2. **Highlight Key Traits:** Emphasize specific traits that define your leadership, such as empathy, decisiveness, and strategic thinking. This gives a clear picture of how you lead and manage a team.

3. **Provide Examples:** Use examples from your past to demonstrate the effectiveness of your leadership style. This adds credibility and shows that your approach is not just theoretical but has practical, successful applications.

4. **Connect to the Role:** Align your leadership style with the needs of the job you are applying for. Highlight how your approach will contribute positively to the organization's goals, showing that you are well-suited for the role.

72. HOW DO YOU HANDLE DELEGATING TASKS?

Tips

1. **Understand Strengths and Weaknesses:** To delegate effectively, it's essential to know the strengths and weaknesses of your team members. This allows you to assign tasks to the most qualified individuals, ensuring that work is completed efficiently and to a high standard. By aligning tasks with each team member's capabilities, you also enhance their job satisfaction and performance.

2. **Clear Communication:** When delegating, clear communication is key. Provide detailed instructions, outline the expected outcomes, and set clear deadlines. This reduces the likelihood of

misunderstandings and ensures that everyone knows what is expected. Clear communication helps in aligning the team's efforts with the project's objectives.

3. **Trust and Empowerment:** Trust your team members to execute their tasks effectively. Empower them by giving them the autonomy to make decisions and providing the necessary resources. This approach not only fosters a sense of ownership but also boosts confidence and encourages creativity. Empowered team members are often more motivated and deliver better results.

4. **Monitor Progress and Provide Feedback:** Regularly check in with your team to monitor progress and provide feedback. This helps to ensure that the work stays on track and meets quality standards. Timely feedback allows for course corrections and helps team members improve continuously. Monitoring progress without micromanaging is essential for maintaining a productive and motivated team.

Response Framework

1. **Assessing Team Members:** Start by explaining how you assess the strengths, skills, and current workload of each team member before delegating tasks. Emphasize the importance of aligning tasks with the team members' abilities and interests to ensure that the work is both engaging and manageable. Highlight that this thoughtful assessment leads to higher quality outcomes and greater job satisfaction, as team members are more likely to excel when tasks match their skills.

2. **Clear Communication:** Next, focus on the importance of clear communication in the delegation process. Describe how you ensure that each team member fully understands the task, the expected results, and the deadlines. Explain that providing clear and detailed instructions helps minimize confusion and aligns the team's efforts with the overall project goals. By prioritizing structured communication, you make the delegation process smoother and more effective, reducing the likelihood of misunderstandings.

3. **Empowerment and Trust:** Discuss how you empower your team members by trusting them with the autonomy to complete their tasks. Explain that while you provide the necessary resources and support, you also give them the freedom to innovate and make decisions. Highlight that this sense of empowerment fosters ownership and drives motivation, leading to higher performance and creative contributions. When team members feel trusted, they are more invested in their work and committed to delivering quality results.

4. **Monitoring and Feedback:** Conclude by describing your approach to monitoring progress and providing feedback. Explain that you conduct regular check-ins to ensure that tasks are progressing as planned and offer constructive feedback to help maintain the quality of work. Emphasize that feedback is crucial for team members' growth and improvement. By continuously monitoring progress and offering guidance, you ensure that the team remains aligned with project objectives and consistently improves in their roles.

Key Takeaways

1. **Understand Strengths and Weaknesses:** Tailor task assignments to match the individual strengths and workload of your team members. This maximizes efficiency and ensures high-quality outcomes.

2. **Clear Communication:** Provide clear and detailed instructions along with well-defined expectations to avoid misunderstandings and ensure alignment with project goals.

3. **Trust and Empowerment:** Empower your team members by giving them the autonomy to complete tasks and make decisions. This fosters ownership, motivation, and innovative thinking.

4. **Monitor Progress and Provide Feedback:** Regular check-ins and constructive feedback help maintain the quality of work, address issues early, and promote continuous improvement within the team.

73. HOW DO YOU MANAGE TEAM PERFORMANCE?

Tips

1. **Set Clear Goals:** Establishing clear, measurable goals is crucial for aligning your team's efforts with the organization's objectives. Clear goals provide direction and allow each team member to understand their role in contributing to the team's success. When goals are well-defined, they serve as a roadmap that fosters collaboration, accountability, and motivation among team members.

2. **Regular Check-Ins:** Frequent check-ins with team members are essential for monitoring progress and offering support. These meetings help identify potential challenges early, allowing for timely adjustments to keep the project on track. Regular check-ins also promote open communication, which is vital for maintaining team morale and ensuring that everyone is aligned with the goals.

3. **Provide Feedback:** Constructive feedback is a key driver of continuous improvement. Regular feedback sessions help team members understand their strengths and areas where they can improve. By providing specific, actionable insights, you can guide your team towards better performance and foster a culture of ongoing learning and development.

4. **Recognition and Rewards:** Recognizing and rewarding achievements is crucial for maintaining high levels of motivation and performance. Acknowledging both individual and team successes reinforces positive behavior and encourages continued excellence. Recognition can take many forms, from formal awards to simple expressions of appreciation, and it plays a significant role in fostering a positive work environment.

Response Framework

1. **Setting Clear Goals:** Start by explaining the importance of establishing clear, measurable goals that are aligned with the organization's broader objectives. Discuss how you collaborate with team members to define these goals, ensuring that each person understands their individual responsibilities and how their work contributes to the team's success. Emphasize that this clarity provides direction and keeps the team focused and motivated throughout the project.

2. **Regular Check-Ins:** Describe your approach to maintaining regular check-ins, which are essential for effective performance management. Highlight the importance of scheduling frequent meetings, both one-on-one and with the entire team, to review progress, address obstacles, and make any necessary adjustments to the plan. Explain that these check-ins foster open communication, allowing issues to be resolved before they escalate and ensuring that the team stays on track with deadlines and quality standards.

3. **Providing Feedback:** Discuss the role of regular, constructive feedback in managing team performance. Explain how you conduct performance reviews and provide actionable feedback to help team members build on their strengths and improve in areas that need development. Emphasize that this continuous feedback loop fosters a culture of learning and development, encouraging the team to grow and achieve higher performance levels over time.

4. **Recognition and Rewards:** Conclude by discussing the importance of recognizing and rewarding team members to maintain high morale and motivation. Explain that you prioritize celebrating both individual and team achievements, whether through formal recognition programs or simple gestures of appreciation. Highlight that this recognition reinforces positive behaviors and contributes to a supportive, motivated team environment, ultimately driving everyone to strive for excellence.

Key Takeaways

1. **Set Clear Goals:** Establishing clear, measurable goals is essential for aligning the team's efforts and ensuring everyone works towards the same objectives.

2. **Regular Check-Ins:** Frequent check-ins help monitor progress, provide support, and address challenges early, keeping the team on track.

3. **Provide Feedback:** Regular feedback sessions promote continuous improvement by helping team members understand their strengths and areas for development.

4. **Recognition and Rewards:** Acknowledging achievements boosts morale and encourages continued excellence, creating a positive and motivated team environment.

74. WHAT STEPS DO YOU TAKE TO DEVELOP YOUR TEAM MEMBERS?

Tips

1. **Assess Individual Strengths and Weaknesses:** Understanding each team member's unique capabilities is essential for effective development. By assessing their strengths and areas for improvement, you can tailor development plans that maximize their potential and align with their career goals. This personalized approach ensures that development efforts are focused and relevant, increasing both engagement and performance.

2. **Set Clear Development Goals:** Establishing clear and achievable development goals is critical for guiding your team members' growth. These goals should be Specific, Measurable, Achievable, Relevant, and Time-bound (SMART) to provide a clear roadmap for development. Aligning these goals with both the team's objectives and the individual's career aspirations helps to maintain motivation and ensure progress.

3. **Provide Training and Resources:** Offering access to training and development resources is a key component of fostering continuous learning. Providing opportunities such as workshops, online courses, and access to relevant materials not only enhances skills but also shows a commitment to your team's professional growth. Ensuring that team members have the tools they need to succeed is essential for their development.

4. **Mentorship and Coaching:** Mentorship and coaching are powerful tools for personal and professional development. By offering one-on-one coaching and pairing team members with mentors, you create an environment of support and continuous learning. Mentorship helps team members navigate challenges, gain insights from experienced colleagues, and achieve their development goals more effectively.

Response Framework

1. **Assess Individual Strengths and Development Needs:** Begin by outlining the importance of understanding each team member's unique strengths and areas for growth. Explain that you conduct regular one-on-one meetings to discuss their skills, experiences, and career aspirations. Additionally, highlight the use of performance reviews and peer feedback to gain a comprehensive understanding of their capabilities. This thorough assessment allows you to create personalized development plans that leverage their strengths while addressing areas that need improvement.

2. **Set Clear and Achievable Development Goals:** Describe how you work collaboratively with team members to set Specific, Measurable, Achievable, Relevant, and Time-bound (SMART) goals that align with both their personal career objectives and the team's overall goals. Emphasize the importance of these goals in providing a clear direction for their development, keeping them motivated and focused.

Mention the regular review of these goals to monitor progress, make adjustments as needed, and ensure that their development remains aligned with changing team needs.

3. **Provide Access to Training and Resources:** Discuss the importance of equipping team members with the necessary tools and resources for their development. Highlight your role in facilitating access to relevant workshops, online courses, industry events, and internal training programs. Explain how these resources support the acquisition of new skills and knowledge, which not only benefits the individual's growth but also enhances the team's overall performance.

4. **Offer Mentorship and Coaching:** Focus on the significance of mentorship and coaching in your approach to developing team members. Explain how you provide personalized coaching sessions to address specific challenges and guide their professional growth. Additionally, describe the process of pairing team members with mentors who can offer valuable insights and advice based on their experiences. Emphasize that this mentoring relationship fosters trust, knowledge transfer, and continuous professional development, creating a supportive environment conducive to learning and growth.

Key Takeaways

1. **Assess Individual Strengths and Weaknesses:** Tailoring development opportunities based on individual strengths and areas for growth ensures a more focused and effective approach to team development.

2. **Set Clear Development Goals:** Establishing SMART goals provides direction and motivation, aligning personal development with team objectives and ensuring continuous progress.

3. **Provide Training and Resources:** Offering access to relevant training and resources supports ongoing skill acquisition and demonstrates a commitment to professional growth.

4. **Mentorship and Coaching:** Creating a supportive environment through mentorship and coaching fosters continuous learning and helps team members navigate challenges effectively.

75. DESCRIBE A TIME WHEN YOU HAD TO MAKE A DIFFICULT DECISION AS A LEADER.

Tips

1. **Be Relevant:** Focus on a decision that highlights skills directly relevant to the role you are applying for. Emphasize qualities like strategic thinking, decisiveness, and ethical judgment. Tailoring your response to align with the job description will demonstrate your fit for the position and make your answer more compelling.

2. **Be Concise:** Clearly articulate the situation, your decision-making process, the actions you took, and the outcome. Avoid unnecessary details that may detract from the impact of your story. Practicing your response will help you deliver it smoothly and ensure all key points are covered.

3. **Show Impact:** Illustrate the positive outcomes of your decision. Use specific metrics or examples to demonstrate the tangible benefits your leadership brought to the team or organization. This will showcase your ability to make effective decisions under pressure.

4. **End with Reflection:** Reflect on what you learned from the experience and how it has shaped your approach to leadership. This shows your capacity for growth and self-improvement, which are valuable traits in any leadership role.

Response Framework

1. **Clearly Define the Situation:** Start by setting the context of the difficult decision. Explain the background and the challenges that led to the need for a critical decision. Highlight the specific circumstances that made the decision particularly tough, such as tight deadlines, high stakes, or conflicting priorities. This helps the interviewer understand the gravity of the situation and the factors you needed to consider.

2. **Outline the Decision-Making Process:** Describe the steps you took to arrive at your decision. Emphasize the importance of gathering all relevant information and consulting with key stakeholders, including your team, senior management, or external partners. Discuss how you evaluated the potential risks and benefits of each option, weighing the short-term challenges against the long-term impact on the project or organization. This demonstrates your analytical skills and your ability to involve others in the decision-making process.

3. **Explain the Action Taken:** Once you made your decision, detail the actions you took to implement it. Explain how you communicated the decision to the team and other stakeholders, ensuring everyone understood the rationale and the expected outcomes. Discuss any plans you developed to manage the transition or mitigate risks, and how you provided support to your team during the implementation. This showcases your leadership in executing difficult decisions effectively.

4. **Describe the Outcome and Impact:** Reflect on the results of your decision. Highlight the positive outcomes, such as meeting revised deadlines, improving the quality of the work, or receiving positive feedback from stakeholders. Discuss how your decision ultimately benefited the project or the organization. This reinforces your ability to make tough decisions that lead to successful outcomes.

5. **Reflect on the Learning Experience:** Conclude by reflecting on what you learned from the experience. Discuss how the situation influenced your approach to leadership and decision-making. Mention any specific lessons, such as the importance of thorough analysis, stakeholder engagement, or clear communication, that you have applied in subsequent leadership roles. This demonstrates your ability to grow and adapt as a leader based on your experiences.

Key Takeaways

1. **Be Relevant:** Choose a decision-making scenario that aligns with the job you're applying for, focusing on the skills and qualities the employer values.

2. **Be Concise:** Provide a clear and focused explanation of the situation, your decision-making process, the action taken, and the outcome.

3. **Show Impact:** Use specific examples and metrics to demonstrate the positive results of your decision, showing your effectiveness as a leader.

4. **End with Reflection:** Reflect on the lessons learned from the experience and how they have influenced your leadership style, emphasizing your ability to grow and adapt.

76. HOW DO YOU HANDLE UNDERPERFORMING TEAM MEMBERS?

Tips

1. **Be Empathetic:** Approach the situation with understanding and compassion. Recognize that underperformance can stem from various factors, such as personal issues, lack of skills, or unclear

expectations. Showing empathy helps build trust and encourages open communication, which is vital for addressing the problem effectively.

2. **Be Proactive:** Address underperformance as soon as it becomes apparent. Delaying the conversation can allow the issue to worsen, potentially affecting the entire team's morale and productivity. Regular check-ins and performance reviews are essential for identifying and resolving issues before they escalate.

3. **Be Clear:** Provide specific, constructive feedback that focuses on behaviors and outcomes, not personal attributes. Set clear, achievable goals to help the team member understand what is expected of them. Use measurable criteria to track progress, ensuring that both you and the team member are aligned on what success looks like.

4. **Offer Support:** Provide the necessary resources and support to help the team member improve. This could include additional training, mentorship, or adjustments to their workload. Demonstrating your commitment to their development can motivate them to make the necessary improvements.

Response Framework

1. **Conduct an Initial Assessment:** Start by identifying and understanding the reasons behind the underperformance. This involves observing the team member's work, reviewing their output, and gathering feedback from colleagues or supervisors. Schedule a one-on-one meeting with the individual to discuss their performance openly. During this conversation, aim to uncover whether the issue stems from a lack of skills, unclear expectations, personal challenges, or other factors. A thorough assessment is crucial for determining the most effective way to address the situation.

2. **Provide Constructive Feedback:** Once the root cause is identified, provide the team member with clear and constructive feedback. Highlight specific instances where their performance has fallen short and explain the impact this has on the team and the project. It's essential to deliver this feedback in a supportive and non-confrontational manner, focusing on behaviors and outcomes rather than personal traits. The goal is to ensure the team member understands the areas needing improvement without feeling criticized or demoralized.

3. **3. Set Clear Goals and Expectations:** Collaborate with the team member to establish clear, measurable, and achievable goals aimed at improving their performance. Outline specific targets and set a realistic timeline for achieving these objectives. Involving the team member in this process helps to foster a sense of ownership and accountability. Implement a performance improvement plan (PIP) if necessary, and schedule regular follow-up meetings to monitor progress and provide ongoing support.

4. **Offer Support and Resources:** Provide the necessary support to help the team member meet their goals. This could include additional training, mentorship, or adjustments to their workload to focus on skill development. Ensure they have access to the resources they need to succeed, which might involve pairing them with a more experienced colleague or offering time to focus on learning. Demonstrating that you are invested in their growth can boost their confidence and motivation.

5. **Monitor Progress and Adjust Plans:** Regularly monitor the team member's progress through scheduled check-ins and performance reviews. During these sessions, discuss their achievements, any ongoing challenges, and whether any adjustments are needed to their improvement plan. If they show progress, provide positive reinforcement and gradually increase their responsibilities. If progress is insufficient, reassess the situation to identify any additional support they might need. This ongoing monitoring ensures that the team member remains on track and receives the encouragement and guidance necessary to improve.

Key Takeaways

1. **Be Empathetic:** Understand the root causes of underperformance and approach the situation with compassion.

2. **Be Proactive:** Address issues early to prevent them from affecting team morale and overall project outcomes.

3. **Be Clear:** Provide specific, constructive feedback and set clear, achievable goals to guide improvement.

4. **Offer Support:** Provide the necessary resources and support to help team members improve and succeed.

77. WHAT IS YOUR APPROACH TO GIVING FEEDBACK?

Tips

1. **Be Specific:** Effective feedback should be precise and focused on specific behaviors or actions. Avoid generalizations and provide clear examples that illustrate the points you're addressing. Specific feedback helps the recipient understand exactly what needs to be improved or continued, making the feedback more actionable.

2. **Be Timely:** Deliver feedback as soon as possible after the behavior or event. This ensures that the details are fresh and relevant, allowing for immediate adjustments. Timely feedback also demonstrates your attentiveness and commitment to continuous improvement.

3. **Be Constructive:** Frame your feedback in a way that is positive and focused on growth. Instead of simply pointing out what went wrong, provide suggestions on how the recipient can improve. Constructive feedback encourages development and helps build a positive, supportive work environment.

4. **Be Balanced:** Balance your feedback by highlighting both what the individual is doing well and areas for improvement. This approach motivates the recipient by acknowledging their strengths while also guiding them towards better performance.

Response Framework

1. **Start with Positives:** Begin the feedback session by acknowledging the individual's strengths and recent successes. This approach sets a positive tone for the conversation and reassures the individual that their contributions are recognized and valued. Starting with positive feedback helps build rapport and makes the recipient more receptive to the constructive feedback that follows. For instance, acknowledge their recent achievements or highlight areas where they consistently excel.

2. **Be Specific and Clear:** When delivering constructive feedback, focus on specific actions or behaviors rather than making general statements. Clearly articulate what needs improvement and why it is important. By being precise and objective, you ensure that the individual understands the exact areas that require attention. This clarity helps them grasp the feedback and provides a clear direction for making improvements. Avoid vague language and aim to provide examples that illustrate the points you're addressing.

3. **Offer Constructive Suggestions:** Alongside identifying areas for improvement, offer actionable and practical suggestions for how the individual can enhance their performance. This could involve recommending resources, suggesting alternative approaches, or providing additional support. Offering

concrete advice shows your commitment to their development and gives them the tools they need to succeed. Ensure that your suggestions are realistic and tailored to the individual's role and capabilities.

4. **Encourage Two-Way Dialogue:** Promote a two-way conversation by inviting the individual to share their thoughts and challenges. This dialogue helps you understand their perspective, uncover any underlying issues, and collaboratively explore solutions. By fostering an open exchange, you demonstrate respect for their input and encourage active participation in their own development. This collaborative approach can lead to more effective problem-solving and stronger buy-in from the individual.

5. **Follow-Up and Support:** Conclude the feedback session by outlining a plan for follow-up and continued support. Schedule future check-ins to monitor progress, address any new challenges, and reinforce positive changes. These follow-up meetings underscore that feedback is part of an ongoing development process and not just a one-time conversation. By offering ongoing support, you help the individual stay on track and continue to grow, ensuring that the feedback leads to sustained improvement.

Key Takeaways

1. **Be Specific:** Offer clear, focused feedback with concrete examples to ensure the recipient understands and can act on it.

2. **Be Timely:** Provide feedback soon after the event to ensure it's relevant and can be implemented quickly.

3. **Be Constructive:** Frame your feedback positively, offering practical suggestions for improvement and support.

4. **Be Balanced:** Combine positive feedback with constructive criticism to motivate and guide the recipient towards better performance.

78. HOW DO YOU ENSURE YOUR TEAM MEETS DEADLINES?

Tips

1. **Be Proactive:** Start with thorough planning to anticipate potential challenges. This includes breaking down the project into smaller tasks and setting realistic deadlines. Regular check-ins and monitoring can help identify obstacles early, allowing you to address them before they impact the timeline.

2. **Set Clear Expectations:** Clearly communicate the project goals, deadlines, and individual responsibilities to the team. Ensure everyone understands their role and how their contributions fit into the overall project. This clarity prevents misunderstandings and aligns the team towards the same objectives.

3. **Use Tools and Systems:** Implement project management tools like Asana, Trello, or Microsoft Teams to track tasks, deadlines, and overall progress. These tools promote transparency, accountability, and efficiency by allowing everyone to see what needs to be done and by when.

4. **Prioritize Communication:** Maintain open communication channels within the team. Encourage regular updates, and be available for any questions or concerns. This approach helps in quickly addressing issues and keeping the team aligned with the project's goals.

Response Framework

1. **Begin with Detailed Planning:** The foundation for meeting deadlines is thorough and strategic planning. I start by breaking down the overall project into smaller, manageable tasks, each with its own specific deadline. This approach creates a clear roadmap and ensures that every team member knows what is expected of them from the outset. By setting these smaller milestones, the project becomes more manageable, and progress can be tracked more effectively. This planning stage is crucial for aligning the team's efforts and preventing last-minute rushes.

2. **Set Clear Expectations:** Setting clear expectations is essential for maintaining focus and ensuring deadlines are met. I clearly define the scope, objectives, and timelines for each task, making sure that every team member understands their role and responsibilities. This clarity helps prevent misunderstandings and keeps everyone aligned with the project's goals. By outlining these expectations early on, the team can work more efficiently and stay focused on the end goal, reducing the risk of delays.

3. **Utilize Project Management Tools:** I leverage project management tools like Trello, Asana, or similar platforms to monitor progress and maintain transparency. These tools provide a visual overview of the project, helping the team stay organized and on track. They allow for real-time updates and enable the team to see what tasks are pending, in progress, or completed. This transparency fosters accountability and ensures that deadlines are not missed due to oversight or miscommunication.

4. **Prioritize Regular Communication:** Effective communication is key to keeping the team on track. I hold regular check-ins, whether weekly or bi-weekly, to discuss progress, address challenges, and adjust plans if necessary. These meetings keep the team informed, engaged, and aligned with the project's objectives. Open communication also provides a platform for team members to voice concerns or offer suggestions, which can be crucial for overcoming obstacles and staying on schedule.

5. **Monitor Progress and Offer Support:** Continuous monitoring of progress is vital to ensuring deadlines are met. I track the team's progress through regular updates and am proactive in offering support when needed. If any team member is struggling or if unforeseen issues arise, I step in to provide assistance, reallocate resources, or adjust timelines as necessary. This proactive approach helps maintain momentum and ensures that the team can meet deadlines without compromising on quality.

Key Takeaways

1. **Be Proactive:** Start with detailed planning and anticipate challenges early on. Regular monitoring helps prevent issues from escalating.

2. **Set Clear Expectations:** Clearly define goals, responsibilities, and deadlines to align the team's efforts and avoid confusion.

3. **Use Tools and Systems:** Leverage project management tools to enhance transparency, accountability, and efficiency throughout the project.

4. **Prioritize Communication:** Maintain open communication channels to keep the team informed, engaged, and aligned with project objectives.

79. DESCRIBE A TIME WHEN YOU HAD TO MANAGE A CONFLICT WITHIN YOUR TEAM.

Tips

1. **Be Specific:** Choose a specific example that clearly illustrates your approach to managing conflict. This helps to showcase your skills in a real-world context and provides a concrete demonstration of your effectiveness.

2. **Focus on Resolution:** Highlight the steps you took to resolve the conflict, emphasizing the process you followed and the positive outcomes. This shows your ability to navigate difficult situations and lead your team to a successful resolution.

3. **Show Empathy:** Demonstrate your ability to understand and consider different perspectives. Addressing the emotional aspects of the conflict is crucial in showing that you can manage not just the practical, but also the interpersonal dimensions of conflict.

4. **Highlight Leadership:** Use the example to showcase your leadership skills, particularly in ensuring fairness, maintaining team cohesion, and fostering a positive work environment even during challenging times.

Response Framework

1. **Introduction to the Conflict:** Begin by acknowledging that conflicts are a natural part of team dynamics and require effective management to maintain productivity and harmony. Introduce the scenario by briefly explaining the nature of the conflict, ensuring to highlight the key issues at play without diving into specifics.

2. **Identify the Core Issue:** Clearly outline the root cause of the conflict. This could involve differing work styles, priorities, or communication breakdowns among team members. Emphasize the impact of the conflict on team morale, productivity, or project progress. Identifying the core issue is crucial for demonstrating your analytical abilities in conflict resolution.

3. **Approach to Resolution:** Describe the steps you took to address the conflict. Start by explaining how you gathered information, such as by meeting with each team member involved to understand their perspectives. Highlight your use of active listening and empathy to ensure that all parties felt heard. Then, detail how you facilitated a constructive dialogue between the conflicting parties, ensuring a neutral and supportive environment where each person could express their concerns and viewpoints.

4. **Implementing a Solution:** Explain how you guided the team towards a resolution. Focus on how you helped the team members identify common ground, explore compromises, and agree on a solution that balanced the differing priorities. Describe any specific strategies or plans put in place to ensure the agreed-upon solution was followed, such as setting milestones or checkpoints to monitor progress and adherence to the resolution.

5. **Outcome and Reflection:** Conclude by discussing the outcome of the conflict resolution process. Emphasize how the conflict was resolved and the positive effects on the team's collaboration and overall project success. Reflect on the key lessons learned from the experience, such as the importance of open communication, empathy, and a structured approach to conflict resolution. Highlight how this experience has strengthened your skills in managing team dynamics and maintaining a productive work environment.

Key Takeaways

1. **Be Specific:** Choose a concrete example that clearly illustrates your conflict management skills, giving a clear picture of your approach and effectiveness.

2. **Focus on Resolution:** Emphasize the steps you took to resolve the conflict and the positive outcomes that resulted from your actions.

3. **Show Empathy:** Highlight your ability to understand and consider different perspectives, addressing both practical and emotional aspects of the conflict.

4. **Highlight Leadership:** Showcase your leadership skills in managing conflict, ensuring fairness, and maintaining team cohesion, ultimately leading to a positive and productive outcome.

80. HOW DO YOU SET AND COMMUNICATE TEAM GOALS?

Tips

1. **Be Clear and Specific:** When setting team goals, clarity and specificity are paramount. Ensure that the goals are well-defined and directly aligned with the broader organizational objectives. This clarity helps team members understand exactly what is expected of them, creating a shared sense of purpose and direction.

2. **Use SMART Criteria:** Utilize the SMART criteria—Specific, Measurable, Achievable, Relevant, and Time-bound—to create effective goals. This framework ensures that goals are not only clear but also realistic and time-bound, which facilitates easier tracking and achievement.

3. **Involve the Team:** Engage your team in the goal-setting process. By involving team members, you ensure that the goals are realistic and attainable, while also fostering a sense of ownership and commitment. This collaborative approach makes the team more invested in the success of the project.

4. **Communicate Regularly:** Regular communication is key to keeping the team on track. Use multiple channels such as meetings, emails, and project management tools to share updates, provide feedback, and celebrate milestones. Consistent communication helps maintain momentum and ensures everyone stays informed about progress and any necessary adjustments.

Response Framework

1. **Introduction:** Begin by emphasizing the importance of setting and communicating clear team goals for achieving success and driving performance. Explain that your approach involves a structured and inclusive process that ensures alignment with broader organizational objectives while fostering team engagement and accountability.

2. **Setting Goals:** Describe your goal-setting process by first ensuring that the goals align with the organization's overall objectives. Break down these larger objectives into specific, actionable targets that are relevant to your team's responsibilities. Apply the SMART criteria (Specific, Measurable, Achievable, Relevant, Time-bound) to create goals that are clear and measurable. This method provides a structured roadmap that helps the team stay focused and track progress effectively.

3. **Involving the Team:** Highlight the importance of involving the team in the goal-setting process. Explain that you facilitate collaborative brainstorming sessions where team members can contribute their ideas and perspectives. This involvement not only ensures that the goals are realistic and attainable but also fosters a sense of ownership among the team. When team members are actively involved in setting the goals, they are more committed to achieving them.

4. **Communicating Goals:** Detail your approach to communicating the goals clearly and consistently. Explain that you use a combination of team meetings, email updates, and project management tools to ensure that everyone is aware of the goals and understands their roles in achieving them. This approach maintains transparency and ensures that the entire team is aligned and working towards the same objectives.

5. **Progress and Providing Feedback:** Discuss the importance of regularly tracking progress and providing feedback. You schedule periodic check-ins and review meetings to assess the team's progress, address any challenges, and celebrate milestones. Providing constructive feedback and recognizing achievements are key to maintaining motivation and encouraging continuous improvement. This ongoing support helps the team stay on track and adapt to any changes or obstacles that arise.

Key Takeaways

1. **Be Clear and Specific:** Define team goals clearly and align them with the organization's objectives to ensure that everyone understands what is expected.

2. **Use SMART Criteria:** Ensure that goals are Specific, Measurable, Achievable, Relevant, and Time-bound to facilitate effective tracking and achievement.

3. **Involve the Team:** Engage team members in the goal-setting process to foster a sense of ownership and commitment, which enhances motivation.

4. **Communicate Regularly:** Maintain regular communication through various channels to share updates, provide feedback, and celebrate milestones, keeping the team aligned and focused.

CHAPTER 9
CAREER DEVELOPMENT AND LEARNING

81. HOW DO YOU SET CAREER GOALS?

Tips

1. **Be Self-Aware:**
Self-awareness is crucial when setting career goals. Reflect on your strengths, weaknesses, passions, and core values. This understanding will help you identify what you truly want to achieve and ensure your goals are aligned with both your personal and professional aspirations. Setting goals that resonate with who you are increases your motivation and commitment to achieving them.

2. **Use SMART Criteria:**
Applying the SMART criteria—Specific, Measurable, Achievable, Relevant, and Time-bound—can help you craft well-defined and realistic career goals. This framework ensures that your goals are clear, actionable, and easy to track over time, which enhances your chances of success. For instance, instead of a vague goal like "advance in my career," aim for something specific like "secure a leadership role within two years by completing relevant certifications."

3. **Research and Plan:**
Thorough research is essential for effective career goal setting. Investigate your desired career path, industry trends, and the skills required to advance. Understanding the landscape will help you identify the steps needed to achieve your goals and create a realistic plan. This planning phase is crucial for setting goals that are both ambitious and attainable.

4. **Set Short-term and Long-term Goals:**
Balancing short-term and long-term goals is key to sustained career progress. Short-term goals provide immediate steps you can take, such as completing a course or gaining experience in a specific

area. Long-term goals, like reaching a senior management position, give you a broader vision to work towards. Together, these goals keep you motivated and focused on your career journey.

Response Framework

1. **Introduction:** Begin by highlighting the importance of setting career goals for personal and professional growth. Explain that your approach to goal setting is structured and intentional, involving a combination of self-assessment, strategic planning, and the application of the SMART criteria. This method ensures that your career goals are both clear and achievable, keeping you focused and motivated.

2. **Self-Assessment:** Start with self-assessment as the foundation of your career goal-setting process. Describe how you reflect on your strengths, areas for improvement, passions, and core values. This introspective analysis helps you align your goals with what is truly meaningful to you, ensuring that your career path is both fulfilling and strategically aligned with your long-term aspirations.

3. **Applying SMART Criteria:** Discuss how you apply the SMART criteria—Specific, Measurable, Achievable, Relevant, and Time-bound—to each of your career goals. This approach ensures that your goals are well-defined, realistic, and time-bound, making them easier to track and achieve. For example, rather than setting a broad goal like "advance in my career," you would specify "achieve a promotion to a management position within the next 12 months by completing relevant leadership training and demonstrating project management skills."

4. **Research and Planning:** Explain the importance of research and planning in your goal-setting process. Describe how you analyze industry trends, consult with professionals in your field, and review job descriptions to understand the necessary skills and qualifications. This research informs your goals and helps you create a detailed action plan, outlining the specific steps needed to advance in your career.

5. **Balancing Short-term and Long-term Goals:** Emphasize the need to balance short-term and long-term goals. Short-term goals provide immediate milestones that keep you engaged and motivated, such as acquiring a new certification or developing a specific skill. Long-term goals, like reaching a senior leadership position or starting your own business, give you a clear direction and purpose, ensuring that your efforts are aligned with your ultimate career aspirations.

Key Takeaways

1. **Be Self-Aware:** Understand your strengths, weaknesses, passions, and values to set career goals that are truly aligned with your personal and professional aspirations.

2. **Use SMART Criteria:** Apply the SMART criteria to ensure your goals are Specific, Measurable, Achievable, Relevant, and Time-bound, making them clear and attainable.

3. **Research and Plan:** Conduct thorough research on your chosen career path and industry trends to inform your goal-setting and create a realistic, actionable plan.

4. **Set Short-term and Long-term Goals:** Balance short-term and long-term goals to maintain motivation and focus, providing both immediate steps to take and a clear vision for the future.

82. WHAT ARE YOU CURRENTLY DOING TO IMPROVE YOUR SKILLS?

Tips

1. **Be Proactive:** When responding to this question, highlight the steps you are actively taking to enhance your skills. This could include enrolling in courses, attending workshops, or seeking mentorship. Showing that you are continuously improving your abilities reflects a growth mindset and a commitment to professional development.

2. **Focus on Relevance:** Ensure that the skills you mention are relevant to the job or industry you are pursuing. Emphasize how these skills will benefit the company and align with your career goals. This demonstrates that you are strategically improving areas that will directly contribute to your success in the role.

3. **Balance Hard and Soft Skills:** Showcase both hard skills (technical abilities specific to your field) and soft skills (interpersonal abilities like communication, leadership, or teamwork). A well-rounded approach to skill development indicates that you are not only focusing on technical expertise but also on becoming a more effective collaborator and leader.

4. **Mention Continuous Learning:** Highlight your commitment to lifelong learning. Mentioning how you stay updated with industry trends, whether through reading, attending seminars, or participating in professional networks, shows that you are dedicated to staying ahead in your field.

Response Framework

1. **Introduction:** Begin by emphasizing the importance of continuous skill improvement in your professional development. Explain that you view learning as an ongoing process that is essential for staying competitive and effective in your field. This sets the stage for a focused discussion on the specific steps you are taking to enhance your skills.

2. **Proactive Skill Development:** Discuss the proactive measures you are taking to improve your skills. Highlight the specific areas you are focusing on and the methods you are using to develop these skills. For instance, mention if you are enrolled in courses, pursuing certifications, or participating in workshops. You could also talk about how you are seeking mentorship or gaining hands-on experience through challenging projects. This shows that you are taking deliberate actions to grow professionally.

3. **Alignment with Career Goals:** Explain how the skills you are developing align with your long-term career goals and the demands of your industry. Describe how improving these skills will enhance your ability to contribute to your current role and prepare you for future opportunities. This demonstrates that your efforts are strategic and focused on adding value to your career and organization.

4. **Balancing Hard and Soft Skills:** Detail your holistic approach to skill improvement by addressing both hard and soft skills. Mention how you are working on technical skills, such as mastering new technologies or tools, while also investing time in developing soft skills like leadership, communication, and teamwork. This balanced approach ensures you are well-rounded and can effectively navigate various professional situations.

5. **Commitment to Continuous Learning:** Conclude by highlighting your commitment to continuous learning. Describe how you stay updated on industry trends and advancements through reading, attending webinars, participating in professional networks, or engaging in other educational activities. This ongoing effort to stay informed and adaptable underscores your dedication to professional growth and readiness to meet new challenges.

Key Takeaways

1. **Be Proactive:** Demonstrate that you are actively improving your skills through courses, mentorship, and hands-on experience. Show that you are committed to ongoing professional development.

2. **Focus on Relevance:** Highlight how the skills you are developing are directly relevant to your career goals and the industry you are in. This shows that your efforts are strategic and aligned with your professional aspirations.

3. **Balance Hard and Soft Skills:** Emphasize a balanced approach to skill development, focusing on both technical expertise and interpersonal abilities. This illustrates that you are well-rounded and prepared to excel in various aspects of your role.

4. **Mention Continuous Learning:** Show your dedication to lifelong learning by mentioning how you stay informed about industry trends and continuously seek new knowledge. This reflects your commitment to staying competitive and effective in your career.

83. DESCRIBE A TIME WHEN YOU TOOK INITIATIVE TO LEARN SOMETHING NEW.

Tips

1. **Be Specific:** Clearly describe the skill or knowledge you pursued and why it was important for your career. Focus on the relevance of what you learned to your professional growth and how it addressed a specific gap in your expertise.

2. **Highlight the Process:** Detail the steps you took to acquire the new skill or knowledge. This demonstrates your proactive approach and commitment to learning. Mention the resources you used, such as courses, books, or mentorship, to show how you structured your learning journey.

3. **Show Impact:** Explain how this new skill or knowledge made a tangible difference in your work. Highlight any improvements in performance, efficiency, or outcomes that resulted from your initiative. This illustrates the practical benefits of your learning efforts and your ability to apply new knowledge effectively.

Response Framework

1. **Introduction:** Begin by emphasizing the importance of taking initiative in learning new skills for professional development. Explain that you actively seek opportunities to expand your knowledge and capabilities, especially when it comes to areas that are critical for your role or career advancement. This sets the stage for discussing a specific instance where you proactively pursued learning.

2. **Identifying the Need:** Describe the specific situation that prompted you to take initiative. Explain how you identified a gap in your knowledge or skills that needed to be addressed. This could be due to changes in your role, industry trends, or a desire to enhance your effectiveness in your current position. Highlight the importance of this skill or knowledge in the context of your professional goals.

3. **Learning Process:** Detail the steps you took to acquire the new skill or knowledge. Outline your structured approach, which might include enrolling in courses, seeking mentorship, dedicating time for self-study, or engaging in hands-on practice. Mention any specific resources you used, such as online platforms, workshops, or networking with experts. This section should convey your proactive attitude and commitment to learning.

4. **Implementation and Impact:** Explain how you applied the new skills or knowledge in your work. Discuss the tangible results or improvements that occurred as a result of your initiative. This could include enhanced performance, successful completion of a project, or contributions that positively impacted your team or organization. Highlight the value that your newly acquired skills brought to your professional environment.

5. **Reflection and Future Learning:** Conclude by reflecting on the experience and its significance in your career. Emphasize how this initiative reinforced your belief in the importance of continuous learning. Discuss how you plan to continue seeking out new learning opportunities that align with your long-term career goals, ensuring that you remain a valuable asset to your team and organization.

Key Takeaways

1. **Be Specific:** Identify the new skill or knowledge you pursued and its relevance to your career. Specificity shows a targeted approach to your professional development.

2. **Highlight the Process:** Detail the steps you took to learn the new skill, showcasing your proactive and structured approach to learning. This demonstrates your commitment to personal and professional growth.

3. **Show Impact:** Emphasize the positive impact of your new skill on your job or organization, illustrating the practical benefits of your initiative. This highlights your ability to apply what you learn effectively.

84. WHAT PROFESSIONAL DEVELOPMENT OPPORTUNITIES ARE YOU SEEKING?

Tips

1. **Be Specific:** When discussing professional development, be clear about the specific opportunities you are pursuing. This demonstrates that you have a well-thought-out plan for your career advancement. Specificity also shows that you are actively seeking ways to enhance your skills and stay competitive in your field.

2. **Align with Career Goals:** Ensure that the professional development opportunities you mention are directly aligned with your long-term career goals. This alignment demonstrates strategic thinking and a clear vision for your career path. Employers value candidates who are proactive about their growth and can articulate how these opportunities will benefit both them and the organization.

3. **Show Enthusiasm:** Express genuine enthusiasm for continuous learning and self-improvement. Employers appreciate candidates who are committed to their professional growth and who actively seek out ways to enhance their expertise. Your enthusiasm can also indicate that you will bring new ideas and skills to the organization, contributing positively to its success.

Response Framework

1. **Introduction:** Begin by expressing your commitment to continuous professional development as a key element of maintaining relevance and effectiveness in your field. Emphasize that you actively seek opportunities that align with your career goals and enhance your ability to contribute to your organization.

2. **Specific Areas of Interest:** Identify the specific areas in which you are seeking professional development. This might include certifications, specialized training, leadership development programs, or acquiring new technical skills. Highlight how these areas are relevant to your current role and future aspirations. For example, mention certifications or courses that will help you gain expertise in emerging trends or enhance your leadership capabilities.

3. **Learning Approach and Strategy:** Outline your approach to professional development, which could involve a mix of formal education, such as enrolling in courses or certification programs, and experiential learning, such as participating in industry conferences, attending workshops, or engaging

in mentorship. This demonstrates your proactive approach and dedication to gaining both theoretical knowledge and practical experience.

4. **Application and Anticipated Impact:** Discuss how you plan to apply the new skills and knowledge in your current role. Explain how these professional development efforts will enhance your performance and contribute to the success of your team or organization. For example, acquiring a specific certification might enable you to take on more complex projects or lead initiatives that drive business growth.

5. **Long-Term Career Goals:** Conclude by connecting your professional development efforts to your long-term career goals. Explain how these opportunities will prepare you for future roles, such as taking on more strategic responsibilities or advancing into leadership positions. Emphasize your ambition to become a thought leader in your field, driving innovation and contributing to your organization's long-term success.

Key Takeaways

1. **Be Specific:** Clearly define the professional development opportunities you are pursuing. This shows that you have a focused and proactive approach to career growth.

2. **Align with Career Goals:** Ensure that your professional development plans are aligned with your long-term career aspirations. This demonstrates that you are strategic in your approach to growth and are committed to achieving your career goals.

3. **Show Enthusiasm:** Express your enthusiasm for continuous learning and self-improvement. This indicates your commitment to your career and your willingness to bring new skills and ideas to your role.

85. HOW DO YOU KEEP UP WITH INDUSTRY CHANGES?

Tips

1. **Be Proactive:** Staying ahead of industry changes is vital for remaining competitive and relevant in your field. Demonstrate a proactive approach by consistently seeking out new information, whether through formal education, industry events, or other reliable sources. Being proactive not only keeps your knowledge up to date but also shows employers that you are committed to continuous improvement.

2. **Utilize Multiple Sources:** Highlight the diverse range of resources you use to stay informed. This could include industry publications, online courses, professional networks, and social media platforms. By using multiple sources, you can gain a well-rounded perspective on industry trends and best practices. This approach also helps you stay informed about emerging technologies and methodologies that could impact your field.

3. **Regular Engagement:** Discuss the activities you regularly engage in to maintain your industry knowledge. These might include attending webinars, participating in online forums, joining professional associations, or following industry thought leaders on social media. Regular engagement ensures that you are continuously exposed to new ideas and innovations, which can inspire your work and keep you ahead of the curve.

Response Framework

1. **Introduction:** Begin by emphasizing the importance of staying current with industry changes to remain competitive and effective in your role. Mention that your approach is multifaceted, combining continuous learning, networking, and active engagement in industry activities to stay well-informed about the latest trends and best practices.

2. **Utilizing Diverse Information Sources:** Explain that you rely on a variety of sources to keep up with industry developments. This includes regularly reading trade journals, white papers, and subscribing to newsletters from reputable organizations. Additionally, you follow industry blogs and online publications to receive timely updates on emerging trends. This diverse approach ensures that you are well-informed about the latest advancements in your field.

3. **Engaging in Continuous Learning:** Highlight your commitment to continuous education as a key component of staying up to date with industry changes. Mention that you frequently enroll in relevant online courses and attend webinars to deepen your understanding of new technologies and methodologies. Specify that you use platforms like Coursera, LinkedIn Learning, or other industry-specific resources to expand your skill set and stay current with the latest knowledge in your field.

4. **Networking and Professional Associations:** Discuss the importance of networking and being an active member of professional associations. Explain that you attend industry conferences, seminars, and events, which provide valuable opportunities to learn from experts, exchange ideas with peers, and discuss the latest developments. Engaging with these communities helps you stay connected to industry changes and build a network of professionals who can provide insights and support.

5. **Regular Industry Engagement:** Mention that you participate in online forums and discussion groups, particularly on platforms like LinkedIn, where you can exchange insights, ask questions, and share your own experiences. This active participation allows you to remain connected with your professional community and gain diverse perspectives on industry changes, ensuring you are aware of any shifts that could impact your work.

6. **Applying Acquired Knowledge:** Conclude by stressing that staying updated is not just about acquiring knowledge but also about applying it in your work. Explain that you actively seek opportunities to implement new ideas, technologies, or methodologies in your role. This practical application helps you understand the real-world impact of industry changes, keeps your skills sharp, and ensures that you can contribute effectively to your team and organization.

Key Takeaways

1. **Be Proactive:** Highlight the importance of proactively staying ahead of industry changes to remain competitive and relevant. Being proactive shows your commitment to ongoing learning and adaptation.

2. **Utilize Multiple Sources:** Demonstrate the value of using a variety of sources to stay informed. This ensures a well-rounded understanding of industry trends and helps you stay up to date with emerging developments.

3. **Regular Engagement:** Emphasize the importance of regular engagement with industry activities, such as webinars, forums, and networking events. Continuous engagement keeps you connected and informed, allowing you to apply new insights to your work effectively.

86. WHAT ARE YOUR SHORT-TERM CAREER GOALS?

Tips

1. **Be Specific:** When discussing your short-term career goals, it's crucial to be clear and specific. Avoid vague statements and instead focus on concrete objectives that are measurable and time-bound. This shows your potential employer that you have a clear plan for your career and that you are focused on achieving specific outcomes.

2. **Align with Role:** Make sure that your short-term goals align with the responsibilities and expectations of the role you are applying for. This alignment demonstrates that you have carefully considered how the position fits into your broader career plans and that you are ready to contribute meaningfully to the organization.

3. **Show Immediate Impact:** Highlight how achieving your short-term goals will allow you to make an immediate positive impact in the role. Employers value candidates who can hit the ground running and contribute to the company's success from the start. Your goals should reflect your intention to add value to the team and the organization as a whole.

Response Framework

1. **Introduction:** Begin by emphasizing the importance of setting clear and actionable short-term career goals that align with both personal growth and the needs of the organization. Highlight that your focus is on rapidly contributing to the team's success while also laying the groundwork for long-term career development.

2. **Developing Expertise:** State that one of your primary short-term goals is to quickly develop proficiency in the specific skills, processes, or technologies required for the role. Explain that you plan to engage in relevant training programs and actively apply what you learn to real-world tasks. By focusing on mastering the tools and methodologies critical to your role, you aim to enhance your effectiveness and efficiency early in your tenure.

3. **Aligning with Organizational Goals:** Explain that you intend to align your efforts with the organization's strategic objectives. This involves understanding how your role contributes to broader company goals and prioritizing projects that support key initiatives. For example, if the company is focused on innovation or market expansion, you would aim to contribute to projects that advance these priorities, ensuring your work has a direct and positive impact.

4. **Demonstrating Immediate Value:** Mention that you are keen on achieving quick wins to demonstrate your ability to contribute immediately. This could involve identifying areas for improvement, streamlining processes, or introducing new strategies that yield measurable results. Achieving these short-term successes will help you build credibility and establish your value within the team from the outset.

5. **Expanding Professional Networks:** Discuss your goal to expand your professional network both within the company and in the industry at large. Building strong relationships with colleagues, attending industry events, and participating in professional associations will enhance your knowledge, open up opportunities for collaboration, and support your career growth. This networking will also facilitate your integration into the company culture and the broader professional community.

6. **Continuous Learning:** Conclude by highlighting your commitment to continuous learning. State that you plan to regularly seek out opportunities for professional development, such as attending workshops, webinars, or pursuing certifications relevant to your role. This dedication to growth will ensure that you remain adaptable and capable of meeting the evolving demands of your position.

Key Takeaways

1. **Be Specific:** Clearly define your short-term career goals, ensuring they are specific and measurable. This demonstrates your focus and determination to achieve tangible outcomes.

2. **Align with Role:** Ensure that your goals are closely aligned with the role you are applying for. This shows that you have thoughtfully considered how the position fits into your overall career strategy.

3. **Show Immediate Impact:** Emphasize how achieving your short-term goals will enable you to make an immediate positive impact in your new role. This conveys your commitment to contributing to the company's success from the outset.

87. HOW DO YOU HANDLE PROFESSIONAL SETBACKS?

Tips

1. **Acknowledge the Setback:** The first step in effectively handling a professional setback is to recognize it and understand its impact. Acknowledging the situation demonstrates self-awareness and an honest assessment of the challenges faced. This also shows maturity in dealing with adverse situations, which is crucial in any professional environment.

2. **Learn from the Experience:** Every setback provides valuable lessons. Emphasize the importance of analyzing what went wrong and identifying areas for improvement. This approach highlights your ability to learn from mistakes and take proactive steps to avoid similar issues in the future. By showing that you use setbacks as opportunities for growth, you demonstrate a mindset focused on continuous improvement.

3. **Stay Positive and Resilient:** Maintaining a positive attitude and resilience in the face of setbacks is essential. Demonstrate your ability to stay motivated and focused on the bigger picture, even when things don't go as planned. This resilience shows that you can handle adversity without letting it derail your progress or dampen your enthusiasm.

Response Framework

1. **Acknowledge the Setback:** Begin by acknowledging the setback in a realistic and objective manner. Explain that recognizing and accepting the situation is the first crucial step. Assess the impact of the setback on your goals or projects and understand the areas that need improvement. This acknowledgment is essential for laying the groundwork for a constructive response.

2. **Analyze and Learn from the Experience:** Discuss the importance of viewing setbacks as learning opportunities. After acknowledging the setback, conduct a thorough analysis of the factors that contributed to it. This might involve reviewing processes, decisions, and strategies to identify what went wrong and why. The goal is to extract valuable lessons that can be applied to future situations, turning the setback into a stepping stone for growth.

3. **Develop a Concrete Action Plan:** Outline the steps for creating an action plan that addresses the root causes of the setback. This plan should include specific, actionable steps and clear timelines to correct the issues and prevent similar setbacks in the future. Emphasize that the plan should not only focus on rectifying the immediate problem but also on implementing strategies that enhance overall performance and resilience.

4. **Maintain a Positive and Resilient Attitude:** Highlight the importance of staying positive and resilient in the face of setbacks. A positive mindset helps you remain motivated and keeps team morale high. Discuss how you use setbacks as opportunities to build resilience, encouraging yourself and your team

to see challenges as part of the learning process. This resilience is key to bouncing back stronger and staying focused on long-term goals.

5. **Seek Feedback and Support:** Emphasize the value of seeking feedback and support from colleagues, mentors, or supervisors after experiencing a setback. Explain how gaining additional perspectives can provide new insights and help refine your strategies. Being open to feedback fosters a culture of continuous improvement and collaboration, ensuring that you and your team are better equipped to handle future challenges.

Key Takeaways

1. **Acknowledge the Setback:** Recognizing and understanding the impact of a setback demonstrates self-awareness and an honest approach to problem-solving.

2. **Learn from the Experience:** Analyzing what went wrong and identifying areas for improvement showcases your ability to turn challenges into learning opportunities.

3. **Develop an Action Plan:** Creating a concrete plan to address issues and prevent future setbacks highlights your proactive and strategic approach.

4. **Stay Positive and Resilient:** Maintaining a positive attitude and resilience demonstrates your ability to stay motivated and proactive, even in difficult situations.

5. **Seek Feedback and Support:** Using feedback and support from colleagues and mentors to refine your approach underscores your commitment to continuous improvement.

88. WHAT HAS BEEN YOUR BIGGEST LEARNING EXPERIENCE?

Tips

1. **Be Reflective:** When answering this question, it's important to choose a learning experience that significantly impacted your professional growth. Reflect deeply on the situation, considering how it shaped your career and personal development. This reflection will help you convey genuine insights that demonstrate your capacity for self-awareness and continuous learning.

2. **Be Specific:** Provide clear and detailed information about the experience, focusing on what you learned and how it influenced your professional development. Specific examples will make your response more engaging and credible, helping the interviewer understand the context and significance of the learning experience.

3. **Show Growth:** Emphasize how this experience contributed to your growth as a professional. Highlight the skills or perspectives you gained and how they have influenced your approach to work. This not only shows that you learn from challenges but also that you actively apply these lessons to improve your performance and decision-making in the future.

Response Framework

1. **Introduction:** Begin by introducing the context of your learning experience. Explain that it was a significant event or project in your career that presented unique challenges. This could be an instance where you were faced with high stakes, tight deadlines, or unexpected obstacles. Set the stage by indicating that this experience had a profound impact on your professional development.

2. **Identify the Challenges Faced:** Clearly outline the key challenges or obstacles you encountered during this experience. These might include technical difficulties, resource constraints, or complex team dynamics. Emphasize the gravity of the situation and how these challenges tested your skills, decision-making, and resilience. This helps to illustrate why this experience was a pivotal learning moment.

3. **Lessons Learned:** Discuss the specific lessons you learned from navigating these challenges. Focus on the key takeaways that had a lasting impact on your approach to work. For example, you might mention the importance of adaptability, effective communication, or strategic problem-solving. Highlight how these lessons shifted your perspective or enhanced your professional skills.

4. **Application of Learnings:** Explain how you have applied these lessons in your subsequent roles or projects. This could involve changes in your approach to project management, leadership, or teamwork. Describe how the insights gained from this experience have influenced your decision-making, improved your performance, or contributed to your professional growth. This demonstrates your ability to learn from experience and apply that knowledge effectively.

5. **Outcome and Impact:** Conclude by reflecting on the overall outcome of the experience and its impact on your career. If the project or situation was successful, mention how it benefited the organization and solidified your confidence in handling similar challenges in the future. If it involved setbacks, discuss how the experience helped you grow and become more resilient. This final reflection ties the experience back to your ongoing career development and illustrates your commitment to continuous learning and improvement.

Key Takeaways

1. **Be Reflective:** Choose a learning experience that had a significant impact on your professional growth, demonstrating self-awareness and a commitment to learning.

2. **Be Specific:** Provide detailed and specific examples of the situation, what you learned, and how it influenced your development. This adds credibility and depth to your response.

3. **Show Growth:** Highlight how the experience contributed to your growth and how you have applied these lessons in your career. This shows your ability to learn from challenges and continuously improve your performance.

89. DESCRIBE A TIME WHEN YOU HAD TO ADAPT TO A NEW SKILL QUICKLY.

Tips

1. **Be Specific:** hen describing a situation where you had to adapt to a new skill quickly, it's important to provide specific details about the context and the skill involved. This specificity helps to make your story more engaging and relatable to the interviewer. Focus on what prompted the need for the new skill, the environment you were in, and why it was crucial to adapt quickly.

2. **Highlight Challenges:** Make sure to emphasize the challenges you encountered while learning this new skill. Whether it was a lack of time, resources, or prior knowledge, explaining these obstacles shows your ability to overcome difficulties and adapt under pressure. This also demonstrates resilience and problem-solving skills, which are highly valued by employers.

3. **Demonstrate Impact:** After discussing the process of learning the new skill, it's essential to highlight the positive impact it had on your work or project. This shows that your quick adaptation wasn't just

about learning something new, but about applying it effectively to achieve tangible results. This part of your answer should illustrate the value you bring to the table in terms of adaptability and effectiveness.

Response Framework

1. **Introduction:** Start by briefly introducing the context in which you had to adapt to a new skill quickly. Highlight the importance of the situation and why it was critical for you to learn the new skill in a short timeframe. Emphasize that this scenario was pivotal to the success of a project or a significant responsibility in your role.

2. **Challenges Faced:** Detail the specific challenges you faced during this period of rapid learning. These could include the complexity of the new skill, the limited time available, and the potential risks involved if you didn't adapt quickly. This section should convey the urgency and difficulty of the situation, setting the stage for how you approached the challenge.

3. **Learning Process:** Describe the strategies you employed to learn the new skill quickly. This could involve using a variety of resources, such as online courses, tutorials, and hands-on practice. Mention any proactive steps you took, such as seeking advice from colleagues or experts, or dedicating extra time outside of work to master the skill. This part of the framework should demonstrate your resourcefulness and commitment to learning under pressure.

4. **Application of New Skill:** Explain how you applied the new skill in your work. Focus on how you integrated what you learned into your project or tasks, ensuring that you met the necessary deadlines and maintained quality. If relevant, discuss how you helped others adapt to the change, perhaps by leading training sessions or providing support to your team. This demonstrates your ability to not only learn quickly but also to lead and support others during transitions.

5. **Outcome and Impact:** Conclude by discussing the positive outcomes that resulted from your quick adaptation to the new skill. Highlight how your efforts contributed to the success of the project, improved team efficiency, or led to recognition from management. Reflect on how this experience reinforced the importance of adaptability and continuous learning in your professional growth.

Key Takeaways

1. **Be Specific:** Detail the situation and the skill you had to learn, making your example relatable and concrete.

2. **Highlight Challenges:** Focus on the obstacles you faced and how you overcame them, showcasing your problem-solving and adaptability skills.

3. **Demonstrate Impact:** Emphasize the positive outcomes that resulted from quickly adapting to the new skill, illustrating the value of your adaptability and effectiveness in your role.

90. HOW DO YOU PLAN YOUR CAREER DEVELOPMENT?

Tips

1. **Be Strategic:** When discussing career development, it's essential to focus on outlining a clear and strategic plan. Emphasize your long-term vision for your career and the specific steps you are taking to achieve it. A well-thought-out plan shows that you are goal-oriented and have a roadmap for your professional growth.

2. **Show Initiative:** Highlight how you proactively seek opportunities for growth and learning. This demonstrates your commitment to continuous improvement and your drive to advance in your career. Employers appreciate candidates who take charge of their professional development and are motivated to enhance their skills and knowledge.

3. **Reflect on Achievements:** Reflecting on your achievements and setbacks is crucial in career planning. Mention how you use these reflections to refine your career path continuously. This shows your ability to learn from your experiences and adapt your strategies to achieve your career objectives.

Response Framework

1. **Self-Assessment and Goal Setting:** Begin your career development planning with a comprehensive self-assessment. This involves evaluating your strengths, areas for improvement, and career aspirations. Utilize tools such as SWOT analysis and seek feedback from mentors or colleagues to gain a clear understanding of your current professional standing. Based on this self-assessment, set specific, measurable, and realistic goals that align with your long-term career objectives. These goals should guide your efforts and provide a roadmap for your professional growth.

2. **Creating a Structured Roadmap:** Once you have established your career goals, develop a detailed roadmap to achieve them. This roadmap should outline both short-term and long-term objectives, along with clear milestones and timelines. Break down your goals into manageable steps, ensuring that each step contributes to your overall career progression. This structured approach helps maintain focus and direction, allowing you to track your progress and stay on course towards achieving your career aspirations.

3. **Prioritizing Continuous Learning:** Continuous learning is a key element of effective career development. Actively seek out opportunities to enhance your skills and stay updated with industry trends. Enroll in relevant courses, attend workshops, and participate in conferences to expand your knowledge and expertise. By committing to lifelong learning, you ensure that you remain competitive in your field and are prepared to adapt to new challenges and opportunities as they arise.

4. **Networking and Mentorship:** Networking and mentorship are crucial components of your career development strategy. Engage with industry peers, join professional associations, and attend networking events to build meaningful relationships. Seek out mentors who can offer guidance, share their experiences, and help you navigate your career path. These connections not only open doors to new opportunities but also provide valuable insights and advice that can shape your career trajectory.

5. **Regular Review and Adaptation:** Regularly review and adjust your career development plan to ensure it remains aligned with your evolving goals and the changing landscape of your industry. Periodically assess your progress, celebrate your achievements, and make any necessary adjustments to your plan. This iterative process allows you to stay flexible and responsive, ensuring that your career development efforts remain relevant and effective in helping you achieve your long-term objectives.

Key Takeaways

1. **Be Strategic:** Develop a clear and strategic career development plan that includes a long-term vision and actionable steps, ensuring you stay focused on your goals.

2. **Show Initiative:** Demonstrate a proactive approach by seeking out growth and learning opportunities, showcasing your commitment to continuous professional development.

3. **Reflect on Achievements:** Regularly reflect on your progress, using your experiences to refine and adapt your career path, which underscores your ability to learn and evolve in your career.

CHAPTER 10

ETHICS AND INTEGRITY

91. DESCRIBE A TIME WHEN YOU FACED AN ETHICAL DILEMMA AT WORK.

Tips

1. **Understand the Importance:** Ethical dilemmas challenge your values and test your integrity. Employers look for candidates who can handle such situations with a strong sense of ethics. It's important to demonstrate that you can make difficult decisions while upholding ethical standards, even when there are significant consequences. Show that you understand the gravity of these situations and how they impact both your work and the organization.

2. **Be Honest:** Choose a real-life example that authentically represents an ethical dilemma you faced. Your response should reflect your genuine experience and decision-making process. Honesty in your example will not only demonstrate your integrity but also your ability to navigate complex situations with authenticity and moral clarity.

3. **Highlight Your Decision-Making Process:** When discussing your approach to the dilemma, explain how you identified the ethical issue, considered your options, and made your decision. Break down the steps you took, the factors you considered, and why you chose the path you did. This part of your response is crucial as it shows your thought process and ability to handle ethical challenges.

4. **Show the Outcome:** Discuss the results of your decision, including any actions you took to resolve the situation and what you learned from the experience. Emphasize the positive outcomes, such as strengthened ethical practices or personal growth, to illustrate the lasting impact of your decision-making.

Response Framework

1. **Introduction to the Ethical Dilemma:** Begin by clearly defining the ethical dilemma you encountered. This should include a concise explanation of the conflicting values, principles, or interests at stake. For instance, discuss a situation where you faced a decision that challenged your ethical standards, highlighting the tension between professional obligations and moral considerations. This sets the context for the interviewer, helping them understand the complexity of the situation you were in.

2. **Decision-Making Process:** Next, outline the steps you took to navigate the ethical dilemma. Describe how you assessed the situation, including the ethical considerations you weighed and the potential consequences of different actions. Explain your thought process, such as consulting with relevant policies, seeking advice from trusted colleagues, or reflecting on your own moral principles. This part of your response should demonstrate your ability to think critically and ethically under pressure.

3. **Actions Taken:** Detail the specific actions you decided to take to resolve the dilemma. This could involve directly addressing the issue with those involved, reporting the situation to higher authorities, or implementing corrective measures. Be clear about how you balanced the need to maintain professional standards with the potential impacts of your decision. This section should emphasize your commitment to ethical integrity and responsible decision-making.

4. **Outcome and Reflection:** Conclude by discussing the results of your actions and what you learned from the experience. Reflect on how the situation was resolved, including any positive changes that occurred as a result of your decision. Highlight the lessons you took away from the experience, such

as the importance of transparency, the need for ethical vigilance, or the value of courage in standing up for what is right. This reflection demonstrates your growth and commitment to maintaining high ethical standards in your professional life.

Key Takeaways

1. **Understand the Importance:** Show that you recognize the significance of ethical dilemmas and their potential impact on your work and the organization.

2. **Be Honest:** Choose a real and relevant example that reflects your authenticity and integrity, ensuring your response is genuine.

3. **Highlight Your Decision-Making Process:** Explain how you approached the dilemma, considering all factors, and made a principled decision that upheld ethical standards.

4. **Show the Outcome:** Discuss the results of your actions, focusing on the positive outcomes and the lessons learned, emphasizing how the experience contributed to your professional growth.

92. HOW DO YOU HANDLE CONFIDENTIAL INFORMATION?

Tips

1. **Understand the Importance:** Confidential information is essential to a company's operations, and mishandling it can lead to severe consequences. When answering this question, emphasize your understanding of why confidentiality is critical in your role. Show that you are aware of the legal, ethical, and competitive implications of protecting sensitive information and how it impacts the organization's success and reputation.

2. **Show Your Experience:** Provide examples from your career where you have handled sensitive or confidential information. By discussing real-life situations, you demonstrate your practical experience and reassure potential employers that you can be trusted with sensitive data. This helps to build confidence in your ability to manage confidential matters effectively.

3. **Explain Your Methods:** Detail the specific procedures and practices you follow to protect confidential information. This can include digital security measures, such as using encrypted communication tools and secure storage systems, as well as physical measures, like secure document storage. Clearly outline how you follow company policies and ensure that only authorized personnel have access to sensitive information.

4. **Highlight Ethical Standards:** Reinforce your commitment to ethical standards and integrity when dealing with confidential information. Emphasizing your dedication to maintaining confidentiality as part of your professional ethics will underline your reliability and professionalism.

Response Framework

1. **Acknowledge the Importance of Confidentiality:** Begin by demonstrating your understanding of the critical importance of confidentiality in your role. Explain how maintaining the privacy and security of sensitive information is essential for the success of the organization and the trust placed in you by clients, colleagues, and stakeholders. This shows that you recognize the gravity of handling confidential data and its potential impact on the company.

2. **Adherence to Policies and Procedures:** Describe your commitment to following established policies and procedures for handling confidential information. Mention how you ensure that you are always

up-to-date with the company's protocols regarding data protection, document handling, and information sharing. Emphasize your diligence in adhering to these guidelines to maintain the security of sensitive information at all times.

3. **Secure Practices and Tools:** Outline the specific practices and tools you use to manage confidential information securely. Discuss your use of secure systems, such as password-protected files, encrypted communication channels, and secure storage solutions. Highlight your attention to detail in ensuring that only authorized personnel have access to confidential data, and that information is only shared through secure and approved methods.

4. **Handling Sensitive Situations:** Provide an overview of how you approach situations where confidentiality is paramount. Discuss your approach to ensuring that sensitive information is discussed only in secure environments and shared with those who have a legitimate need to know. Mention how you manage confidentiality in various scenarios, such as handling personnel records, financial data, or strategic business plans.

5. **Ethical Responsibility and Integrity:** Conclude by emphasizing your personal commitment to ethical behavior in handling confidential information. Highlight your integrity and the trustworthiness you bring to your role. Reinforce your understanding that maintaining confidentiality is not just a procedural requirement, but a fundamental aspect of your professional responsibilities. This commitment ensures that you consistently protect the integrity and reputation of the organization.

Key Takeaways

1. **Understand the Importance:** Highlight your awareness of the critical nature of handling confidential information and its impact on the organization's success and reputation.

2. **Show Your Experience:** Use real-life examples to demonstrate your experience and reliability in managing sensitive information, ensuring you can be trusted in this capacity.

3. **Explain Your Methods:** Clearly outline the specific steps and practices you follow to secure confidential information, reinforcing your methodical approach to this responsibility.

4. **Highlight Ethical Standards:** Emphasize your commitment to ethical behavior and integrity, showing that confidentiality is a key component of your professional values.

93. WHAT STEPS DO YOU TAKE TO ENSURE ACCURACY IN YOUR WORK?

Tips

1. **Understand the Importance:** Accuracy is crucial in maintaining the integrity and reliability of your work. It directly impacts decision-making, trust, and overall performance within an organization. When discussing this topic, emphasize your understanding of how accuracy influences your role and the broader business objectives. Show that you prioritize accuracy as a key element of your professional responsibilities.

2. **Show Your Methods:** To ensure accuracy, it's essential to highlight the specific techniques and tools you use. These might include double-checking your work, using specialized software, and adhering to detailed processes that minimize the risk of errors. Explain how these methods contribute to consistently accurate results in your work.

3. **Provide Examples:** Including examples from your past experience is an effective way to demonstrate your commitment to accuracy. Discuss situations where maintaining accuracy was particularly

challenging or critical, and how your approach ensured successful outcomes. This adds credibility to your response by showing practical application.

4. **Commitment to Continuous Improvement:** Emphasize your dedication to improving your accuracy and efficiency over time. This could involve ongoing training, learning from past mistakes, or staying informed about the latest best practices in your field. Continuous improvement shows that you are proactive in maintaining high standards in your work.

Response Framework

1. **Understanding the Importance of Accuracy:** Start by explaining the significance of accuracy in your role and its impact on the organization. Highlight how maintaining high accuracy standards is crucial for ensuring the reliability of your work and the trust that clients and colleagues place in you. For instance, emphasize that accuracy is vital for maintaining data integrity, supporting informed decision-making, and safeguarding the organization's reputation.

2. **Methodical Approach and Processes:** Outline the systematic approach you use to ensure accuracy in your work. Describe the processes you follow, such as double-checking your work, using automated tools for verification, and adhering to industry best practices. Mention specific steps, such as creating and following checklists, conducting peer reviews, and using software tools designed to minimize errors. This methodical approach demonstrates your commitment to delivering precise and error-free results.

3. **Use of Technology and Tools:** Discuss the technology and tools you utilize to maintain accuracy. Highlight how you leverage software applications, data validation techniques, and other digital tools to cross-check information and identify potential discrepancies. Explain how these tools enhance your ability to detect and correct errors before they can impact the final outcome, ensuring that your work is consistently accurate.

4. **Continuous Monitoring and Quality Control:** Describe how you continuously monitor the accuracy of your work throughout a project. Explain your practice of conducting regular audits, spot checks, and reviews to catch any issues early on. Discuss the importance of quality control measures in maintaining high standards of accuracy and how these practices are integrated into your daily workflow to prevent errors from slipping through the cracks.

5. **Commitment to Ongoing Improvement:** Conclude by emphasizing your dedication to continuous improvement in maintaining accuracy. Explain how you seek out professional development opportunities, such as attending workshops, gaining certifications, or staying current with industry trends, to refine your skills and enhance your accuracy. This ongoing commitment to learning and self-improvement ensures that you are always striving to uphold and exceed accuracy standards in your work.

Key Takeaways

1. **Understand the Importance:** Recognize the critical nature of accuracy and its significant impact on decision-making, trust, and overall organizational performance.

2. **Show Your Methods:** Highlight specific techniques and tools you use to ensure accuracy, such as automated tools, manual checks, and detailed processes.

3. **Provide Examples:** Use real-life examples to demonstrate your experience and commitment to maintaining high levels of accuracy in your work.

4. **Commitment to Improvement:** Emphasize your dedication to continuous learning and improvement, showing that you proactively work to enhance accuracy and efficiency in your professional responsibilities.

94. DESCRIBE A TIME WHEN YOU HAD TO STAND UP FOR WHAT YOU BELIEVED IN.

Tips

1. **Be Authentic:** When discussing a situation where you stood up for your beliefs, it's essential to choose an experience that genuinely reflects your values. Authenticity in your response will demonstrate your integrity and commitment to your principles. Avoid embellishing the story; instead, focus on sharing a real-life scenario that had a significant impact on you.

2. **Context Matters:** Providing sufficient background information is crucial to helping the interviewer understand the stakes involved in the situation. Clearly explain the context in which the ethical dilemma arose, including the specific circumstances and the potential consequences. This sets the stage for why your decision was important and what was at risk.

3. **Actions Taken:** Detail the specific steps you took to address the situation. Describe your thought process, how you communicated your beliefs to others, and the actions you implemented to uphold your values. This section should convey your problem-solving skills and how you navigated the challenges posed by the dilemma.

4. **Outcome:** Whether the outcome was positive or negative, it's important to focus on the results of your actions and what you learned from the experience. Highlight the impact your decision had on the situation, the people involved, and how it reinforced your values. This reflection demonstrates your ability to learn and grow from challenging experiences.

Response Framework

1. **Setting the Scene:** Begin by briefly introducing the context of the situation. Clearly outline the scenario where your values or beliefs were challenged. This could involve an ethical dilemma, a disagreement with a decision, or a situation where you felt it was necessary to defend a principle you strongly believed in. For example, you might say, "In a previous role, I was faced with a situation where the company's approach to handling a client issue conflicted with my commitment to transparency and fairness."

2. **The Challenge or Ethical Dilemma:** Describe the challenge or ethical dilemma that prompted you to take a stand. Provide enough detail to convey the gravity of the situation and why it was significant to you. This could involve a scenario where there was pressure to compromise on quality, honesty, or ethical standards. It's important to explain what was at stake and why the situation was challenging, as this helps to frame the importance of your actions.

3. **The Decision-Making Process:** Detail your thought process and the factors you considered before taking action. Explain how you weighed the potential risks and benefits, and why you ultimately decided to stand up for your belief. This section should highlight your commitment to your principles, even in the face of potential adversity. For example, you might describe how you sought advice, considered the long-term implications, and carefully chose the best course of action to address the issue.

4. **Actions Taken:** Explain the specific actions you took to stand up for what you believed in. This could involve voicing your concerns, proposing an alternative solution, or taking steps to ensure that your principles were upheld. Be clear about how you communicated your stance and the steps you took to address the situation. This demonstrates your ability to act decisively and ethically under pressure.

5. **Outcome and Reflection:** Conclude by discussing the outcome of your actions and what you learned from the experience. Reflect on how the situation was resolved, the impact of your decision on the team or organization, and any positive changes that resulted from your actions. Highlight any lessons learned, such as the importance of integrity, the value of ethical leadership, or the need for open communication in difficult situations. This reflection reinforces your commitment to your values and demonstrates your ability to learn and grow from challenging experiences.

Key Takeaways

1. **Be Authentic:** Choose a real experience where you stood up for your beliefs, demonstrating your integrity and commitment to your values. Authenticity resonates and adds credibility to your story.

2. **Context Matters:** Provide sufficient background to set the scene and help the interviewer understand the stakes involved. Clear context allows the interviewer to grasp the significance of the ethical dilemma.

3. **Actions Taken:** Detail the specific steps you took to uphold your values, showing your problem-solving skills and how you effectively navigated the challenges.

4. **Outcome:** Highlight the results of your actions, focusing on what you learned from the experience. Whether the outcome was positive or challenging, emphasize the growth and reaffirmation of your values.

95. HOW DO YOU HANDLE PRESSURE TO COMPROMISE YOUR VALUES?

Tips

1. **Stay Firm:** Emphasize the importance of maintaining your principles, even under pressure. Show that you prioritize integrity and ethical behavior over short-term gains.

2. **Be Reflective:** Reflect on past experiences where you faced similar pressures. Sharing real-life examples can illustrate your commitment to your values.

3. **Detail Actions:** Describe the steps you take to handle these situations. This shows your proactive approach and problem-solving skills.

4. **Outcome and Learning:** Highlight the outcomes and what you learned. This demonstrates your ability to handle difficult situations and grow from them.

Response Framework

1. **Introduction:** Begin by setting the stage with a brief statement that underscores your commitment to maintaining your values and integrity in the workplace. For example, "Maintaining my integrity and upholding ethical standards are non-negotiable aspects of my professional conduct, even when faced with pressure to compromise."

2. **Describe the Situation:** Clearly outline a specific scenario where you encountered pressure to compromise your values. Provide enough context to help the interviewer understand the nature of the situation, the source of the pressure, and why it was significant. This could involve a request from a supervisor, a challenging project requirement, or a situation involving ethical gray areas. For example, "In a previous role, I was pressured to adjust project timelines in a way that would mislead stakeholders about the project's progress."

3. **Analyze the Pressure:** Explain how you recognized the pressure and the potential consequences of compromising your values. Discuss the thought process you went through to assess the situation, including any ethical considerations, potential risks, and the long-term impact on the organization or your career. This demonstrates your ability to think critically and ethically under pressure.

4. **Take Action:** Describe the specific actions you took to address the pressure without compromising your values. This might include having a difficult conversation, proposing alternative solutions, or seeking guidance from a mentor or ethics committee. Highlight your assertiveness in standing by your principles and your ability to navigate the situation diplomatically.

5. **Outcome and Reflection:** Conclude by discussing the outcome of your actions and what you learned from the experience. Reflect on how your decision impacted the team or organization, and how it reinforced your commitment to ethical behavior. This section should emphasize the positive results of maintaining your integrity, such as earning respect from colleagues or contributing to a more transparent and ethical work environment.

6. **Lessons Learned:** Finally, touch on how this experience has shaped your approach to similar situations in the future. Discuss how it strengthened your resolve to uphold your values and how it has prepared you to handle any potential pressures that may arise in your career.

Key Takeaways

1. **Stay Firm:** Emphasize the importance of maintaining your principles, even under pressure. Show that you prioritize integrity and ethical behavior over short-term gains.

2. **Be Reflective:** Reflect on past experiences where you faced similar pressures. Sharing real-life examples can illustrate your commitment to your values.

3. **Detail Actions:** Describe the steps you take to handle these situations. This shows your proactive approach and problem-solving skills.

4. **Outcome and Learning:** Highlight the outcomes and what you learned. This demonstrates your ability to handle difficult situations and grow from them.

96. WHAT WOULD YOU DO IF YOU SAW A COLLEAGUE DOING SOMETHING UNETHICAL?

Tips

1. **Stay Firm:** Emphasize the importance of adhering to your principles, even in situations where you might be pressured to compromise. Show that you prioritize integrity and ethical behavior over short-term gains or appeasing others. Employers value candidates who are committed to maintaining high standards, especially when it's difficult.

2. **Be Reflective:** Think back to instances where you encountered pressure to act against your values. Reflecting on these experiences allows you to provide real-life examples that illustrate your commitment to your principles. This helps to demonstrate that you can stand by your values even in challenging circumstances.

3. **Detail Actions:** Clearly describe the steps you took when faced with the pressure to compromise your values. This shows your proactive approach to handling difficult situations and your problem-solving skills. Outline your decision-making process and how you communicated your stance to others involved.

4. **Outcome and Learning:** Conclude by discussing the outcome of your actions and the lessons you learned. This reinforces your ability to navigate ethical dilemmas successfully and highlights your commitment to continuous personal and professional growth. Show that you emerged from the situation with strengthened resolve and valuable insights.

Response Framework

1. **Introduction:** Begin by emphasizing your commitment to ethical behavior in the workplace. For example, "Upholding ethical standards and integrity is a core principle of my professional conduct. When faced with unethical behavior, I believe it is crucial to address the issue promptly and appropriately."

2. **Assess the Situation:** Describe how you would first assess the situation to understand the nature and extent of the unethical behavior. Explain the importance of gathering facts and not jumping to conclusions. For example, "Upon noticing something that appears unethical, my first step would be to assess the situation carefully. I would ensure that I have all the relevant facts and fully understand the context before taking any action."

3. **Address the Behavior Directly:** If appropriate, describe how you would approach the colleague directly to discuss your concerns. This step shows that you are willing to handle issues at the source, giving your colleague the opportunity to explain or correct their behavior. For example, "If the situation allows, I would approach the colleague privately to discuss my concerns. This conversation would be conducted respectfully, with the goal of understanding their perspective and encouraging them to rectify the situation if necessary."

4. **Escalate if Necessary:** Explain how, if the issue persists or if the unethical behavior is severe, you would escalate the matter to a higher authority, such as a manager or HR department. Emphasize the importance of following company protocols to handle such situations effectively and maintaining confidentiality throughout the process. For example, "If the unethical behavior continued or if it involved a serious breach, I would escalate the issue to my manager or HR. I would follow company protocols to ensure that the matter is addressed properly and confidentially."

5. **Reflect on the Importance of Integrity:** Conclude by reflecting on why addressing unethical behavior is critical for maintaining a positive and ethical workplace culture. Discuss how you believe this approach reinforces trust and integrity within the organization. For example, "Addressing unethical behavior is essential for maintaining trust and integrity within the organization. By taking action, I would not only protect the company's interests but also contribute to a work environment where ethical standards are upheld by all."

Key Takeaways

1. **Stay Firm:**
Highlight the importance of maintaining your principles, even under significant pressure. Demonstrating your commitment to ethical behavior is crucial for building trust with employers.

2. **Be Reflective:**
Reflect on past experiences where you encountered similar challenges. Sharing these stories adds credibility to your response and shows your ability to navigate complex situations with integrity.

3. **Detail Actions:**
Clearly outline the steps you took to handle the pressure without compromising your values. This demonstrates your proactive approach and problem-solving abilities.

4. **Outcome and Learning:**
Conclude by discussing the results of your actions and what you learned. Emphasizing growth from

137

these experiences shows that you are capable of handling difficult situations while staying true to your principles.

97. HOW DO YOU ENSURE YOUR WORK ADHERES TO LEGAL AND ETHICAL STANDARDS?

Tips

1. **Understand Regulations:** Familiarize yourself with the specific regulations and company policies relevant to your industry. This foundational knowledge ensures that your work consistently meets legal requirements. Employers want to see that you are proactive in staying informed about the rules that govern your work, as this reduces risks and enhances compliance.

2. **Ongoing Education:** Commit to continuous learning to keep up with the latest legal and ethical standards. This can be achieved through attending courses, webinars, or industry events. Staying informed about changes in regulations and best practices is crucial for maintaining compliance and ethical integrity in your work.

3. **Ethical Decision-Making:** Develop and use a structured approach to ethical decision-making. Consider the potential impact of your actions on all stakeholders, including colleagues, customers, and the broader community. Employers value employees who can make sound decisions that align with both legal standards and ethical principles.

4. **Consult Experts:** When faced with complex or unclear situations, consult with legal or compliance experts. This step ensures that your actions align with current legal and ethical guidelines, minimizing the risk of errors or non-compliance. Seeking expert advice demonstrates your commitment to making well-informed decisions.

5. **Documentation:** Keep thorough records of your processes and decisions. Documentation is essential for transparency and accountability, especially during audits or reviews. Well-maintained records provide a clear trail of compliance, showcasing your commitment to upholding legal and ethical standards.

Response Framework

1. **Commitment to Compliance and Ethics:** Begin by emphasizing your dedication to maintaining high legal and ethical standards in your work. For example, "Adhering to legal and ethical standards is fundamental to my professional integrity. I am committed to ensuring that every aspect of my work aligns with the relevant regulations and ethical guidelines."

2. **Staying Informed and Updated:** Explain how you keep yourself informed about the latest regulations and ethical practices in your industry. This could involve regularly reviewing legal updates, attending compliance training, or participating in industry forums. For example, "I stay informed by regularly reviewing updates from regulatory bodies, attending industry-specific training sessions, and subscribing to legal and ethical guidelines updates. This helps me stay current with any changes that could affect my work."

3. **Continuous Learning and Professional Development:** Describe your commitment to continuous learning and how it plays a role in ensuring adherence to standards. For example, "To ensure my knowledge remains current, I engage in continuous professional development through online courses, certification programs, and webinars. This ongoing education enables me to adapt to new legal requirements and uphold the highest ethical standards in my work."

4. **Ethical Decision-Making Process:** Discuss the approach you take when faced with ethical dilemmas or complex situations. Explain how you consider the impact on stakeholders and ensure that your decisions align with both legal requirements and ethical principles. For example, "In situations where ethical dilemmas arise, I apply a structured decision-making process, weighing the potential impacts on all stakeholders. This ensures that my actions not only comply with legal requirements but also uphold the ethical standards of my profession."

5. **Seeking Expert Guidance:** Highlight the importance of consulting with experts when necessary to navigate complex legal or ethical issues. For example, "When faced with complex legal or ethical challenges, I consult with legal advisors or compliance officers to ensure that my actions are fully aligned with current standards. This collaboration helps me address any uncertainties with confidence."

6. **Documentation and Accountability:** Emphasize the role of thorough documentation in ensuring compliance and transparency. For example, "I meticulously document all processes and decisions related to legal and ethical matters. This practice not only ensures accountability but also provides a clear audit trail, demonstrating my commitment to maintaining compliance and upholding ethical standards."

Key Takeaways

1. **Understand Regulations:** Stay informed about industry-specific regulations and company policies to ensure your work consistently meets legal requirements.

2. **Ongoing Education:** Commit to continuous learning to stay updated with the latest legal and ethical standards, which is essential for maintaining compliance.

3. **Ethical Decision-Making:** Develop and utilize a structured approach to ethical decision-making, ensuring your actions consider the impact on all stakeholders.

4. **Consult Experts:** When in doubt, seek guidance from legal or compliance experts to ensure your decisions align with the most current standards.

5. **Documentation:** Maintain thorough and accurate records of your processes and decisions to provide transparency and accountability in all your professional activities.

98. DESCRIBE A SITUATION WHERE YOU HAD TO ACT WITH INTEGRITY.

Tips

1. **Be Specific:** When discussing a situation where you acted with integrity, choose a clear and specific example that highlights your commitment to ethical behavior. Provide enough detail to paint a vivid picture of the situation and your actions. This specificity will help your response stand out and demonstrate your reliability.

2. **Explain the Situation:** Clearly outline the context and the ethical dilemma you faced. Providing a thorough explanation allows the interviewer to grasp the significance of the situation and the potential consequences. It's important to show that the stakes were high and that your decision required careful consideration.

3. **Describe Your Actions:** Detail the steps you took to address the issue, focusing on how you adhered to ethical principles. Emphasize any challenges you encountered, such as pressure from others or

potential risks, and how you navigated these obstacles while maintaining your integrity. This demonstrates your ability to act ethically, even in difficult circumstances.

4. **Highlight the Outcome:** Explain the results of your actions, whether it was a positive resolution, recognition from leadership, or simply the satisfaction of knowing you did the right thing. If possible, quantify the impact of your decision, as this can help convey the significance of your actions.

5. **Reflect on the Experience:**
   Discuss what you learned from the situation and how it has influenced your professional behavior moving forward. This reflection shows your ability to grow from experiences and your ongoing commitment to ethical conduct, which is a valuable trait for any role.

Response Framework

1. **Introduction:** Start with a concise statement that sets the stage for your response. For instance, "Acting with integrity is a core value in my professional life, and I faced a situation that truly tested my commitment to this principle."

2. **Setting the Scene:** Describe the context of the situation that required you to demonstrate integrity. Provide enough detail to help the interviewer understand the stakes involved. For example, "I was managing a crucial project where the stakes were high, and every decision had significant implications for the company's finances and reputation."

3. **Identifying the Ethical Dilemma:** Clearly explain the ethical dilemma you encountered. This should include the conflicting pressures or challenges you faced. For example, "During a routine review of project expenses, I noticed a discrepancy in the financial records. It appeared that a vendor had submitted an invoice with inflated charges, which could have easily gone unnoticed, leading to a substantial financial loss for the company."

4. **Actions Taken:** Detail the specific actions you took to address the situation. Explain how you prioritized ethical considerations and transparency in your decision-making process. For example, "I immediately flagged the issue, halted the payment process, and informed my supervisor. I then conducted a thorough audit of all related transactions and engaged in direct communication with the vendor to correct the billing errors."

5. **Outcome:** Discuss the results of your actions, focusing on how integrity prevailed. Highlight any positive outcomes that resulted from your decision to act ethically. For example, "My actions led to the recovery of the overcharged amount and prompted the vendor to revise their billing practices. Senior management recognized my efforts to uphold the company's ethical standards, which reinforced our commitment to financial integrity."

6. **Reflection and Lessons Learned:** Conclude with a reflection on the importance of integrity and how this experience has shaped your professional behavior. For example, "This experience reaffirmed my belief in the importance of vigilance and transparency in all financial matters. It has strengthened my resolve to consistently act with integrity, ensuring that ethical considerations guide every decision I make, no matter the circumstances."

Key Takeaways

1. **Be Specific:** Choose a specific instance that highlights your commitment to integrity, providing enough detail to give a comprehensive understanding of the situation and your actions.

2. **Explain the Situation:** Clearly outline the context and the ethical dilemma you faced, helping the interviewer understand the gravity of the situation and the stakes involved.

3. **Describe Your Actions:** Detail the steps you took to address the issue, emphasizing your adherence to ethical principles and the challenges you overcame.

4. **Highlight the Outcome:** Explain the results of your actions, including any positive impact or recognition you received, to demonstrate the significance of your ethical decision.

5. **Reflect on the Experience:** Discuss what you learned from the situation and how it has shaped your approach to professional conduct, showing your growth and commitment to ethical behavior.

99. HOW DO YOU BALANCE COMPANY LOYALTY WITH ETHICAL STANDARDS?

Tips

1. **Be Clear About Values:** Start by emphasizing that maintaining both company loyalty and ethical standards is crucial for long-term success. Explain that ethical behavior builds trust and sustainability within the organization, which ultimately benefits the company. Make it clear that your approach to loyalty is intrinsically linked to your commitment to ethics.

2. **Use Specific Examples:** When discussing how you balance loyalty and ethics, provide a specific example that demonstrates your thought process and actions. Avoid generalities and focus on a real situation where you had to navigate this balance. This concrete example will make your response more relatable and credible.

3. **Show Your Decision-Making Process:** Detail the steps you took to weigh the factors involved. Explain how you considered the consequences of both loyalty to the company and adherence to ethical standards. Mention any frameworks or guiding principles you used to make your decision, such as company policies, legal standards, or personal values.

4. **Emphasize Communication:** Highlight the importance of open and honest communication when ethical concerns arise. Discuss how you engaged with superiors or colleagues to address the issue, ensuring that all perspectives were considered and that the final decision was made with integrity.

5. **Reflect on Outcomes:** Conclude by discussing the outcomes of your actions. Whether the result was positive or challenging, focus on the lessons learned and how your actions contributed to improving company culture or practices. This reflection shows your ability to grow from experiences and reinforces your commitment to ethical behavior.

Response Framework

1. **Introduction:** Start by acknowledging the importance of maintaining both company loyalty and ethical standards. For example, "Balancing company loyalty with ethical standards is crucial because it ensures that the organization operates with integrity, which is essential for long-term success and maintaining trust with stakeholders."

2. **Understanding the Conflict:** Explain the inherent tension that can arise between company loyalty and ethical considerations. For example, "There are times when loyalty to the company might seem to conflict with the need to adhere to ethical standards, such as when pressure is applied to meet certain targets or achieve specific outcomes."

3. **Decision-Making Process:** Describe your approach to navigating situations where company loyalty and ethics might conflict. For example, "When faced with such a dilemma, I first consider the long-term implications of my actions on both the company's reputation and my own professional integrity. I

analyze the potential consequences of compromising ethical standards versus finding a solution that upholds those standards while still supporting the company's goals."

4. **Open Communication:** Emphasize the importance of communicating your concerns when ethical standards are at risk. For example, "I believe in addressing such issues proactively by engaging in open and honest communication with relevant stakeholders. This often involves having a candid conversation with my supervisor or team to discuss the potential ethical concerns and explore alternative approaches that align with both company goals and ethical principles."

5. **Finding a Resolution:** Discuss how you strive to find a resolution that upholds ethical standards without compromising company loyalty. For example, "In most cases, it's possible to find a solution that satisfies both ethical obligations and company objectives. By proposing alternatives that maintain integrity while achieving the desired outcomes, I contribute to a culture of transparency and trust within the organization."

6. **Reflect on the Outcome:** Conclude by reflecting on the positive outcomes that can result from prioritizing ethical standards. For example, "By consistently upholding ethical standards, I've found that not only does it protect the company's reputation, but it also fosters a work environment built on trust and respect. This approach ultimately strengthens both individual and organizational integrity, leading to sustainable success."

Key Takeaways

1. **Be Clear About Values:** Emphasize the importance of both company loyalty and ethical standards, and explain how upholding ethics is critical to long-term success.

2. **Use Specific Examples:** Provide a specific example where you had to balance loyalty and ethics, showing your decision-making process and actions.

3. **Show Your Decision-Making Process:** Detail the steps you took to make an ethical decision, highlighting the frameworks or principles that guided you.

4. **Emphasize Communication:** Discuss the role of open communication in addressing ethical concerns and ensuring that decisions are made with integrity.

5. **Reflect on Outcomes:** Explain the outcomes of your actions and how they contributed to improving company culture or practices, demonstrating your commitment to ethical behavior.

100. WHAT DOES INTEGRITY MEAN TO YOU?

Tips

1. **Be Personal and Reflective:** When answering this question, it's important to relate integrity to your personal values and experiences. Explain how integrity influences your actions and decisions, both in your professional and personal life. This not only makes your response more genuine but also demonstrates how deeply rooted this value is in your character.

2. **Use Examples:** Illustrate your understanding of integrity with specific examples from your career or personal life. These examples should clearly show how you have upheld ethical standards and made decisions that align with your principles, even in challenging situations.

3. **Highlight Its Importance:** Discuss why integrity is essential in the workplace, focusing on how it fosters trust, strengthens relationships, and supports a positive reputation for both individuals and organizations. Emphasize that integrity is foundational to effective leadership and team collaboration.

4. **Connect to the Role:** Align your commitment to integrity with the values of the company you are applying to. Show that your understanding of integrity is not only a personal commitment but also a professional one that will benefit the organization.

5. **Show Consistency:** Make it clear that integrity is a consistent part of your behavior, not just something you consider in certain situations. Highlight your ongoing commitment to ethical behavior and how it has shaped your career.

Response Framework

1. **Defining Integrity:** Begin by clearly defining what integrity means to you. For example, "Integrity, to me, is the unwavering commitment to doing what is right, even in the face of challenges or when no one is observing. It involves maintaining a strong moral compass, ensuring that my actions are always aligned with ethical standards and personal values."

2. **The Role of Integrity in the Workplace:** Explain why integrity is essential in a professional setting. For example, "In the workplace, integrity is the foundation of trust and credibility. It underpins every decision and action, ensuring that interactions with colleagues, clients, and stakeholders are honest and transparent. Upholding integrity builds a culture of accountability and respect, which is crucial for long-term success and a positive work environment."

3. **Demonstrating Integrity:** Outline how you consistently demonstrate integrity in your professional life. For example, "I demonstrate integrity by being truthful in my communications, owning up to mistakes, and ensuring that my work meets the highest ethical standards. This means making decisions that reflect honesty and fairness, even if it involves taking a more challenging or less popular path."

4. **Handling Ethical Dilemmas:** Discuss your approach to situations where your integrity might be tested. For example, "When faced with ethical dilemmas, I carefully consider the potential impact of my actions on all stakeholders. I make decisions that align with both my personal values and the ethical guidelines of the organization. I also believe in transparent communication, openly discussing any concerns with relevant parties to find the most ethical solution."

5. **Commitment to Continuous Integrity:** Conclude by emphasizing your ongoing commitment to integrity in your career. For example, "Integrity is not just a one-time act but a continuous commitment to ethical behavior. Throughout my career, I have made it a priority to uphold this value in all my professional interactions, ensuring that I contribute positively to the organization's reputation and culture."

Key Takeaways

1. **Be Personal and Reflective:** Relate integrity to your personal values and experiences, showing how it guides your actions and decisions in both professional and personal contexts.

2. **Use Examples:** Provide specific examples that illustrate your understanding and commitment to integrity, making your response more tangible and credible.

3. **Highlight Its Importance:** Emphasize the critical role that integrity plays in building trust, fostering collaboration, and maintaining a positive reputation in the workplace.

4. **Connect to the Role:** Align your commitment to integrity with the values of the company, demonstrating how your principles will benefit the organization.

5. **Show Consistency:** Demonstrate that integrity is a consistent part of your behavior, highlighting your ongoing commitment to ethical standards in all aspects of your work.

CHAPTER 11
MISCELLANEOUS QUESTIONS

101. WHAT DO YOU DO FOR FUN OUTSIDE OF WORK?

Tips

1. **Be Personal and Authentic:** When responding to this question, share activities that genuinely interest you. This gives the interviewer insight into your personality, helping them see you as a well-rounded individual. Authenticity in your response ensures that your interests align naturally with your character, making your answer more relatable and sincere.

2. **Connect to Soft Skills:** Consider highlighting hobbies or interests that help develop skills relevant to your professional life. For instance, activities that involve teamwork, creativity, problem-solving, or leadership can be subtly tied to your professional strengths. This connection can demonstrate that you are continuously growing both personally and professionally.

3. **Show Balance:** It's important to illustrate that you maintain a healthy work-life balance. Discuss activities that help you relax and recharge outside of work. This indicates that you have effective time management skills and know how to alleviate stress, which can enhance your productivity and resilience at work.

4. **Relate to Company Culture:** If possible, align your interests with the company's culture or values. This not only shows that you fit well with the team but also that you are likely to thrive in the company's environment. For example, if the company values community involvement, mention any volunteer work or community service you are involved in.

5. **Be Positive:** Choose activities that reflect positively on your character. Avoid hobbies that could be seen as controversial or overly time-consuming. Instead, focus on interests that demonstrate qualities such as discipline, creativity, or social engagement, which are likely to be appreciated by employers.

Response Framework

1. **Brief Introduction:** Start by giving an overview of your interests outside of work. For example, "Outside of work, I enjoy a variety of activities that help me stay balanced and energized. These hobbies not only provide relaxation but also contribute to my overall well-being."

2. **Discuss Hobbies:** Mention specific hobbies or activities that you are passionate about. For instance, "One of my favorite activities is hiking. I love exploring new trails and immersing myself in nature. It's a great way to stay physically active and clear my mind."

3. **Connect to Soft Skills:** Relate your hobbies to skills that are beneficial in a professional context. For example, "In addition to hiking, I enjoy playing chess, which sharpens my strategic thinking and problem-solving skills. These are abilities that I find valuable in my professional life as well."

4. **Show Balance:** Illustrate how your activities contribute to a well-rounded lifestyle. For instance, "I also spend time volunteering at a local food bank. This experience has taught me the importance of empathy and community engagement, which are values I bring to my work environment."

5. **Relate to Company Culture:** If relevant, connect your hobbies to the company's culture or values. For example, "I noticed that your company values teamwork and community involvement, which resonates with my own commitment to volunteering and collaborative activities."

6. **Conclude Positively:** End on a positive note by reflecting on how these activities benefit your professional life. For example, "These activities not only provide me with a healthy work-life balance but also allow me to return to work with renewed focus and a fresh perspective, which enhances my productivity and creativity."

Key Takeaways

1. **Be Personal and Authentic:** Choose activities that genuinely interest you to provide the interviewer with a glimpse of your true personality and how you maintain balance in your life.

2. **Connect to Soft Skills:** Highlight hobbies that develop skills relevant to your professional life, subtly demonstrating that you are continually growing both personally and professionally.

3. **Show Balance:** Demonstrate that you have a healthy work-life balance, which suggests good time management skills and the ability to manage stress effectively.

4. **Relate to Company Culture:** If possible, align your interests with the company's culture and values to show that you would be a good fit for the organization.

5. **Be Positive:** Share activities that reflect positively on your character, emphasizing qualities like discipline, creativity, and social engagement, which are likely to be valued by employers.

102. HOW DO YOU HANDLE WORK-LIFE BALANCE?

Tips

1. **Prioritize and Plan:** Start by emphasizing the importance of setting clear priorities and planning your schedule. This ensures that you can allocate sufficient time for both your work responsibilities and personal life. Highlight how proactive planning helps you stay organized, avoid last-minute rushes, and maintain a balanced lifestyle.

2. **Set Boundaries:** Discuss the significance of setting boundaries between work and personal life. Clear boundaries help prevent burnout by allowing you to disconnect from work and focus on your personal well-being. Explain how maintaining these boundaries ensures you remain productive during work hours and fully engaged in your personal life.

3. **Time Management:** Effective time management is crucial for maintaining work-life balance. Share the strategies you use to prioritize tasks and manage your time efficiently. Discuss tools or techniques like to-do lists, project management apps, or breaking down tasks into smaller steps that help you stay on track and avoid feeling overwhelmed.

4. **Use Technology Wisely:** Explain how you use technology to streamline your work and personal commitments. Tools such as calendar apps, reminders, and communication platforms can help you stay organized and manage your time more effectively. This also includes knowing when to unplug from technology to maintain a healthy balance.

5. **Self-Care:** Emphasize the role of self-care in maintaining work-life balance. Engaging in activities that promote your well-being, such as exercise, meditation, or hobbies, helps you recharge and stay mentally and physically fit. Highlight how prioritizing self-care enhances your performance both at work and in your personal life.

Response Framework

1. **Prioritize and Plan:** Start by emphasizing the importance of careful prioritization and planning in managing work-life balance. Explain how you organize your week in advance, allocating specific times for work tasks, meetings, and personal activities. This structured approach helps you ensure that neither work nor personal commitments are overlooked. By anticipating busy periods and making necessary adjustments, you maintain a healthy balance between your professional and personal life.

2. **Set Boundaries:** Discuss the importance of setting clear boundaries between work and personal life. Explain how you establish specific work hours and make a conscious effort to disconnect from work during personal time. This could include not checking work emails or taking work calls after a certain hour and reserving weekends for relaxation and family activities. By maintaining these boundaries, you can be fully present in both your work and personal life, helping you recharge and stay productive.

3. **Effective Time Management:** Highlight the role of time management in achieving work-life balance. Describe how you prioritize tasks based on urgency and importance, using tools like to-do lists and project management apps to stay organized. Breaking down larger tasks into manageable steps helps you efficiently complete work assignments without feeling overwhelmed, ensuring you have time for personal pursuits and relaxation.

4. **Leverage Technology:** Explain how you use technology to streamline work processes and manage commitments effectively. Mention tools like calendar apps, reminders, and communication platforms that help you stay organized and coordinate tasks efficiently. For example, you might use calendar notifications to remind you of important deadlines and meetings, ensuring you stay on top of work responsibilities. Additionally, discuss how productivity apps help you manage personal tasks, aiding in maintaining a balance between work and personal life.

5. **.Prioritize Self-Care:** Discuss the significance of self-care in your work-life balance strategy. Share how you engage in activities that promote well-being, such as regular exercise, meditation, and spending quality time with loved ones. Prioritizing self-care ensures that you remain physically and mentally fit, positively impacting your performance at work and your overall quality of life.

Key Takeaways

1. **Prioritize and Plan:** Prioritizing and planning your schedule is crucial to ensuring that both work and personal activities receive the attention they need. A structured approach allows for better organization and prevents last-minute stress.

2. **Set Boundaries:** Establishing clear boundaries between work and personal life is essential to avoid burnout and maintain productivity. Boundaries help you stay fully engaged in your personal life and recharge for work.

3. **Time Management:** Effective time management enables you to complete work tasks efficiently while still having time for personal activities. Prioritizing tasks and breaking them down into manageable steps helps avoid feeling overwhelmed.

4. **Use Technology Wisely:** Leveraging technology to streamline work processes and manage commitments helps maintain a healthy work-life balance. It also involves knowing when to unplug to ensure proper rest.

5. **Self-Care:** Prioritizing self-care is key to maintaining balance and overall well-being. Engaging in activities that promote physical and mental health enhances performance in both work and personal life.

103. WHAT IS YOUR FAVORITE BOOK AND WHY?

Tips

1. **Choose a Meaningful Book:** Select a book that has had a significant impact on your life. It should align with your values, interests, or professional aspirations. This choice will reflect on your character and what you prioritize in both your personal and professional life.

2. **Be Concise:** While sharing your thoughts, keep the response focused and direct. Clearly articulate why the book is meaningful to you without deviating from the main point. A concise answer shows that you can communicate effectively and stay on topic.

3. **Connect to Personal Growth:** Highlight how the book has contributed to your development. Whether it's through lessons learned, inspiration gained, or perspectives changed, showing personal growth demonstrates that you are reflective and value self-improvement.

4. **Relate to the Role:** If applicable, draw connections between the themes of the book and the role you are applying for. This can demonstrate how the book's lessons have practical applications in your professional life, showing your ability to apply knowledge in real-world scenarios.

5. **Show Passion:** Express your enthusiasm for the book. Genuine passion can make your response more engaging and memorable, leaving a lasting impression on the interviewer.

Response Framework

1. **Brief Introduction:** Begin by introducing the book you've chosen and offering a concise explanation of its significance to you. For example, "My favorite book is 'Sapiens: A Brief History of Humankind' by Yuval Noah Harari. This book has deeply influenced my understanding of human history, culture, and the evolution of societies."

2. **Key Themes and Impact:** Discuss the central themes or ideas presented in the book and how they have impacted your thinking or worldview. For instance, "The book's exploration of how human societies have evolved, particularly the ways in which culture, economics, and science intersect, has broadened my perspective on the complexities of modern civilization. It has made me more aware of the underlying forces that shape our world."

3. **Connection to Personal Development:** Explain how the book has contributed to your personal or professional growth. "Reading 'Sapiens' has made me more reflective about my role in society and more critical in my thinking. It has encouraged me to approach problems with a broader, more holistic perspective, which has been invaluable in my decision-making processes both personally and professionally."

4. **Relevance to the Role:** If applicable, relate the book's themes to the job you are applying for. "The book's insights into human behavior and societal trends are particularly relevant to the role I am pursuing in [industry/field]. Understanding these dynamics is crucial for anticipating market shifts and making informed strategic decisions, skills that are essential in this position."

5. **Passion and Enthusiasm:** Conclude by expressing your genuine enthusiasm for the book and how it continues to inspire you. "I am passionate about 'Sapiens' because it challenges me to think critically about the world and my place in it. The depth of its insights keeps me engaged, and it's a book I revisit regularly to gain fresh perspectives on the challenges we face as a society."

Key Takeaways

1. **Choose a Meaningful Book:** Select a book that reflects your values and has made a significant impact on your life.

2. **Be Concise:** Communicate your thoughts clearly and stay focused on why the book is meaningful to you.

3. **Connect to Personal Growth:** Highlight how the book has influenced your personal or professional development.

4. **Relate to the Role:** If possible, link the book's themes to the job you're applying for, demonstrating practical applications.

5. **Show Passion:** Express genuine enthusiasm for the book, making your response engaging and memorable.

104. WHO IS YOUR ROLE MODEL?

Tips

1. **Be Genuine:** Select a role model who truly inspires you and whose qualities you genuinely admire. This could be a public figure, a mentor, or even someone from your personal life. Authenticity in your choice will make your response more compelling and relatable.

2. **Explain Why:** Clearly explain why this person is your role model. Focus on specific traits, values, or achievements that resonate with you and align with your own goals. This demonstrates thoughtful reflection on what qualities you value most.

3. **Relate to Personal Growth:** Highlight how your role model has influenced your personal or professional development. Discuss how their example has shaped your actions, decisions, and overall growth. This shows that you are committed to learning from others and continuously improving yourself.

4. **Connect to the Role:** If possible, connect the qualities of your role model to the job you're applying for. This shows that the attributes you admire are relevant to the position and that you are likely to bring similar qualities to your role.

5. **Show Passion:** Let your admiration for your role model come through in your response. Enthusiasm and respect for your role model can make your answer more engaging and memorable, leaving a positive impression on the interviewer.

Response Framework

1. **Brief Introduction:** Start by introducing your role model and explaining why they inspire you. For instance, "My role model is [Name], someone whose leadership and dedication to [specific cause or field] have greatly influenced my own professional journey."

2. **Impact and Lessons:** Discuss the key qualities, actions, or accomplishments of your role model that have had a significant impact on you. "Their commitment to [specific values or actions] taught me the importance of [related principles, such as integrity, perseverance, or innovation]. These lessons have shaped my approach to both my career and personal life."

3. **Connection to Personal Growth:** Explain how your role model's influence has contributed to your personal and professional development. "Inspired by [Name], I have sought to [specific actions, such

as taking on leadership roles, pursuing advanced education, or advocating for important issues]. Their example has pushed me to grow in areas that are vital to my success and fulfillment."

4. **Relate to the Role:** Connect the traits or values of your role model to the job you are applying for. "The qualities I admire in [Name]—such as [courage, determination, empathy, etc.]—are directly relevant to the role I'm pursuing. In my current and previous roles, I've drawn on these qualities to [specific job-related actions or successes], demonstrating my alignment with both their values and the demands of this position."

5. **Passion and Enthusiasm:** Conclude by expressing your deep admiration for your role model and how they inspire you daily. "The impact that [Name] has had on my life extends beyond just admiration; it's a constant source of motivation. Their example reminds me of the importance of [specific values or actions], which I strive to embody in my work and interactions every day."

Key Takeaways

1. **Be Genuine:** Choose a role model who genuinely inspires you, and share why they are significant to you.

2. **Explain Why:** Clearly articulate the specific traits or achievements of your role model that resonate with you.

3. **Relate to Personal Growth:** Highlight how your role model has influenced your development, demonstrating your commitment to growth.

4. **Connect to the Role:** Relate the qualities of your role model to the job you are applying for, showing how these traits are relevant to your professional life.

5. **Show Passion:** Express your admiration and respect for your role model with enthusiasm, making your response engaging and memorable.

105. WHAT ARE YOUR HOBBIES?

Tips

1. **Be Honest:** Choose hobbies that you genuinely enjoy and can speak about with enthusiasm. Authenticity makes your response more engaging and relatable to the interviewer. Avoid mentioning activities that you don't actually engage in, as this could lead to awkwardness if the topic is explored further.

2. **Be Relevant:** If possible, mention hobbies that demonstrate skills or qualities relevant to the job. For example, if you enjoy team sports, this can highlight your teamwork and collaboration skills. If you enjoy puzzles or strategy games, this could showcase your problem-solving abilities.

3. **Show Balance:** Highlight a range of activities to show that you have a well-rounded life outside of work. Including physical activities, creative pursuits, and social or volunteer engagements demonstrates that you maintain a healthy balance between work and personal life.

4. **Keep It Concise:** Provide enough detail to make your hobbies interesting, but keep your response focused and to the point. Avoid going off on tangents or including too much unrelated information, as this can make your answer less impactful.

Response Framework

1. **Brief Introduction:** Start by providing a general overview of your hobbies and their significance in your life. For example, "I engage in several hobbies that help me relax, stay balanced, and foster my personal growth. These activities not only bring me joy but also enhance various skills that I apply in my professional life."

2. **Physical Activity:** Discuss a hobby that involves physical activity and how it benefits you. "One of my key hobbies is [e.g., running, yoga, or playing sports], which helps me stay physically active and mentally focused. This activity improves my stamina and resilience, which are crucial for maintaining productivity and managing stress in the workplace."

3. **Creative Pursuits:** Highlight a creative hobby and its impact on your professional abilities. "I also enjoy [e.g., painting, writing, or playing a musical instrument], which allows me to express creativity and think outside the box. This hobby sharpens my ability to approach problems from different angles and fosters innovative thinking, both of which are essential in my role."

4. **Social and Volunteer Activities:** Include hobbies that involve social interaction or community involvement. "I am actively involved in [e.g., volunteering, group activities, or social clubs], which enhances my teamwork and leadership skills. These experiences help me build strong relationships, communicate effectively, and work collaboratively, all of which are vital in a professional setting."

5. **Intellectual Hobbies:** Discuss any hobbies that contribute to your intellectual growth. "Reading is another passion of mine, particularly books on [e.g., business, technology, or personal development]. This hobby broadens my knowledge base and strengthens my analytical thinking, enabling me to make informed decisions and stay updated on industry trends."

6. **Balancing Hobbies and Work:** Conclude by explaining how your hobbies contribute to your overall well-being and work performance. "Engaging in these hobbies allows me to maintain a well-rounded life, ensuring that I can recharge and bring fresh perspectives to my work. This balance helps me manage stress effectively and demonstrates my ability to prioritize and manage my time efficiently."

Key Takeaways

1. **Be Honest:** Choose hobbies that you genuinely enjoy and can discuss with enthusiasm, ensuring authenticity in your response.

2. **Be Relevant:** Mention hobbies that highlight skills or qualities relevant to the job, showing how your personal interests align with professional attributes.

3. **Show Balance:** Highlight a range of activities that demonstrate a well-rounded life outside of work, contributing to a balanced and healthy lifestyle.

4. **Keep It Concise:** Provide enough detail to make your hobbies interesting, but stay focused and avoid unnecessary tangents, making your response clear and impactful.

106. DESCRIBE A TIME WHEN YOU WENT ABOVE AND BEYOND YOUR JOB DUTIES.

Tips

1. **Be Specific:** When discussing a time you went beyond your job duties, focus on a particular instance that clearly demonstrates your commitment and initiative. Specific examples make your story more engaging and memorable, helping the interviewer to see the tangible impact of your efforts.

2. **Highlight Impact:** Emphasize the positive outcomes and results of your actions. This could be a significant achievement, a problem solved, or a project that benefited from your extra effort. Demonstrating the tangible impact of your work shows the value you bring to the organization.

3. **Show Initiative:** Highlight your proactive approach in identifying a need or opportunity to contribute beyond your regular responsibilities. This demonstrates your dedication and willingness to go the extra mile for the benefit of the team or organization.

4. **Connect to Skills:** Relate your actions to the skills and competencies that are relevant to the job you are applying for. This helps to illustrate how your initiative aligns with your professional abilities and how it can be an asset to your potential employer.

Response Framework

1. **Brief Introduction:** Start by setting the context for the situation where you went above and beyond. "In a previous role, I had an opportunity to exceed my regular responsibilities when a critical project faced unforeseen challenges that required additional support."

2. **Identifying a Need:** Explain how you recognized a gap or a need that required extra effort. "During the project, I identified a significant communication gap between our development and client-facing teams, which was hindering the project's progress and could have compromised its success."

3. **Taking Initiative:** Describe the specific actions you took that were beyond your job duties. "Recognizing the importance of seamless communication, I took the initiative to act as a liaison between the teams. I organized cross-departmental meetings, developed a communication plan, and ensured that both teams were aligned on goals and expectations. This role was not part of my job description, but I understood its critical importance to the project's success."

4. **. Impact and Results:** Highlight the positive outcomes that resulted from your efforts. "As a result of my proactive involvement, the project timeline was back on track, and the teams were able to collaborate more effectively. This led to the successful completion of the project, which received positive feedback from both the client and senior management, and contributed to a long-term contract extension."

5. **Skills Demonstrated:** Connect your actions to key professional skills that were showcased. "This experience highlighted my ability to take initiative, communicate effectively, and solve problems under pressure. It also demonstrated my leadership and ability to collaborate across different departments, all of which are crucial skills in driving successful project outcomes."

Key Takeaways

1. **Be Specific:** Select a clear example where you went beyond your regular duties to make your response more memorable.

2. **Highlight Impact:** Focus on the positive outcomes of your actions to demonstrate the value of your extra efforts.

3. **Show Initiative:** Emphasize your proactive approach and willingness to take on additional responsibilities.

4. **Connect to Skills:** Link your actions to relevant skills and competencies, showing how your initiative aligns with your professional abilities.

107. WHAT DO YOU THINK IS YOUR BIGGEST CONTRIBUTION TO YOUR CURRENT JOB?

Tips

1. **Be Specific:** When answering this question, focus on a particular achievement or contribution that had a significant impact on your team or organization. Specific examples help make your response more credible and memorable. Choose a contribution that showcases your strengths and aligns with the key requirements of the role you are applying for.

2. **Highlight Impact:** Emphasize the positive outcomes of your contribution. If possible, use specific metrics or examples to illustrate the benefits. This could include improvements in productivity, revenue growth, or enhanced customer satisfaction. Demonstrating tangible results shows the value you bring to your role.

3. **Show Initiative:** Highlight how you took the initiative to go beyond your standard responsibilities to make a difference. This reflects your commitment to the organization and your proactive approach to problem-solving and innovation.

4. **Connect to Skills:** Link your contribution to relevant skills and competencies. This helps demonstrate how your actions align with your professional strengths and how they are applicable to the job you are targeting. This connection is crucial in convincing potential employers that you have the necessary experience and skills to excel in their organization.

Response Framework

1. **Introduction:** Begin by providing a brief overview of your role within the organization and the context in which your contribution was made. For example, "In my current position as a [Job Title], I have focused on making a meaningful impact by addressing key challenges within the department."

2. **Identifying a Key Contribution Area:** Outline the specific area where you believe you've made the most significant contribution. This might involve identifying a critical gap, opportunity, or challenge within the organization. "Early in my tenure, I recognized that [specific issue or opportunity] was a pressing concern that needed to be addressed to improve [a specific outcome or area]."

3. **Taking Action:** Detail the actions you took to address the identified need or opportunity. This section should highlight your proactive approach and any strategic decisions you made. "I took the lead in [describe the actions you took, such as implementing a new strategy, leading a project, or introducing a new process], which required collaboration with various teams and a clear focus on [specific objectives or goals]."

4. **Impact and Results:** Discuss the measurable outcomes or results of your contribution. Highlight how your efforts positively impacted the organization, whether in terms of financial performance, efficiency, customer satisfaction, or other key metrics. "As a result of my initiatives, we achieved [specific results, such as increased revenue, improved processes, or enhanced team performance], which significantly contributed to [overall company success or department improvement]."

5. **Skills Demonstrated:** Link your contribution to the relevant skills that were essential for achieving these results. This could include leadership, strategic thinking, problem-solving, or technical expertise. "This contribution demonstrated my strengths in [mention specific skills, such as leadership, strategic planning, or collaboration], which were critical in driving these successful outcomes and advancing our organizational goals."

6. **Reflection and Continued Impact:** Conclude by reflecting on how this contribution aligns with your broader goals within the organization and how you plan to continue delivering value. "Looking ahead, I

am committed to [mention your continued focus or next steps], ensuring that my contributions continue to support the long-term success of the company."

Key Takeaways

1. **Be Specific:** Choose a specific contribution that had a significant impact on your team or organization to make your response more memorable.

2. **Highlight Impact:** Use specific metrics or examples to emphasize the positive outcomes of your contribution, demonstrating the value you bring to your role.

3. **Show Initiative:** Demonstrate how you took the initiative to go beyond your standard responsibilities, reflecting your commitment and proactive approach.

4. **Connect to Skills:** Link your contribution to relevant skills and competencies to show how your experience and abilities align with the job you are applying for.

108. HOW DO YOU DEAL WITH STRESS?

Tips

1. **Understand Your Triggers:** To effectively manage stress, it's essential to recognize the specific situations or tasks that trigger it. Knowing your triggers allows you to anticipate and prepare for stressful moments, helping you to manage them proactively rather than reactively. Common triggers might include tight deadlines, high-pressure projects, or complex problem-solving tasks.

2. **Develop Coping Strategies:** Implementing practical stress management techniques is crucial. Time management is one key strategy, where you prioritize tasks and break down larger projects into smaller, more manageable steps. Mindfulness practices, such as deep breathing exercises and meditation, can help maintain your focus and calmness under pressure. Regular physical activity is another effective method to reduce stress and improve overall well-being.

3. **Seek Support:** Don't hesitate to reach out to colleagues, friends, or professionals when dealing with stress. Sharing your concerns can provide new perspectives and possible solutions. Collaboration often leads to a more supportive work environment, where stress is more manageable. Building a network of support is essential for maintaining mental and emotional health.

4. **Maintain Work-Life Balance:** Balancing work demands with personal life is crucial for avoiding burnout. Setting clear boundaries between work and leisure, and prioritizing self-care activities, helps ensure that you have the energy and focus needed for both personal and professional responsibilities. Regularly engaging in activities that you enjoy, whether it's spending time with loved ones, exercising, or pursuing hobbies, is essential for maintaining overall well-being.

Response Framework

1. **Understanding Stress Triggers:** Begin by acknowledging that everyone experiences stress and that understanding your specific triggers is the first step in managing it effectively. For example, "I start by identifying the situations that typically cause stress, such as tight deadlines, high-stakes projects, or balancing multiple priorities. Recognizing these triggers allows me to anticipate and prepare for them, reducing their impact on my performance."

2. **Developing Coping Strategies:** Discuss the techniques you employ to manage and alleviate stress. "I use a combination of time management strategies and relaxation techniques to handle stress. By

breaking down large tasks into smaller, more manageable steps and prioritizing them based on urgency, I reduce the feeling of being overwhelmed. Additionally, I practice mindfulness and deep breathing exercises, which help me maintain focus and calm during stressful moments."

3. **Seeking Support and Collaboration:** Highlight the importance of seeking support when needed and collaborating with others. "I also believe in leveraging the support of my colleagues when dealing with stress. Sharing my workload when appropriate and discussing challenges with team members not only helps distribute the pressure but also fosters a collaborative environment where we can support each other in finding effective solutions."

4. **Maintaining a Healthy Work-Life Balance:** Emphasize the significance of balancing work demands with personal well-being. "To effectively manage stress, I prioritize maintaining a healthy work-life balance. I set clear boundaries between work and personal time, ensuring that I engage in activities that help me relax and recharge, such as exercising, spending time with family, and pursuing hobbies. This balance enables me to return to work with renewed energy and focus."

5. **Continuous Learning and Adaptation:** Conclude by expressing your commitment to continuously improving your stress management strategies. "I am committed to continuously refining my stress management techniques by learning from past experiences and adapting to new challenges. This proactive approach helps me stay resilient and maintain high performance, even in demanding situations."

Key Takeaways

1. **Understand Your Triggers:** Identify the specific situations or tasks that lead to stress. This awareness allows for proactive management of stressful situations.

2. **Develop Coping Strategies:** Implement practical techniques, such as time management and mindfulness practices, to maintain focus and calm under pressure.

3. **Seek Support:** Reach out to colleagues, friends, or professionals when needed. Building a support network is essential for managing stress effectively.

4. **Maintain Work-Life Balance:** Ensure a balance between work and personal life to prevent burnout. Regularly engage in activities that help you recharge and maintain overall well-being.

109. WHAT ARE YOUR PASSIONS?

Tips

1. **Be Genuine:** When discussing your passions, choose something that genuinely excites you. Authenticity in your response will make your passion more compelling and relatable to the interviewer. Avoid choosing a passion just because it sounds impressive; instead, focus on what truly drives you.

2. **Align with the Role:** If possible, align your passions with the job or the company's culture. This demonstrates that your interests naturally complement the role you are applying for. For instance, if you are passionate about technology and the job involves tech innovation, highlight this connection.

3. **Show Enthusiasm:** Express your enthusiasm when talking about your passions. This shows that you are a motivated and engaged individual, which can be appealing to potential employers. Your excitement can make a lasting impression, making you stand out as a candidate who brings energy and dedication.

4. **Provide Examples:** Support your discussion with specific examples of how you pursue your passions. This makes your response more concrete and relatable, helping the interviewer to visualize your commitment. Whether it's a hobby, volunteer work, or a personal project, examples can strengthen your narrative.

Response Framework

1. **Brief Introduction:** Start by explaining why having passions is important in your life. For instance, "Pursuing my passions is essential because it not only enriches my personal life but also fuels my motivation and creativity in my professional life. Engaging in activities I am passionate about helps me stay balanced, energized, and focused."

2. **Identifying a Key Passion:** Select one of your primary passions and describe it in detail. "One of my core passions is [specific passion, e.g., mentoring young professionals]. I dedicate time to guiding and supporting emerging talent, helping them navigate their career paths and achieve their goals. This passion stems from my belief in the power of knowledge-sharing and the importance of fostering the next generation of leaders."

3. **Connecting Passion to Professional Life:** Link your passion to the role or company you're applying for. "This passion for mentoring aligns with my professional values and the role I am pursuing, where leadership and the development of others are key components. My experiences in mentoring have honed my communication, empathy, and leadership skills, which I am eager to bring to this position."

4. **Demonstrating Enthusiasm:** Express your genuine enthusiasm for your passion. "My commitment to [specific passion] goes beyond personal satisfaction—it's about making a meaningful impact. I find great fulfillment in seeing others grow and succeed, and this drives my continued involvement and dedication."

5. **Providing Additional Examples:** Offer more examples to demonstrate the depth of your commitment. "In addition to mentoring, I am passionate about continuous learning. I regularly participate in professional development courses and attend industry conferences to stay at the forefront of my field. This passion for learning ensures that I am always growing and can contribute fresh perspectives to my work.

Key Takeaways

1. **Be Genuine:** Choose a passion that truly excites you, ensuring your response is authentic and engaging.

2. **Align with the Role:** Highlight how your passion aligns with the job or the company's culture, demonstrating a natural fit.

3. **Show Enthusiasm:** Express your enthusiasm to showcase your motivation and engagement.

4. **Provide Examples:** Use specific examples to make your passion more concrete and relatable, strengthening your response.

110. IF YOU COULD HAVE ANY JOB IN THE WORLD, WHAT WOULD IT BE?

Tips

1. **Be Honest:** When answering this question, it's crucial to be genuine about your dream job. This reflects your true aspirations and gives the interviewer insight into what truly drives you. Honesty also makes your response more relatable and engaging.

2. **Show Alignment:** Whenever possible, try to align your dream job with the role you're applying for. This demonstrates that you've carefully considered your career path and how this position fits into your long-term goals. Even if your dream job is somewhat different, find common ground that relates to the skills or values required in the role.

3. **Reflect Your Values:** Choose a job that embodies your core values and interests. This shows that you have a clear understanding of what's important to you in your professional life and how you want to contribute to your field or society.

4. **Highlight Skills:** Discuss how the skills and experiences you're currently developing are helping prepare you for your dream job. This shows that you're not just daydreaming—you're actively working towards that goal, which indicates foresight and a commitment to continuous growth.

Response Framework

1. **Brief Introduction:** Begin by emphasizing the importance of aligning your dream job with your passions and long-term career goals. For example, "When envisioning my ideal job, I consider roles that align with my deepest interests and where I can make the most meaningful impact. My dream job would combine my passion for [specific area, e.g., technology, creativity, social impact] with my desire to drive positive change."

2. **Define the Dream Job:** Clearly articulate what your dream job would be, focusing on the elements that most excite and motivate you. "If I could choose any job in the world, I would aspire to be a [specific role, e.g., Chief Innovation Officer, Social Entrepreneur, Research Scientist]. This role would allow me to lead initiatives that [explain the core responsibilities and impact of the job], harnessing my skills to address challenges and create solutions that make a difference."

3. **Show Alignment with Current Role:** Connect your dream job to the role you are currently pursuing or your career trajectory. "The aspirations I have for this dream role are closely aligned with the position I am applying for, which also emphasizes [key elements like innovation, leadership, strategic thinking]. The experience and skills I am building now, such as [mention relevant skills, e.g., project management, leadership, creative problem-solving], are preparing me to pursue my ultimate career goals."

4. **Reflect Your Core Values:** Explain how your dream job reflects your personal and professional values. "This ideal role perfectly embodies my core values of [mention values, e.g., creativity, continuous learning, making a positive impact]. I believe that [discuss the significance of these values in the context of your dream job], and in this role, I could fully dedicate myself to work that not only excites me but also contributes to the greater good."

5. **Highlight Skills and Preparation:** Describe how your current efforts and skills are positioning you for this dream role in the future. "In my current role, I actively seek out opportunities to develop the skills necessary for this dream job. Through [mention specific experiences, e.g., leading innovative projects, participating in advanced training], I am honing the strategic thinking, leadership, and technical expertise that will be essential for excelling in such a position."

Key Takeaways

1. **Be Honest:** Be genuine about your dream job to reflect your true aspirations. This honesty will make your response more authentic and relatable.

2. **Show Alignment:** Align your dream job with the position you are applying for, demonstrating thoughtful career planning and how this role fits into your long-term goals.

3. **Reflect Your Values:** Choose a job that reflects your core values and interests, showing that you have a clear understanding of what is important to you professionally.

4. **Highlight Skills:** Mention how your current skills and experiences are preparing you for your dream job, indicating foresight and a commitment to growth.

111. DO YOU HAVE ANY QUESTIONS FOR ME?

Tips

1. **Show Genuine Interest:** Asking insightful and thoughtful questions is a great way to demonstrate your genuine interest in the role and the company. This approach shows that you are engaged, have done your research, and are serious about the opportunity. Your questions should reflect curiosity about the role, the team, and the company's future.

2. **Focus on the Future:** Inquire about the company's long-term goals, growth opportunities, and how the role you're applying for fits into the broader organizational strategy. This demonstrates that you're thinking beyond the immediate responsibilities and are interested in contributing to the company's success over time.

3. **Clarify Expectations:** Asking questions about job expectations, team dynamics, and performance metrics is crucial to understanding what will be expected of you. This helps you gauge how you can excel in the role and provides clarity on what success looks like in the short and long term.

4. **Cultural Fit:** Understanding the company's culture is essential to determine if it aligns with your values and work style. Asking about team collaboration, company values, and the work environment helps you assess whether this is a place where you can thrive.

5. **Professional Development:** Inquire about opportunities for growth and professional development. This shows that you are committed to continuous learning and are looking for a role where you can evolve and advance your career.

Response Framework

1. **Show Genuine Interest:** Start by expressing your appreciation for the opportunity to interview and convey your genuine interest in the company and the role. This sets a positive tone and demonstrates that you're engaged and thoughtful about your potential future with the organization. For example, "Thank you for the opportunity to discuss this role. I do have a few questions that will help me better understand the company's vision and how I can contribute effectively."

2. **Focus on the Company's Future:** Ask about the company's long-term goals and how the position you're applying for fits into those plans. This shows that you're thinking strategically about your role in the organization's future. For instance, "Could you share more about the company's long-term objectives and how this role contributes to achieving those goals?"

3. **Inquire About Career Growth:** Demonstrate your interest in career development by asking about growth opportunities within the company. This highlights your ambition and commitment to long-term success. For example, "I'm very interested in understanding the potential for career progression within this role. Could you provide some insight into the pathways for advancement and how the company supports professional development?"

4. **Clarify Role Expectations:** It's important to understand what success looks like in the role, so ask about the key performance indicators (KPIs) and expectations. This shows that you're proactive and keen to meet or exceed expectations. "Could you elaborate on the key performance indicators for this position and what success would look like within the first six months to a year?"

5. **Explore Company Culture:** Cultural fit is crucial for job satisfaction and success, so inquire about the team dynamics and company culture. This reflects your awareness of the importance of a supportive work environment. "Company culture is very important to me. Can you describe the team dynamics and how the company fosters collaboration on projects?"

6. **Ask About Professional Development:** Show your commitment to continuous learning by asking about opportunities for professional development. This signals that you're eager to grow and improve your skills. "I prioritize continuous learning and skill development. What opportunities does the company offer for professional growth, and are there specific programs that support ongoing employee development?"

Key Takeaways

1. **Show Genuine Interest:** Demonstrate your engagement and seriousness about the role by asking thoughtful and insightful questions that reflect your research and curiosity.

2. **Focus on the Future:** Inquire about the company's future plans and how the role fits into the broader strategy to show that you're thinking long-term and are eager to contribute to the company's success.

3. **Clarify Expectations:** Seek to understand job expectations and performance metrics so you can align your efforts with what is most valued in the role.

4. **Cultural Fit:** Ask questions to assess whether the company's culture aligns with your values and work style, ensuring it's a place where you can thrive.

5. **Professional Development:** Show your commitment to continuous learning and career advancement by asking about opportunities for growth, professional development, and company initiatives that support employee advancement.

<u>**Appendix No 1**</u>

Thank You for Reading!

I hope you found valuable insights and guidance in this book that will help you on your journey to mastering job interviews and securing your dream job.

As you reach the end of this book, I would greatly appreciate it if you could take a moment to share your thoughts. Your review can help other readers discover this resource and benefit from it just as you have.

Leaving a review is quick and easy—simply scan the QR code below to be taken directly to the review page.

Your feedback is incredibly valuable and will help improve future editions of this book. Thank you for your time, and I wish you all the best in your job search.

Warm regards,

Mauricio

PS. If you're looking to elevate your job search and interview preparation, our latest book is a must-have. It offers a step-by-step guide on harnessing the power of Artificial Intelligence and ChatGPT, specifically tailored for job seekers.

Appendix No 2
Unlock the Power of Real-World Examples

Congratulations on taking a significant step toward mastering your job interviews. To fully prepare and excel, it's essential to see how the strategies you've learned are applied in real-world scenarios. That's why I'm offering you exclusive access to practical examples for each of the 111 questions in this book.

Why access the examples?

- **Real-world application:** Understand how to tailor your responses with examples that bring the concepts to life.
- **Boost your confidence:** Reviewing well-crafted answers will give you the edge you need to stand out.
- **Personalized preparation:** Adapt these examples to fit your experiences and the specific roles you're targeting.

Maximize your preparation

The difference between a good and a great interview lies in the details. These examples will give you the clarity and confidence to navigate any question with ease.

Scan the QR code now to take your preparation to the next level and secure your path to success.

Made in the USA
Las Vegas, NV
12 January 2025

16250435R00090